CONTEMPORARY'S

PRE-GED

SCIENCE

 Wright Group

Wright Group

Send all inquiries to:
Wright Group/McGraw-Hill
130 E. Randolph, Suite 400
Chicago, IL 60681

ISBN 0-07-252761-7

5 6 7 8 9 10 QPD 08 07 06

Table of Contents

PART ONE: THEMES IN SCIENCE

PART FOUR:
EARTH AND SPACE SCIENCE

To the Student

Contemporary's Pre-GED Science will help you begin to strengthen the skills you need to pass the GED Science Test. This test is based on the National Science Education Standards of the National Academy of Sciences. In accordance with these standards, a major emphasis of the test is on *interdisciplinary* themes—themes that thread through all areas of scientific inquiry.

To answer some questions successfully, you will need to focus on fundamental understandings in the traditional subject areas of science:

- Life Science (Plant and Animal Science; Human Biology)
- Physical Science (Chemistry; Physics)
- Earth and Space Science (Earth Science; Space Science)

For others, you will need to concentrate on the interdisciplinary themes—issues common to all areas of science:

- Unifying Concepts and Processes
- Science as Inquiry
- Science and Technology
- Science in Personal and Social Perspectives
- History and Nature of Science

Before beginning this book, you should take the **Pretest**. This test will help you identify which areas you need to concentrate on most. Use the chart at the end of the Pretest to pinpoint the types of questions you have answered incorrectly and to determine in which areas you need special work. You may decide to concentrate on specific areas or to work through the entire book. We strongly suggest you *do* work through the whole book to build a strong foundation in the areas in which you will be tested.

Contemporary's Pre-GED Science is divided into four parts based upon the organization of the NSES Science Content Standards.

Part One: Themes in Science covers the major interdisciplinary themes that are essential to the general study of science:

- In **Chapter 1: Concepts and Processes in Science**, you will learn about the major concepts and processes necessary for scientific investigation.

- In **Chapter 2: Comprehending and Applying Science**, you will review the basics of scientific inquiry, including how to make inferences and recognize the difference between inductive and deductive reasoning.

- In **Chapter 3: Analyzing and Evaluating Science**, you will learn the more advanced procedures of scientific inquiry, including how to draw conclusions based on evidence, judge the value and adequacy of information, recognize values, and understand the scientific method.

Part Two: Life Science covers the fundamentals of biology:

- In **Chapter 4: Plant and Animal Science**, you will learn about cells, simple organisms, flowering plants, animals, ecology, and evolution.

- In **Chapter 5: Human Biology**, you will learn about human body systems, genetics, and health and disease.

Part Three: Physical Science covers the fundamentals of chemistry and physics.

- In **Chapter 6: Chemistry**, you will learn about matter, atoms, compounds and molecules, chemical reactions and matter, solutions, and organic chemistry.

- In **Chapter 7: Physics**, you will learn about mechanics, forces and machines, energy, heat energy, and wave theory.

Part Four: Earth and Space Science covers the fundamentals of the Earth sciences and astronomy:

- In **Chapter 8: Earth Science**, you will learn about Earth's formation, oceans, and weather.

- In **Chapter 9: Space Science**, you will learn about the objects in the universe, including the Sun, the moon, the planets, and other celestial bodies.

In addition, *Contemporary's Pre-GED Science* has a number of features designed to familiarize you with and prepare you for the GED Test:

- **Pre-GED Practice** exercises appear at the end of every major section to test your knowledge of key concepts as you answer items in GED-format. The Pre-GED Practice at the end of each chapter serves as a review of the skills you have learned.

- **Thinking About Science Exercises** appear immediately after a concept to test your understanding of what you have just read.

- The **Answer Key** gives answers and explanations for all the questions in this book. Use the Answer Key only after you have attempted to answer a set of questions in an exercise.

- The **Glossary** contains a list of key terms found throughout the book.

- The **Index** provides easy access to important terms and concepts.

After you have worked through the book, you should take the **Posttest**. The Posttest will help you to see how well you have learned the skills presented in this book. The Posttest consists of 50 questions—the same amount that will appear on the GED Science Test.

Reading Efficiency Activities

This book contains **Reading Efficiency Activities** to help you practice reading speed and accuracy in order to achieve an optimum reading efficiency level. When you take the GED Test, you will be limited to a certain amount of time for each exam and must receive a minimum passing score to obtain your GED certificate. Because of this, it is important that you read at an acceptable rate while comprehending what you read. The Reading Efficiency Activities provide you with the tools to practice those skills and chart your progress.

There are twelve Reading Efficiency Activities in this book. Each activivty corresponds to one of the interdisciplinary content standards. You can identify the standard by the icon at the upper left corner of the page:

 Unifying Concepts and Processes   Science as Inquiry

 Science and Technology   History and Nature of Science

 Science in Personal and Social Perspectives

For each activity, you should time yourself as you read a 200 to 400-word passage and answer the 5 questions that follow. When you finish, you should record the time it took you to complete the activity and check your answers using the answer key provided in the back of the book.

Efficiency Factor (E-Factor) Chart

Once you complete a Reading Efficiency Activity, you can determine your Efficiency Factor (E-Factor) by using the E-Factor Chart on page 320. This chart provides a quick and easy way for you to determine your level of efficiency for each activity. The E-Factor takes into account an optimum reading rate and score for success on the actual GED Test. By locating your completion time on the vertical axis and your score on the horizontal axis, you can quickly determine your E-Factor. You should aim to achieve an optimum E-Factor of 100 or higher. The optimum range is located in the shaded areas of the chart.

Efficiency Factor Plotting Grid

Once you have located your E-Factor on the chart, you should plot it on the Efficiency Factor Grid on page 321. Possible E-Factor scores are listed on the vertical axis with each activity listed across the horizontal axis. Every point above 100 is shaded so you can instantly see when you have achieved an optimum E-Factor. As each Reading Efficiency Activity is completed and plotted, you can connect the dots to create a graph of your progress.

Good luck with your studies! Keep in mind that an understanding of science fundamentals will help you understand many practical aspects of daily life.

Acknowledgments

Photo on page 76: © NASA

Photo on page 77: © Lester V. Bergman/CORBIS

Photo on page 263: © Ecoscene/CORBIS

Photo on page 278: © NASA

The Pretest that follows is a guide to using this book. Its purpose is to help you determine which skills you need to develop as you prepare for the GED Science Test. You should take the Pretest before you begin working on any of the chapters.

Directions: Choose the <u>one best answer</u> to each question. The questions are based on reading passages, charts, graphs, and maps. Answer each question as carefully as possible. If a question seems to be too difficult, do not spend too much time on it. Work ahead and come back to it later when you can think it through carefully.

Pretest Answer Grid

1	① ② ③ ④ ⑤					10	① ② ③ ④ ⑤					19	① ② ③ ④ ⑤
2	① ② ③ ④ ⑤					11	① ② ③ ④ ⑤					20	① ② ③ ④ ⑤
3	① ② ③ ④ ⑤					12	① ② ③ ④ ⑤					21	① ② ③ ④ ⑤
4	① ② ③ ④ ⑤					13	① ② ③ ④ ⑤					22	① ② ③ ④ ⑤
5	① ② ③ ④ ⑤					14	① ② ③ ④ ⑤					23	① ② ③ ④ ⑤
6	① ② ③ ④ ⑤					15	① ② ③ ④ ⑤					24	① ② ③ ④ ⑤
7	① ② ③ ④ ⑤					16	① ② ③ ④ ⑤					25	① ② ③ ④ ⑤
8	① ② ③ ④ ⑤					17	① ② ③ ④ ⑤						
9	① ② ③ ④ ⑤					18	① ② ③ ④ ⑤						

When you have completed the test, check your work with the answers and explanations on page 10. Use the evaluation chart on page 11 to determine which areas you need to study the most.

Question 1 is based on the following illustration.

Nutrition Facts	Amount/serving	%DV*	Amount/serving	%DV*
Serving Size 1 Bag	**Total Fat** 10g	**15%**	**Total Carb.** 34g	**11%**
Calories 230	Sat. Fat 6g	**30%**	Fiber 1g	**4%**
Fat Calories 90	**Cholest.** 10mg	**3%**	Sugars 31g	
*Percent Daily Values (DV) are based on a 2,000 calorie diet.	**Sodium** 35mg	**1%**	**Protein** 2g	
	Vitamin A**	Vitamin C**	Calcium 4%	Iron 2%
	**Contains less than 2 percent of the Daily Value of these nutrients.			

1. The illustration above shows nutrition facts from a typical chocolate candy. What is the approximate number of calories in a gram of fat?

   (1) 90 calories
   (2) 10 calories
   (3) 9 calories
   (4) 6 calories
   (5) 1 calorie

2. Scientists compare fossil bones to trace how different animals have developed over time. For example, fossil bones of horses have been found in rock layers that were laid down tens of thousands of years ago. These fossil bones are quite different from the bones of modern horses. Scientists have found that ancient horses were about the size of modern-day sheep.

   Which statement is <u>not</u> supported by the information above?

   (1) The bones of ancient horses are smaller than bones of modern horses.
   (2) Over thousands of years, horses have changed in size.
   (3) Horses developed during the last days of the dinosaurs.
   (4) Scientists have found fossils of ancient horses.
   (5) Ancient horses and modern horses have both similarities and differences.

3. People used to think that the Sun went around Earth once a day. That idea probably came from observing the Sun appear low in the eastern sky each morning, traveling across the sky from east to west, and then disappearing low in the western sky each night. Copernicus, however, convinced people that Earth was the moving object. He explained that Earth spins as if it were a child's top. The turning makes it seem as if the Sun is moving across the sky.

   Which of the following ideas is supported by the passage?

   (1) The Sun travels across the daytime sky.
   (2) The Sun rises in the morning.
   (3) The Sun sets in the evening.
   (4) The Sun seems to move only because Earth moves.
   (5) The Sun goes around Earth one time each day.

PRETEST

Question 4 refers to the following diagram.

CLIFF

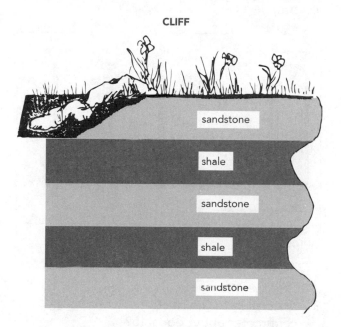

4. The naturally formed cliff shown in the diagram above has alternating layers of sandstone and shale. Which of the following is a reasonable conclusion?

   (1) The layers of shale are older than the sandstone.
   (2) Shale erodes more easily than sandstone.
   (3) The alternating layers indicate intense volcanic activity.
   (4) The layers have undergone tremendous pressures.
   (5) The area was once covered by glaciers.

5. Before people began to worry about the environment and ecology, Rachel Carson wrote a book called *Silent Spring.* The book describes how some chemicals, such as DDT, were being used to protect crops from insects.

   Unfortunately, the chemicals were killing more than bugs. They were also killing birds and other small animals. Chemical companies and the government had declared that these chemicals were safe to use. When people started reading *Silent Spring,* however, the most dangerous chemicals were reexamined and banned from use in this country.

   According to this passage, what does *Silent Spring* describe?

   (1) Rachel Carson's love of nature
   (2) how certain chemicals were harming the environment
   (3) how chemical companies lied to farmers
   (4) how to ban dangerous chemicals
   (5) why robins would no longer sing

6. In the United States, air masses generally move from west to east, creating what are known as prevailing winds.

   In this passage, what does *prevailing* mean?

   (1) moving from west to east
   (2) the most common
   (3) strong
   (4) weak
   (5) changing

Question 7 is based on the following illustration.

PROPANE

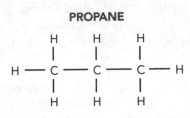

7. The formula illustration represents one molecule of the gas called *propane*.

   Which of the following shows the chemical formula for propane?

   (1) CH
   (2) $8C_3H$
   (3) $3C_8H$
   (4) C_3H_8
   (5) C_8H_3

Questions 8 and 9 refer to the following illustration.

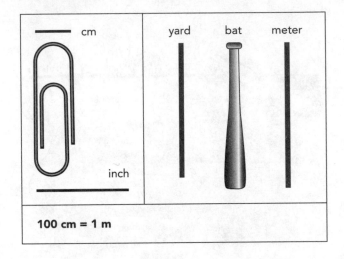

100 cm = 1 m

8. According to the illustration, what is a centimeter about equal to?

   (1) the width of a paper clip
   (2) the length of a baseball bat
   (3) an inch
   (4) a yard
   (5) the length of a paper clip

9. According to the illustration, which of the following is true for a meter?

   A. A meter is about equal to the length of a bat.
   B. A meter is longer than a yard.
   C. A meter is 100 times longer than a centimeter.

   (1) A only
   (2) B only
   (3) C only
   (4) A and B only
   (5) A, B, and C

Questions 10–12 refer to the following passage.

The environment affects the way a plant grows, its rate of growth, its size, and its ability to reproduce. All plants need water, light, a suitable climate, and minerals from the soil to live. Not all plants, however, require exactly the same growing conditions. Some plants, for example, grow best in full sunlight. Others do well in the shade. Some plants require lots of water; others less.

One environmental factor that affects a plant's growth is called *photoperiodism.* A photoperiod is a recurring cycle of light and dark. Some plants, called long-day plants, bloom only if the period of daylight is long. Lettuce is such a plant. Other plants, such as poinsettias and chrysanthemums, are short-day plants. They require a long dark period. Still others, such as marigolds, are day-neutral. They thrive during either long or short days.

Some plants respond to specific factors in their environment by bending. This behavior is called *tropism.* Tropism takes many forms. Response to water is called *hydrotropism.* Response to light is called *phototropism.* Response to Earth's gravity is called *geotropism.* A plant shows positive phototropism if its leaves and stems tend to grow toward the light. Positive geotropism occurs when a plant's roots grow downward toward Earth's center of gravity. When a potted plant is placed on its side, the stem will turn upward within three hours, turning away from the force of gravity. This is negative geotropism.

10. What is the growth of plant roots down toward the center of Earth called?

   (1) hydrotropism
   (2) negative geotropism
   (3) positive geotropism
   (4) negative phototropism
   (5) positive phototropism

11. How will stems and branches that are negatively phototropic react?

   (1) They will grow toward the center of Earth.
   (2) They will attract light.
   (3) They will grow away from a primary light source.
   (4) They will grow best in direct sunlight.
   (5) They can absorb large quantities of water.

12. What does the passage suggest that almost all plant roots would show?

   (1) positive hydrotropism
   (2) negative hydrotropism
   (3) negative geotropism
   (4) positive geotropism
   (5) both positive hydrotropism and geotropism

Question 13 refers to the following illustration.

OBJECT SUSPENDED BY ROPES

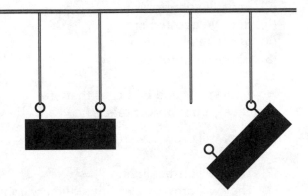

13. One of the objects in the diagram is suspended from the ceiling by two ropes. If one of the ropes is removed so that the object is suspended by only one rope, which of the following will be true?

   (1) The remaining rope bears the same load as it did before the other rope was removed.
   (2) The load on the remaining rope is 50 percent.
   (3) The remaining rope bears twice the load that it did before the other rope was removed.
   (4) The load on the remaining rope is increased by at least 400 percent.
   (5) The load on the remaining rope is reduced by 50 percent.

Questions 14–16 refer to the following passage.

After many years of educating the public on the dangers of cigarette smoking, health advocates seem to have won the battle. Most Americans now realize that smoking can seriously damage their lungs and can greatly increase their chances of getting lung cancer. Only a few people, however, realize that smoking damages the lungs by enlarging the alveoli. As a result, there are fewer places for oxygen to pass from the lungs and into the blood. The lack of oxygen can make the smoker become more easily winded and can decrease the body's ability to fight off diseases such as pneumonia.

14. According to the passage, how does smoking damage the lungs?

   (1) by increasing the oxygen flow
   (2) by decreasing the oxygen flow
   (3) by blackening them
   (4) by enlarging the alveoli
   (5) by shrinking the alveoli

15. According to the passage, what do smokers greatly increase their chances of getting?

   A. lung disease
   B. pneumonia
   C. winded more easily

   (1) A only
   (2) B only
   (3) C only
   (4) A, B, and C
   (5) A and C only

16. According to the passage, which of the following describes how many health advocates feel?

   (1) They feel they're losing the war against smoking.
   (2) They feel they're reaching only a few smokers.
   (3) They feel they're reaching about half of the smokers.
   (4) They feel they're reaching most of the smokers.
   (5) They feel they're winning the war against smoking.

Questions 17–19 refer to the following passage.

Cancer is the term used to describe a group of diseases in which there is an uncontrolled growth of abnormal cells. Masses of these abnormal cells are called tumors. One in six deaths in the United States is caused by cancer, and the number is increasing as people live longer lives. For men, the leading types of cancer are cancers of the lung, prostate, and colon. For women, the leading types of cancer are cancers of the breast, colon, and uterus.

Although scientists have not found out why cancer develops, they have discovered that certain substances play a critical role in causing this disease. For example, tars in tobacco smoke can contribute to lung cancer. Diets that are high in fat can contribute to cancer of the colon. Prolonged exposure to the ultraviolet rays of the Sun can contribute to skin cancer. In addition, hundreds of chemicals have been found to cause cancer. Some of these chemicals have entered our food supply as food additives.

Cancer may be cured by removing or destroying the cancerous growth. Currently, surgery, radiation treatment, and chemotherapy are used to destroy cancer cells. Scientists are also developing several new treatments that may prove to be effective as cancer cures: the use of interferon, heat therapy, and nutrition counseling.

17. Which of the following is <u>not</u> mentioned as a possible cause of cancer?

(1) chemicals in food
(2) tar in tobacco smoke
(3) diets high in fat
(4) exposure to the Sun's ultraviolet rays
(5) air pollution

18. According to the passage, which of the following has been associated with cancer of the colon?

(1) diets high in fat
(2) tars in tobacco smoke
(3) exposure to asbestos
(4) food additives
(5) exposure to ultraviolet rays

19. Which of the following best represents the author's opinion about the increasing number of cancer-related deaths?

(1) The FDA has been lax in notifying the public of possible carcinogenic substances.
(2) The number of chemical additives in our food is increasing.
(3) As people live longer, they are exposed to more cancer-causing agents.
(4) Since more and more people smoke, the incidence of lung cancer has increased.
(5) More cancer patients are using "quack" cures that only aggravate their conditions and postpone proper treatment.

Questions 20–22 refer to the following passage.

When ocean water is heated by the Sun, water from the surface evaporates and becomes an invisible gas known as water vapor, which mixes with the air. As the air moves in currents or winds, the air rises and is cooled.

Cooling decreases the air's ability to hold water. At a certain temperature, known as the dew point, the air cannot hold any more water vapor. Water droplets form. When these become too heavy, gravity takes over, and the particles fall from clouds as rain or snow.

Part of the water that reaches the ground is used by plants and evaporates without ever reaching the sea. Some of the water runs directly into streams. Some water sinks to the level of saturated ground. This groundwater and the streams it feeds eventually flow back to the ocean to complete the water cycle.

20. Which of they following is a probable effect of insufficient rainfall?

(1) Streams overflow.
(2) Evaporation doesn't take place.
(3) The air becomes saturated.
(4) The ground does not become saturated enough to feed streams.
(5) Plants continue to release water vapor as usual.

21. Which of the following pairs of terms have the same meaning?

(1) dew point and temperature
(2) evaporated water and water vapor
(3) cloud and particle
(4) evaporation and condensation
(5) precipitation and infiltration

22. What is the main idea of this passage?

(1) Water travels in an endless cycle of evaporation and condensation.
(2) Clouds are formed when air is saturated and can hold no more water vapor.
(3) Oceans are fed through rivers and streams.
(4) Water condenses when saturated air is cooled to the dew point.
(5) Plants give off water vapor in a process called photosynthesis.

PRETEST

Questions 23–25 refer to the following passage.

Have you ever wondered how a photograph is made? What actually happens when you push the camera's button to record an image? When you push the button, the shutter opens, allowing light to strike the film in the camera. The film is usually coated with silver bromide. The light rays strike the film and reduce the silver bromide, making it less stable. The chemical reaction looks like this:

$$AgBr \xrightarrow{\text{light}} Ag + Br$$

silver bromide   silver   bromine

In black-and-white film, the silver bromide particles that are struck by light turn black when the film is developed. Particles that have not been struck by light will not change in the developer. Since the chemical reduction depends on the intensity of the light, the film becomes a detailed "chemical picture" of the object being photographed. The developing process converts the "chemical picture" into film negatives.

23. What serves as the agent in reducing silver bromide to silver and bromine?

   (1) the camera's shutter
   (2) the lens on the camera
   (3) film
   (4) developer
   (5) light

24. What could you conclude if a negative turned out to be completely black?

   (1) The silver and bromine had been resynthesized into silver bromide.
   (2) The light rays were not strong enough to reduce the silver bromide.
   (3) The film had not been developed.
   (4) The film was underexposed to light.
   (5) The film was overexposed to light.

25. Which of the following would be a good title for this passage?

   (1) "How to Take Pictures"
   (2) "Silver Bromide"
   (3) "The Chemistry of Photography"
   (4) "How to Develop Film"
   (5) "Light and Shadows"

Answers are on page 10.

PRETEST

Answer Key

1. (3) The total calories from fat (90) divided by the total grams of fat (10) equals 9 calories per gram.

2. (3) No mention is made of dinosaurs. Also, the passage states that the horse fossils are tens of thousands of years old. Dinosaurs became extinct 65 million years ago.

3. (4) All the other responses are observations that only seem correct because of Earth's movement.

4. (2) From the diagram, you can conclude that the portions of the cliff that are made of shale have eroded more than the portions made of sandstone. The remaining choices may be correct but cannot be supported by the diagram.

5. (2) Although the other choices are logical topics for *Silent Spring,* this is the only choice actually mentioned in the passage.

6. (2) The key is the word *generally,* which means most common.

7. (4) The diagram shows three atoms of carbon and eight of hydrogen. The correct way to write this is C_3H_8.

8. (1) A comparison of the measures and the objects should show that the paper clip is about 1 cm wide.

9. (5) According to the illustration, the first three choices are all correct.

10. (3) Positive geotropism is defined in the third paragraph.

11. (3) Positive phototropism is described as growing toward a light source. By applying this idea, you can conclude that negative phototropism means growing away from the light.

12. (5) From the passage, you can conclude that tree roots would grow toward the source of water and toward Earth's center.

13. (3) With two ropes attached, each rope bears half the load. If one of the ropes is removed, the other rope must support the entire load (if it is to stay up). This means the remaining rope must support twice the load that it supported when it shared the load with the other rope.

14. (4) The passage states that smoking damages the lungs by enlarging the alveoli.

15. (4) All three effects are mentioned in the passage.

16. (5) The first sentence states that health advocates "seem to have won the battle."

17. (5) In the second paragraph choices, (1), (2), (3), and (4) are mentioned as factors in causing cancer.

18. (1) The fact that colon cancer is associated with diets high in fat is given in the second paragraph.

19. (3) The link between longer lives and the increased cancer death rate is mentioned in the first paragraph.

20. (4) You can conclude that when there is insufficient rainfall, the groundwater will not be sufficient to feed the streams.

21. (2) The passage used evaporation and water vapor to refer to the same process.

22. (1) While choices (2), (3), and (4) are all true, they are too specific to be the main idea. Choice (5) is not discussed.

23. (5) The formula shows that silver bromide, when exposed to light, is reduced to silver and bromine.

24. (5) The last paragraph states that reduced particles of silver bromide turn black when film is developed. If a negative is completely black, then all of the silver bromide must have been reduced by light, indicating exposure to too much light, or overexposure.

25. (3) "The Chemistry of Photography" is the only title that summarizes this passage. The other titles concern a specific topic discussed in the passage.

Evaluation Chart

Theme Subject Area	Fundamental Understandings	Unifying Concepts and Processes (pages 15–30)	Science as Inquiry (pages 31–70)
Life Science (pages 73–172)	7 questions 1, 10, 12, 14, 15 16, 18	2 questions 2, 11	2 questions 17, 19
Physical Science (pages 175–236)	3 questions 7, 13, 25	3 questions 8, 9, 23	1 question 24
Earth and Space Science (pages 239–283)	3 questions 4, 6, 21	2 questions 20, 22	2 questions 3, 5

Themes in Science

- **Concepts and Processes in Science**
- **Comprehending and Applying Science**
- **Analyzing and Evaluating Science**

CHAPTER 1

Concepts and Processes in Science

What is the biggest science classroom in the world? The answer may surprise you. The biggest classroom in which we learn science is the world itself. The world is a place of amazing discoveries. Human beings have long asked questions about the things they see around them. Such questioning has led to discoveries about planet Earth and the forms of life that inhabit it. These questions have also led to findings about the solar system and the universe as a whole.

Questioning, however, is only one part of a whole process that leads to scientific discovery. That process involves the use of the following methods of science:

- **Observing**—noticing things around you and thinking about what you see.

- **Identifying**—asking a question about what you have seen and proposing a possible explanation for it.

- **Describing**—determining what you already know about the subject and researching more information about it.

- **Experimenting**—testing your explanation using orderly steps.

- **Explaining**—gathering results from your experiment and drawing conclusions from them.

- **Communicating**—sharing your experimental results and conclusion with others.

These are the methods that scientists use to explain the things that they observe and the things that are most important to them. These methods help scientists to understand our home here on Earth and to take care of it. These methods help scientists to find answers to our most serious challenges.

Try making the scientific methods a part of your own daily life. You will be amazed at the countless things you will learn about the world in which we live.

Systems, Order, and Organization

The world is too large and complex for us to investigate and comprehend all at once. "Start small" is what that scientists keep in mind as they begin their investigations. Scientists start small by defining small units for investigation. Then they look for similarities that may link the units together.

Systems

Scientists study small units of investigation to gain a better understanding of a larger concept. Each unit of investigation is called a **system.** A system is an organized group of related objects or components that form a whole.

- A system can be an entire living thing, such as the human body. A system can also be a part of a living thing, such as the digestive system, the circulatory system, or the nervous system.

- A system can be the whole Earth. It can also be a part of Earth, such as a river valley or a mountain range.

- A system can include things that we can see and things that we cannot see with our eyes. Our solar system, for example, consists of the Sun, Earth, the Moon, and the other eight planets and other objects that revolve around the Sun.

- A system can be made of things that people have designed, such as a computer system. Parts of the computer system may include a computer, a monitor, a keyboard, a printer, speakers, and a modem.

Systems usually cannot function independently. The well-being of one system often involves the other systems. For example, if you have trouble breathing, your respiratory system is not healthy. The unhealthy respiratory system is likely to cause problems with the other systems in your body.

Order

Through experience we learn that our world has **order**, or properties and behavior that are predictable. For example, our experience tells us that the Sun rises and sets every day. We expect to enjoy more hours of daylight in summer than in winter. We know that an ice cube left at room temperature will melt. We understand that anything we toss up into the air will fall back to the ground.

Order reassures us about our world and gives meaning to our lives. It helps us to structure our time. It gives us things that we can rely on. Because of order, we can predict whether events will or will not occur.

In science, order gives scientists the benefit of knowing that experiments done today in a laboratory will give the same results if they are done at another time in another place. Order lets scientists know that they can trust these results and use them to better understand and help human life on Earth. Order leads to scientific progress that, in turn, leads to technological and cultural advances.

Organization

How do we make sense of the countless facts about our world? To make the study of our world easier, scientists depend on **organization**. One type of organization involves classifying, or organizing, systems to better show their similarities and differences. Scientists have noticed, for example, that some organisms move from place to place and obtain food from outside sources. Scientists have organized these living things in a group called *animals*. Similarly, scientists have noticed that other organisms grow in one place and make their own food. Scientists have organized these living things in a group called *plants*.

The following are other examples of organization by classification:

- Stars are classified into groups according to their color, size, shape, age, and composition.
- Galaxies are classified according to their shape.
- Elements are classified by their number of electrons.
- Organisms are classified by their structure and function.
- Tissues are classified by the type of cells they contain.

Another type of organization results from arranging both living and nonliving things into groups in which they seem to fit naturally.

- A galaxy is a large group of stars.
- The periodic table is made up of all the elements.
- Molecules are made up of atoms.
- Atoms consist of electrons surrounding a central nucleus that contains protons and neutrons.
- The human brain contains many types of tissues.
- A tissue is a group of cells.

Thinking About Science

Directions: Answer each question below.

1. What are the six methods of science?

   OBSERVING, IDENTIF

2. How do scientists "start small" with their investigations?

   SYSTEM

3. In what way does our world have order?

4. What is the term for grouping things based on their similarities and differences?

Answers are on page 303.

PRE-GED PRACTICE

Directions: Choose the <u>one best answer</u> to each question.

Questions 1 and 2 refer to the information on pages 15–17.

1. Which of the following statements about systems is <u>not</u> true?

   (1) A system can be a whole organism made of related parts.
   (2) All systems are organized in the same way.
   (3) A system can be a part of a whole organism.
   (4) A system can include things we can see and things we cannot see.
   (5) A group of related systems are usually interconnected.

2. Which of the following statements best explains how sorting the mail is like scientific organization?

   (1) Mail sorting is based on the time of day in which it is deposited at the post office.
   (2) Mail sorting is based on the color, size, shape, and age of the letters.
   (3) Mail sorting is based on the type of stamp pasted on the upper right corner of the letters.
   (4) Mail sorting is based on the number of post offices the letters pass through.
   (5) Mail sorting is based on similarities and differences in country, state, town, street number, house number, last name, and first name.

Answers are on page 303.

Evidence, Models, and Explanation

Evidence

Scientists base their explanations on **evidence**—the observations and data from experiments. For example, a scientist may believe that heat causes air to expand. What a scientist believes to be true, however, is not a scientific fact. The scientist must base his or her belief on evidence. To obtain evidence, the scientist attaches a balloon over the top of a glass flask and then warms the flask on a burner. If the balloon inflates, the scientist has evidence to support his or her belief. It is this evidence, not the scientist's belief, that is important in scientific investigation.

Models

Scientists often use a **model** to help clarify an explanation. A model is a drawing, a physical object, or a plan that stands for a real thing. A model can help us to picture the way something works. To develop a model, scientists first observe the real thing. Then, they test the model by comparing it with the real thing.

Many computer programs are models of events or situations that are too costly or dangerous to experience firsthand. For example, some computer programs simulate the flight of an airplane. The software allows users to experience what it is like to fly an airplane without the fear of crashing an actual plane.

Architects develop blueprints, or plans, of their ideas for future buildings. Blueprints are models that help prospective homebuyers, for example, to see the layout of a house before they buy it. Blueprints also guide builders, plumbers, and electricians as they construct the house.

Scientists use models to illustrate written explanations. Notice how the illustration helps to clarify the following explanation.

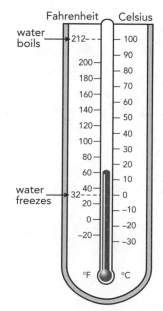

Two different scales can be used to measure temperature. In the United States, we are most familiar with the Fahrenheit scale (°F). On that scale, water freezes at 32°F and boils at 212°F. The Celsius scale is used throughout the rest of the world and in more and more places in the United States. On the Celsius scale, water freezes at 0°C and boils at 100°C.

Explanation

Scientific **explanations** are consistent, logical statements. Explanations include existing scientific facts and new evidence from observation, experiments, and models. Scientists must be careful in their explanations to distinguish among facts, hypotheses, and opinions.

- A **fact** is a conclusion, based on evidence, that scientists agree on. For example, it is a scientific fact, based on fossil evidence, that woolly mammoths once roamed the land in New York State.

- A **hypothesis** is a reasonable explanation of evidence or a prediction based on evidence. Because woolly mammoths were animals well suited for life in a bitterly cold climate, some scientists hypothesize that the climate in New York State once was bitterly cold.

- An **opinion** is a personal belief that is often based on a person's own value system. A person may have the opinion, for example, that the study of Earth's history is a waste of time, resources, and money.

Thinking About Science

Directions: Write *F*, *H*, or *O* on the line preceding each statement below to classify the statement as a fact, hypothesis, or opinion.

_____ **1.** Most scientists believe that the universe is expanding.

_____ **2.** A frog obtains oxygen through its moist skin.

_____ **3.** Many people fear that genetically modified foods will harm the environment and humans.

_____ **4.** Environmentalists say that "environmentally sensitive exploration" in Alaska's Arctic National Wildlife Refuge is laughable.

_____ **5.** Sound travels through air as a compression wave.

Answers are on page 303.

Directions: Choose the <u>one best answer</u> to each question.

Questions 1–3 refer to the information on pages 19–20.

1. A scientist believes that a substance contains sodium chloride (salt). Which of the following would <u>not</u> be evidence to support this belief?

   A. The scientist tastes the substance and it has a salty flavor.
   B. The scientist lets the substance evaporate and discovers tiny crystals of salt at the bottom of the container.
   C. The scientist notices that the substance looks cloudy as if it contained a lot of salt.

   (1) A only
   (2) B only
   (3) C only
   (4) A and B only
   (5) A, B, and C

2. Which of the following is an example of a model?

   (1) a clock
   (2) a video game
   (3) a virtual reality ride
   (4) a lightbulb
   (5) a car

3. A scientist states that by 2010, every person in the United States will have a genetic clone that can be used for lifesaving organ transplants, blood donations, and so on.

   Which of the following best describes this statement?

   (1) a hypothesis
   (2) an opinion
   (3) an explanation
   (4) a fact
   (5) a model

   Answers are on page 303.

Change, Constancy, and Measurement

Change

Some things in the world around us are always changing. Plants and animals grow, for example. Our seasons progress from winter to spring to summer and to fall. Long summer days change into short winter days. The weather changes from sunshine and warm temperatures to cloudy days and cool temperatures. Change is even a property of simple activities, such as bouncing a basketball.

Bouncing a Basketball	
Things That Are Changing	**Things That Are Not Changing**
speed of the ball	shape of the ball
position of the ball on the court	weight of the ball
dust on the ball	material the ball is made from
temperature of the ball	air contained in the ball

Scientists study change to understand why and when it occurs. Some changes, like the bounced basketball, occur only once unless the ball is bounced again. Other changes occur in cycles, happening again and again without human intervention. Scientists examine cyclical changes such as the following:

- Daily changes, including the sunrise and sunset on a predictable time schedule

- Seasonal changes, including mostly hot, dry days in summer and wet, cold days in winter

- Yearly changes, including the migration of butterflies and sea turtles

Constancy

Some events in our world remain constant. **Constancy** is the tendency for things to remain unchanged. Scientists study the constancy of things and events and ask questions. Why, for example, does a bounced basketball maintain its shape and weight? Why doesn't the material from which the ball is made change? Why doesn't the air inside the ball change?

Scientists are very interested in things that remain constant.

- A **law of nature** is a property of nature that does not change. Laws of nature are discovered, not invented, and can often be written as mathematical formulas. The law of gravity, for example, is a law of nature. The law of gravity states that all objects are pulled toward each other by a force that is related to the mass of the objects and to the distance between them. The greater the mass, the greater the pull of gravity toward that mass. The greater the distance between objects, the weaker the pull of gravity.

No one knows for sure why gravity pulls objects to Earth's surface. Experience tells us, however, that gravity exists and that it does not change. Scientists believe that the law of gravity is constant and is the same for all objects in the universe.

- A **biological process** is a fundamental property that is common to all living organisms. One example of a biological process is the property that living things pass on their traits to their offspring through genes. Physical traits, such as body shape and hair color, and behavioral patterns, such as shyness and intelligence, can be passed from one generation to the next.

- A **law of chance** describes the probability of something happening. When a weather forecaster predicts a 40 percent chance of rain, the forecaster bases his or her prediction on such factors as wind patterns, humidity, dew point, and atmospheric pressure. A 40 percent probability of rain means that on four out of ten days in the past, when the measurable conditions were the same as on the day of the prediction, rain has occurred. The insurance industry also determines premium rates based on the laws of chance.

Constancy gives us order in a world of change. This order exists because most changes can be understood and fairly well predicted.

Measurement

We use **measurement** to express an amount of change. For example, you might weigh yourself every day to compare today's weight with your weight on the previous day. A measurement usually has two parts: a number and a unit. A unit of measurement does not change. It is a fixed amount used by all who measure, regardless of their location in the world and time at which they measure. For example, 10°C is the same measure of temperature in Chicago as it is in Japan. Also, 10°C is the same measure of temperature today as it was twenty years ago. The fact that units of measurement don't change is an example of order.

Scientists use measurement to express the amount of change in a system. Today, the United States uses two systems of measurement: the more familiar U.S. customary system and the metric system. Canada and most other industrialized nations of the world use the metric system.

- Familiar units in the U.S. customary systems are inches, feet, yards, miles, fluid ounces, cups, quarts, gallons, pounds, and tons.

- Familiar units in the metric system are centimeters, meters, kilometers, milliliters, liters, grams, and kilograms.

Thinking About Science

Directions: For each action described below, mention two things that change and two things that remain constant.

1. A bicycle tire goes flat.

   a. Change: _____

   b. Remain constant: _____

2. An ice cube in a glass on a counter slowly melts.

   a. Change: _____

   b. Remain constant: _____

Answers are on page 303.

PRE-GED PRACTICE

Directions: Choose the <u>one best answer</u> to each question.

Questions 1 and 2 refer to the information on pages 22–23.

1. Which of the following would be classified as a cyclical change?

   (1) the growth of hair
   (2) the melting of snow
   (3) a tornado
   (4) the changing of tides
   (5) the cheers of a crowd

2. Which of the following best explains why scientists are very interested in things that remain constant?

   (1) Constancy enables scientists to base predictions on scientific facts.
   (2) Constancy helps scientists to guarantee that one generation's traits will be passed on to future generations.
   (3) Constancy lets scientists write laws as mathematical formulas.
   (4) Constancy proves that all objects have gravity.
   (5) Constancy verifies that weather forecasting is a science.

Answers are on page 303.

Evolution and Equilibrium

Evolution

Think about the many breeds and mixed-breeds of dogs in the world. All of these domestic dogs are related to one another. Scientists believe that domestic dogs are descended from a wolflike animal that lived several million years ago. The genetic changes that have produced differences in dogs have taken place over a long period of time. The changes that have taken place in dogs over the years are one example of evolution.

Evolution is a series of changes that occur over time. Evolution can refer to changes taking place in organisms on Earth, on Earth itself, or in the universe as a whole.

- Organisms evolve, or change, over time in response to changes in their natural environment. Scientists believe that organisms evolve in order to increase their chances for survival. According to the modern theory of evolution, many different types of organisms evolved from common ancestors that existed long ago but do not exist today. Similarly, some species that are alive today will become extinct in the future, and new species will take their place.

- Earth evolves by such natural processes as earthquakes, volcanoes, and wind and water erosion. Scientists continue to make discoveries about Earth's evolution. One recent discovery has led scientists to warn us that our actions can affect air quality and possibly influence weather patterns and the evolution of Earth itself.

- The universe is slowly evolving as old stars die and new stars are born. Scientists are just beginning to learn about the complex nature of the universe and its forces.

Equilibrium

Equilibrium is a physical state in which forces and changes occur in opposite and offsetting directions. For example, when a rubber ball is thrown against a wall, the force of the ball hitting the wall is equal to the force that the wall exerts on the ball. You know that the wall exerts an equal and opposing force because the ball bounces off the wall with the same force as when it hit the wall. These two forces, equal in amount and opposite in direction, are said to be in equilibrium.

Chemicals also have equilibrium. When a system is made of various molecules, those molecules might combine in a chemical reaction. The finished reaction results in the formation of new chemicals. For some reason that scientists are not sure about, those new chemicals go through a reverse chemical reaction and become the original molecules. The chemicals are said to be in equilibrium because they are in a state of balance.

Thinking About Science

Directions: Answer each question below.

1. What does the statement "organisms evolve" mean?

   _____

2. What is equilibrium?

   _____

Answers are on page 303.

PRE-GED PRACTICE

Directions: Choose the <u>one best answer</u> to each question.

Questions 1 and 2 refer to the information on page 25.

1. Which of the following is <u>not</u> an example of evolution?

   (1) the warming of Earth
   (2) horses
   (3) continental drift
   (4) cloud formations
   (5) the expanding universe

2. Which of the following explains the state of equilibrium?

   A. Equilibrium occurs in opposite directions.
   B. The forces or changes in equilibrium occur in equal amounts.
   C. All molecules are in a state of equilibrium.

   (1) A only
   (2) B only
   (3) C only
   (4) both A and B
   (5) both B and C

Answers are on page 303.

Form and Function

In the natural world, there is a strong relationship between the **form**, or physical characteristics, of an organism and the **function**, or purpose, served by that form.

- A porpoise is shaped in a way that allows it to swim through water very quickly.

- An eagle has large wings that enable it to glide high above land, searching for prey below.

- A cactus has a stem and branches that are thick and juicy, enabling the plant to survive in the hot, dry desert.

Organisms that are closely related may have slight differences. Closely related animals, such as species of butterflies, may have slightly different body structures. The differing structures are most likely related to the special needs of each animal. The forms differ slightly to better serve slightly differing functions.

What is the main difference between the African elephant and the Asian elephant pictured below?

AFRICAN ELEPHANT　　　　　　　**ASIAN ELEPHANT**

The ears on the African elephant are much larger than those on the Asian elephant. Why is this so? The answer has to do with cooling. Both elephants have large ears that are used for cooling. Ear lobes are full of blood vessels and as an elephant flaps its ears, the blood within the lobes is cooled. The cooled blood circulates through the elephant and helps cool the whole animal.

The difference in ear size is related to the fact that the African elephant lives in a much hotter climate than the Asian elephant. The cooling needs of the African elephant are greater than those of the Asian elephant.

Some related animals have developed quite different uses for very similar body parts. The kiwi, like an eagle, is a bird. An eagle's wings are used for flying. The kiwi, however, is an odd-shaped bird with wings that are too small for flight. An eagle has a large, heavy hooked bill that it uses with its sharp talons to tear apart its prey. The kiwi's bill is long and slender, with nostrils near the tip. Kiwis do something that is very unusual for birds. They locate food by smell.

Learning from Nature

Our observations of nature can often help us to understand how form and function are best related. Then we can use that knowledge in technological designs. For example, consider the similarities in shape between whales and submarines. Also think about the similarities in shape between airplanes and birds. In the natural world, animals have evolved in a way that makes the best use of form and function. Humans, too, have learned to make the best use of form and function in the technological world.

Thinking About Science

Directions: Name a function served by each body part listed below.

1. The tail of a monkey:_____

2. The neck of a giraffe:_____

3. The bill of a pelican:_____

Answers are on page 303.

PRE-GED PRACTICE

Directions: Choose the one best answer to each question.

Questions 1 and 2 refer to the information on pages 27 and 28.

1. Which of the following closely related animals have a different form and function?

   (1) a Labrador retriever and a golden retriever
   (2) a chimpanzee and an orangutan
   (3) a dolphin and a porpoise
   (4) a penguin and a seagull
   (5) a field mouse and a deer mouse

2. Which of the following is true about form and function?

   (1) In nature there is a strong relationship between body shape and weight.
   (2) Related animals always have the same form and function.
   (3) Some physical characteristics of animals are based on the animals' needs.
   (4) Sometimes related animals have no form and function in common.
   (5) Scientists who study form and function in nature are wasting time and money.

   Answers are on page 303.

Concepts and Processes in Science Review

Directions: Choose the <u>one best answer</u> to each question.

Questions 1–6 refer to the information on pages 15–28.

1. Which of the following is <u>not</u> a system?

   (1) a frog
   (2) a galaxy
   (3) a water-purification plant
   (4) a one-dollar coin
   (5) a digestive tract

2. Which of the following does <u>not</u> demonstrate order?

   (1) a scale for weighing
   (2) a physical model
   (3) a rain shower
   (4) insurance rates
   (5) the periodic table of elements

3. Which of the following best explains why scientists depend on organization?

   (1) to make the study of our world easier
   (2) to clear their desks of piles of paper
   (3) to prove that organisms have structure and function
   (4) to group things together
   (5) to make use of the methods of science

4. What are the phases of the Moon an example of?

   A. Constancy
   B. Cyclical change
   C. The laws of chance

   (1) A only
   (2) B only
   (3) C only
   (4) both A and B
   (5) both B and C

5. What are a dark-colored moth and a light-colored moth an example of?

   (1) a state of equilibrium
   (2) a cyclical change
   (3) a biological process
   (4) a law of nature
   (5) an example of evolution

6. Green plants bend toward sunlight. What is this an example of?

   (1) a daily change
   (2) an opinion
   (3) a seasonal change
   (4) a hypothesis
   (5) a yearly change

Questions 7 and 8 refer to the following passage.

In 1938 the biochemist Alexander Oparin suggested that life began when energy from lightning and ultraviolet rays from the Sun combined gases in the early atmosphere into special compounds. The compounds, known as amino acids, fell into the hot seas. There they began to join into more and more complex compounds. Some eventually duplicated themselves. Others attached themselves to other chemicals and used those chemicals for energy. Oparin's suggestion was interesting, but obviously, it was not possible to go back to Earth's origins and test it.

Then in 1953, Stanley Miller broke Oparin's ideas into several more manageable hypotheses. He started devising ways to test these hypotheses in the laboratory. In one experiment, he mixed gases that were present in the early atmosphere and added an electric spark. He left this mixture in his laboratory for one week. When he returned, he found amino acids as well as other compounds that Oparin had predicted would have been formed on Earth at an earlier time.

7. Which of the following statements about Oparin's suggestion is <u>not</u> true?

   (1) He proved it to be a scientific fact.
   (2) His suggestion was a hypothesis.
   (3) He was unable to test it partly because he didn't "start small."
   (4) He was unable to test it partly because he couldn't go back and test something that occurred in history.
   (5) His suggestion was based on scientific facts that existed at the time.

8. Which of the following statements about Miller's experiments is <u>not</u> true?

   (1) He tested his hypotheses with experiments.
   (2) He proved that Oparin's ideas were correct.
   (3) He proved that life could have originated according to Oparin's suggestion.
   (4) He communicated his scientific explanation.
   (5) He used a model to recreate Oparin's suggestion.

Answers are on pages 303–304.

CHAPTER 2

Comprehending and Applying Science

Before scientists test an explanation through experimentation, they gather as much information about the subject as they can. Often they collect and read vast quantities of material written by other scientists. Scientists must think critically to comprehend, or understand, what they read. Thinking critically enables scientists to determine how the information they are reading applies to their investigation.

The GED Science Test will test your critical thinking skills in scientific inquiry. Two very important skills include being able to comprehend science materials and to apply science concepts. You will be tested on reading passages and graphics: drawings, diagrams, and graphs. In this chapter you will practice each of these skills.

Recognizing the Main Idea

A **main idea** can be found in almost everything you read. The main idea is important because it tells what the passage is about. The rest of the passage usually expands on the main idea. Quickly finding and understanding the main idea of a passage is a powerful reading skill. Your understanding of what you read depends greatly on this skill.

Many readers believe that the main idea of a passage is always stated in the first sentence of that passage. This belief is not correct. In fact, the main idea can appear anywhere within the passage. It can be the first sentence, the last sentence, or a sentence in the middle. Sometimes, the main idea may not be stated as a single sentence at all. Instead, you can usually state the main idea as a summary of several points made by the writer.

Every paragraph has a main idea. Usually, the main idea is stated at the beginning of the paragraph. The rest of the paragraph contains details that explain the main idea or prove the point that the main idea expresses.

The best way to be sure that you have found the main idea is to ask yourself: What is the passage about? What is the most important thing the author is saying?

Read the following paragraph. Underline the main idea of the passage. Remember that the main idea can occur anywhere in the passage.

(1) Living things bring about changes as they interact with the environment. (2) For example, when beavers dam a stream, many changes may occur. (3) Before long, land above the dam is flooded. (4) Trees, bushes, and other plant life that once grew in the flooded area die. (5) They are replaced by plants that are able to live in water.

Did you underline the first sentence? Notice that sentence 1 makes a general statement about living things causing changes in the environment. Sentences 2, 3, 4, and 5 give examples of some of those changes—floods, death of vegetation, and growth of new vegetation—that can occur when beavers dam a stream. In this passage, only the first sentence is general enough to include the ideas of the others, so sentence 1 states the main idea.

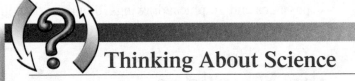

Thinking About Science

Part A

Directions: Find and underline the main idea in the passages below.

1.   (1) Did you know that parents catch most of their colds from their children? (2) Young children between two and six years old usually have twice as many colds as nine-year-old children. (3) Nine-year-olds generally have twice as many colds as twelve-year-olds. (4) Generally speaking, as we get older, we get fewer colds.

2.   (1) Cactuses are remarkable plants, made to live in one of nature's harshest environments. (2) In place of regular leaves, they have needles that also serve as a good defense against hungry animals. (3) Their stems are full of hollow cells that can store enough water to last for months. (4) They can survive the great heat of the desert sun at noon and the bitter cold of the desert night.

Part B

Directions: Read the passage below and put a check in front of the correct answer to each question that follows.

Woods Hole is a resort area in Massachusetts. Bicycling, swimming, and sailing are among the activities that visitors can enjoy.

A variety of scientists also gather at this vacation village. Their activities, however, do not include the usual sun-and-surf relaxation. Geologists dive to the ocean floor to examine underwater mountains and valleys. Oceanographers test the ocean currents. Biologists study the effects of ocean pollution and search for new sources of seafood. Chemists study oil spills and pollutants in the marine food cycle. They also study the chemical interactions among sea creatures.

1. What is the best title for this passage?

_____ **1.** "Mysteries of the Deep"

_____ **2.** "An Exciting Summer Vacation"

_____ **3.** "Hardworking Scientists"

_____ **4.** "Research Activities at Woods Hole"

_____ **5.** "A Massachusetts Vacation Spot"

2. Although Woods Hole is a summer resort, what does the passage emphasize about it?

_____ **1.** A great deal of significant scientific study goes on there.

_____ **2.** Too much scientific activity goes on there.

_____ **3.** People shouldn't vacation there because scientists are polluting the water.

_____ **4.** Many scientists escape from their work and go to Woods Hole.

_____ **5.** It is open year-round for scientific exploration.

Answers are on page 304.

Directions: Choose the <u>one best answer</u> to each question.

Questions 1–3 refer to the following passage.

Although most of our energy comes from Earth, our planet has a major rival. That rival is the Sun. The Sun offers many advantages over geothermal energy, energy from Earth. One advantage is that the Sun's energy is unlimited. A second advantage is that solar energy is pollution-free.

Already the Sun's energy has been used in a limited way. Solar cells that transform sunlight into electric current have been used in the space program. Some people use solar energy to heat and distill water, to cook food, and to heat their homes. Unfortunately, the devices used to accomplish these tasks are far too expensive for widespread use. If solar energy could be converted into electricity and stored on a large scale, however, a solution to our energy crisis would be within our grasp.

1. What is the purpose of this passage?

   (1) to descibe the advantages and uses of solar energy
   (2) to descibe the devices used to harness solar energy
   (3) to descibe the disadvantages of solar energy
   (4) to descibe how to convert solar energy into electricity
   (5) to descibe why geothermal energy is inadequate

2. Which of the following is the best title for the passage?

   (1) "Pollution-free Energy"
   (2) "The Sun"
   (3) "Unlimited Energy"
   (4) "Solar Energy for Tomorrow's Needs"
   (5) "The Disadvantages of Solar Energy"

3. Where is the main idea stated in this passage?

   (1) the first sentence of the first paragraph
   (2) the second sentence of the first paragraph
   (3) the third sentence of the first paragraph
   (4) the first sentence of the second paragraph
   (5) the last sentence of the second paragraph

Questions 4–6 refer to the following passage.

Smog is a type of air pollution that can be seen and felt. It hovers over our major cities. Smog irritates our lungs. It also burns our eyes and even blots out the sunlight. Smog occurs when the incomplete combustion of gasoline releases hydrocarbons and carbon monoxide (CO) into the atmosphere. The CO reduces the amount of oxygen supplied to the body's cells. This makes smog particularly dangerous to people who have heart or lung disease. Because everybody suffers from the health hazards of air pollution, there is an increasing emphasis on strong measures to protect the environment.

4. Which of the following is the main idea of this passage?

    (1) Air pollution can be seen in the smog over our cities.
    (2) Air pollution burns our eyes and irritates our lungs.
    (3) High levels of CO are dangerous to people who have heart and lung disease.
    (4) Air pollution is a health hazard.
    (5) We must protect our environment.

5. What does the passage suggest about the problem of air pollution?

    (1) Smog will continue to increase.
    (2) Government regulations may help us to preserve our environment.
    (3) It is not a serious health hazard.
    (4) It is especially dangerous to people who have heart or lung disease.
    (5) The situation will only get worse.

6. Where is the main idea expressed in this passage?

    (1) the opening sentence
    (2) the fourth sentence
    (3) the fifth sentence
    (4) the last sentence
    (5) not expressed at all

Answers are on page 304.

Finding Supporting Details

You have already learned that the main idea is supported by the details in a passage. When gathering information for an investigation, you may want to find some of these details. When you are looking for supporting details, you do not have to reread an entire paper or article in order to find them. Instead, you may scan the material.

To scan for a detail, run your eyes quickly over the passage. Look for the word or part that relates to your subject. With practice, scanning becomes easy, especially when the detail involves a number or a date.

Scan the following passage and look for supporting details.

> Scientists have been studying the harmful physical effects of long-term space travel. Muscles may atrophy, or waste away, as a result of prolonged weightlessness. Bones can lose 0.5 percent of their calcium each month. The fatigue from space flight causes sleep problems. Pulse rates have been found to increase because the heart shrinks by about 10 percent.

Check each supporting detail that is mentioned as an adverse effect of long-term space travel.

_____ **1.** sleep problems

_____ **2.** acute dizziness

_____ **3.** increased pulse rate

_____ **4.** bones lose calcium

_____ **5.** muscles atrophy

Did you check details 1, 3, 4, and 5 as adverse effects of space travel? Only detail 2, acute dizziness, was not mentioned in the passage.

To be sure that you have found ideas that support the main idea, ask yourself if the facts in the passage explain or illustrate the main idea. If they do, they are supporting details. If they don't, then they are not.

Thinking About Science

Part A

Directions: Read the following passage. In the space provided, briefly describe why climate affects the decay of stone.

Several factors influence the processes that break stone into smaller pieces of matter. Time is one important factor in determining the extent of decay. Climate is another important influence because stone decays faster in moist air than in dry air. Finally, stone that is buried beneath the soil decays more rapidly because acids work on it.

_____

_____

_____

_____

Part B

Directions: Read the following passage and complete each sentence in the space provided.

Loudness depends upon two factors: the frequency of a sound and the intensity of a sound. Sound can be measured in a unit of frequency called a hertz. Intensity is measured in a unit called a decibel. Low-frequency sounds (below 900 hertz) seem softer than high-frequency sounds (between 900 and 5,000 hertz) if the intensity remains the same. A sound-level meter is designed so that tones or narrow bands of noise will all sound the same when their sound levels are at about 40 decibels.

1. Nine hundred hertz is thought to be the lower limit of _____

   _____ .

2. Loudness depends upon _____

   _____ .

Answers are on page 304.

Directions: Choose the <u>one best answer</u> to each question

Questions 1–3 refer to the following passage.

Dioxin is a dangerous chemical that has contaminated hundreds of sites throughout the United States. The Environmental Protection Agency (EPA) orders the cleanup of any site containing more than 1 part per billion of dioxin. One of the first major cleanup sites was at Times Beach, Missouri. There the dioxin levels along some roadways were as high as 100 parts per billion.

The major focus of EPA cleanups is to prevent public exposure to any dangerous chemical. Dioxin has been found along roadways, in the ground, and even inside some homes. The biggest fear is that dioxin will seep through the soil and contaminate the groundwater. Fortunately, dioxin is one of the few chemicals that bonds itself to soil. The bonding reduces the chance that dioxin will contaminate the water supplies.

1. Which of the following is true because dioxin bonds itself to soil?

   (1) It is not dangerous.
   (2) The EPA is investigating it.
   (3) It will definitely contaminate the water system.
   (4) It may not seep into the water system.
   (5) It is in some homes.

2. What was the level of dioxin at Times Beach?

   (1) 100 parts per billion
   (2) 50 parts per billion
   (3) 1 part per billion
   (4) 1 part per million
   (5) less than 1 part per million

3. Where is the main idea expressed in this passage?

   (1) the first sentence of the passage
   (2) the second sentence of the passage
   (3) the first sentence of the second paragraph
   (4) the last sentence of the passage
   (5) It is not stated in the passage.

   Answers are on page 304.

Making Inferences

An **inference** is an educated guess. Some people think of making inferences as "reading between the lines." To make inferences you rely on information found in the passage, as well as prior knowledge, to make an educated guess or interpretation. Before you practice this skill, read the following passage.

> A radiation-thickness gauge is a device used to measure coatings on metals and other materials. Any deviation from the desired width or weight of a given material can be detected immediately by this tool. The detected deviation is relayed to the production foreman so an adjustment can be made. Often, the gauges are hooked up to computers and other mechanisms that automatically make the required adjustments.

Check the statement that is an inference based on the passage.

_____ 1. The radiation thickness is often connected to a manually operated computer.

_____ 2. The radiation is a computer.

_____ 3. The use of a radiation-thickness gauge leads to the production of a highly uniform product.

Did you check statement 3? Since the gauge can detect the slightest deviation in width or weight, its use can lead to products with coatings that always have the same width and weight. Statements 1 and 2 contain incorrect information. The gauge is separate from the computer (sentence 4).

When the main idea is not stated directly, it doesn't mean that a main idea does not exist. It means that you have to "put two and two together" to come up with the main point. You can still find the main idea by asking these three questions:

1. What is the passage about?

2. What is the most important idea the writer suggests about the topic?

3. Do all the ideas in the passage support the main idea?

Thinking About Science

Directions: Read the following passage and put a check in front of the correct answer to the question that follows.

About 1,800 years ago, Ptolemy declared that Earth was the center of the universe. He believed that Earth was stationary and that the Sun revolved around it. Until the sixteenth century, most scientists thought that the sunrise and sunset occurred because the Sun revolved around Earth.

From this passage, what you can infer about Ptolemy's theory?

_____ **1.** It was not proved correct until the sixteenth century.

_____ **2.** It remained the only explanation until the twentieth century.

_____ **3.** It was not believed by anyone else.

_____ **4.** It incorrectly explained the orbiting of the Sun and other bodies.

Answers are on page 304.

PRE-GED PRACTICE

Questions 1 and 2 refer to the following passage.

Aluminum is the most abundant metal in Earth's crust. It is important to the building, automobile, and aircraft industries because it is light in weight. Aluminum can also conduct both heat and electricity. One of aluminum's most important characteristics, however, is its resistance to corrosion.

While other metals often rust when exposed to oxygen, aluminum does not. Aluminum reacts so quickly with oxygen that the two elements combine to form a tough surface film. That film prevents further corrosive action.

1. Why is aluminum important to the automotive and aircraft industries?

   (1) It prevents serious accidents on the ground and in the air.
   (2) It does not conduct electricity.
   (3) It promotes corrosion in automobiles.
   (4) It resists corrosion.
   (5) It makes automobiles better-looking and easier to paint.

2. Which of the following best explains why aluminum is an unusual metal?

   (1) It is used in the manufacturing of cars.
   (2) It is resistant to corrosion.
   (3) It is lightweight.
   (4) It has an adverse reaction to oxygen.
   (5) It is a tough film.

Questions 3 and 4 refer to the following passage.

Although it appears solid, Earth's crust is constantly moving. Under the weight of mountain ranges and continents, rocks creep and flow. The shift of weight causes strains and breaks in Earth's crust.

A change in the crust may take millions of years, or it may occur rapidly. Faults may be created beneath the surface. Sudden shifts at these fault lines can cause earthquakes.

One slow process, called folding, produces mountains. Outstanding examples of folding can be seen where coastlines have risen above sea level. Here, rocks that were originally deposited in horizontal layers have been warped or bent upward and downward by crustal movement. This same effect can often be seen where roads have been cut into a mountainside.

Mountains may rise not only from faulting or folding but also from volcanic activity. The Hawaiian Islands, for example, are being formed by erupting volcanoes. Volcanic change is almost always rapid. Earthquakes are another source of rapid change. The earthquake, however, may be the result of the slow creation of faults beneath Earth's surface.

3. Which of the following can be inferred from the passage?

   (1) The face of Earth is constantly changing.
   (2) All mountains are constantly rising.
   (3) Earth's crust is stable.
   (4) Faulting always results in cliffs.
   (5) Folding occurs only in an upward direction.

4. Which of the following statements is true about Hawaii?

   (1) It is constantly changing.
   (2) It is formed by erupting volcanoes.
   (3) It is still being formed.
   (4) It is an area of rapid change.
   (5) All of the above statements are true.

Answers are on page 305.

Inferring the Meanings of Unknown Words

As you read scientific materials, you will encounter unfamiliar words. The best way to increase your vocabulary is to increase the amount of reading you do. When you read, keep a dictionary handy. Use the dictionary to look up unfamiliar words; then study them and use them in conversation and writing. Although this method may seem tiresome, you will find that it will help you to increase your vocabulary.

Using Prior Knowledge

When a dictionary isn't handy, you can use another method to figure out the meanings of unknown words. Some common words have special meanings in science. Your understanding of the common usage of these words will help you to understand their particular scientific meanings. For example, you may know that a common usage of the word *percolate* means to brew coffee with an old-fashioned percolator pot. As the coffee percolates, the water in the pot boils up and passes through the coffee beans. In a science passage, you can apply your understanding of the word *percolate* to gain meaning.

> **Magma, or molten rock, percolates beneath the earth, then wells up to burn through solid rock.**

You know that the author is not suggesting that coffee gets hot enough to burn through rock. Here, *percolate* is used to describe the formation of a volcano. By applying your prior knowledge of the word *percolate*, you can infer the new meaning: Magma is so hot that it boils, rising up through solid rock.

Using Context Clues

Sometimes you can infer the meanings of unknown words by using context clues. Context is the words and thoughts that surround the unknown word. For example, suppose that you do not know the meaning of *resistance*. Which context clues in the following sentences could help you to infer the meaning of *resistance*?

> **The filament, a thin wire coil, does not permit electricity to flow through it easily. The electricity must overcome resistance in the wire.**

The word *resistance* has a special meaning in science material. The first sentence above provides an excellent context clue to the word's meaning. Electricity is not allowed to flow through easily. Some force is working against it. To move, electricity must overcome this force. Therefore, in this context, *resistance* means "a force that must be overcome."

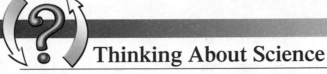

Thinking About Science

<u>Part A</u>

Directions: Read the following paragraph. Look for context clues to fill in the word meanings in the space provided.

The human body has a way of recognizing its enemies. When foreign bodies enter it, the human body attacks the "foe." The most common unwanted bodies are from bacteria, viruses, and other microscopic organisms. The body recognizes these antigens and fights them.

1. You can infer from the paragraph that *antigens* means_____ _____.

2. In the passage, the word *foe* means the _____ _____.

<u>Part B</u>

Directions: Read the following passage and complete the sentences below.

All solids do not liquify at the same temperature. If ice stays at a temperature above 32°F for a period of time, it becomes water. Iron ore, on the other hand, becomes molten at 2,800° to 3,000°F. Wax is solid at room temperature, but liquifies at 90° to 150°F. Liquids shrink when they solidify. A good example of this shrinking is the indentation that appears in the center of a tub of margarine.

1. In this passage, *liquify* means to become _____.

2. According to the passage, *molten* means _____.

3. *Solidify* means _____.

4. An *indentation* is _____.

Answers are on page 305.

Directions: Choose the <u>one best answer</u> to each question.

Questions 1–3 refer to the following passage.

Aquaculture may increase the world's food supply, but there is a danger that it will deplete the ocean's food supply. One popular seafood is the conch, a shellfish. Conchs are an excellent source of protein. Scientists are working to replenish the ocean's supply of conchs. The conchs are grown in laboratories until they have passed the egg and larva stages. They are kept in the laboratory until the conchs are large enough to defend themselves against predators.

1. From the context of the passage, what meaning can you infer for the word *deplete*?

   (1) to eat
   (2) to pollute
   (3) to replenish supplies
   (4) to lower prices
   (5) to use up

2. Since there is a danger of depleting the ocean's supplies, scientists are trying to replenish them. What can you infer *replenish* means?

   (1) to replace them
   (2) to react to them
   (3) to rejoin them
   (4) to repeat them
   (5) to remind them

3. Agriculture means "cultivating or using the soil for food production." What can you infer *aquaculture* means?

   (1) space for food production
   (2) the ocean for laboratory experiments
   (3) the ocean for seawater
   (4) the ocean for food production
   (5) laboratories to produce predators

Questions 4 and 5 refer to the following passage.

Hemophilia is a potentially dangerous condition. A hemophiliac's blood does not coagulate. As a result, even a minor cut can lead to heavy, uncontrolled bleeding. Hemophiliacs must be more cautious in their daily lives than the average person.

4. Based on this passage, what can you assume *coagulate* means?

   (1) to thin
   (2) to turn red
   (3) to flow
   (4) to clot
   (5) to adapt

5. Which of the following statements is true about a hemophiliac?

   (1) A hemophiliac is someone who gets hurt easily.
   (2) A hemophiliac is someone who easily forms scabs.
   (3) A hemophiliac is someone whose blood does not clot.
   (4) A hemophiliac is someone who never hemorrhages.
   (5) A hemophiliac is someone whose veins are too big.

Answers are on page 305.

Applying Scientific Principles

When conducting a scientific investigation, you may need to apply a scientific principle from one science reading to another. You may need to apply the idea to a similar set of circumstances not mentioned in the passage. For example, you may have to analyze a chemical formula and predict what might happen if two substances were mixed. In the following sections, you will practice how to use and apply several scientific principles.

You can apply general scientific principles to a situation described in a science passage. You can also use information that you already have to help you understand a new situation. For instance, you already know that water freezes at 32°F. Read the passage below and put a check in front of the correct answer to the question that follows.

> Snow fell heavily on Saturday morning. During the afternoon, temperatures warmed slightly and the snow changed to sleet, a mixture of snow and rain. The sleet melted some of the snow. By evening, the temperature had dropped to below 30°F.

What was true about the driving conditions on Saturday?

_____ **1.** They were not dangerous because the snow had melted.

_____ **2.** They were difficult because the roads were snow-covered.

_____ **3.** They were dangerous because the sleet and melted snow turned to ice.

_____ **4.** They were unpleasant because the streets were flooded.

Did you check choice 3? When the evening temperature dropped below 30°F, the sleet and melted snow froze. The highways were probably glazed with ice. To answer this question correctly, you had to apply the knowledge that water freezes at 32°F.

As you work through the exercises, think about what scientific principle you are using. By applying concepts that you learn, you are showing that you understand them in a concrete way.

Thinking About Science

Directions: Read the passage below and study the diagram at right to fill in the correct answers in the spaces provided.

Temperature can be measured using two different scales. In the United States, we are more familiar with the Fahrenheit scale (°F). On that scale, water freezes at 32°F and boils at 212°F. The Celsius scale is used throughout the rest of the world and in a growing number of places in the United States. On the Celsius scale, water freezes at 0°C and boils at 100°C.

The thermometer at right compares the Fahrenheit and Celsius scales. The Fahrenheit temperatures are shown on the left and their Celsius equivalents are represented on the right.

You can convert temperatures in degrees Celsius to temperatures in degrees Fahrenheit or vice versa by using these formulas:

Fahrenheit temperature = (Celsius temperature $\times \frac{9}{5}$) + 32

Celsius temperature = (Fahrenheit temperature − 32) $\times \frac{5}{9}$

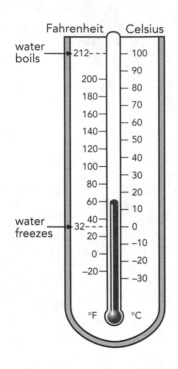

1. Paraffin, a waxy solid, begins to melt at 90°F. On the Celsius scale, that would be a little over _____.

2. Water freezes at 32°F. On the Celsius scale, that would be about

_____.

Answers are on page 305.

PRE-GED PRACTICE

Directions: Choose the <u>one best answer</u> to each question.

Questions 1 and 2 refer to the information on page 45.

1. The normal body temperature for humans is 98.6°F. About what would this be on the Celsius scale?

   (1) 8°C
   (2) 25°C
   (3) 37°C
   (4) 52°C
   (5) 70°C

2. Trichosis is caused by a dangerous parasite that can be transferred to humans by way of undercooked pork. To kill this parasite, the internal temperature of pork must reach at least 137°F. About what would this be on the Celsius scale?

   (1) 2°C
   (2) 28°C
   (3) 43°C
   (4) 57°C
   (5) 64°C

Answers are on page 305.

Inductive and Deductive Reasoning

Inductive Reasoning

Inductive reasoning involves making a generalization based on a specific experience and then applying that generalization to another experience. Since the generalization is made from only one sample, one cannot be sure that the conclusion is absolutely correct. The following reading passage gives an example of inductive reasoning.

> From a distance, the sand on a beach seems to be one large mass. Up close, however, one can see that beach sand is actually made up of many small grains. The water at the beach also seems to be one large mass. Even a drop of water at the beach may be made of smaller units. Perhaps the water drop is made of particles that are too small to see.

The author uses inductive reasoning to conclude that water, like beach sand, is made up of tiny particles. Perhaps that is correct. Actually, the theory of atomism states that all matter is composed of tiny particles. If that theory is correct, the author's inductive reasoning is also correct.

Deductive Reasoning

Deductive reasoning means using a generalization about one thing to draw a conclusion about another. Scientists use deductive reasoning when they apply general principles to specific situations. For example:

Generalization: Scientists have noticed that the increase in oil slicks has hurt birds that depend on the ocean for food.

Conclusion: If the number of oil slicks continues to increase, the number of sea gulls will decrease.

Thinking About Science

Part A

Directions: Read the passage below and put a check in front of the correct generalization.

The American researcher Jonas Salk knew that three types of infectious viruses cause poliomyelitis, also known as infantile paralysis. They are the Brunhilde, the Lansing, and the Leon viruses. He also knew that immunity to one type of these viruses did not ensure immunity to the others. Then Dr. John Enders found a method of growing viruses in cultures outside the human body. Salk used this discovery in his research. He developed a vaccine to protect people from the disease. The vaccine contained inactivated poliomyelitis viruses from each of the three types.

For what purpose did Dr. Salk use Dr. Enders's research?

_____ **1.** To discover an immunity-giving culture that would conquer the Brunhilde virus and, therefore, protect people from poliomyelitis

_____ **2.** To find a way to grow viruses in cultures outside the human body

_____ **3.** To grow polio viruses in laboratory cultures

_____ **4.** To separate the deadly Lansing virus from the Leon virus

Part B

Directions: Read the passage below and answer the questions that follow.

(1) The elements we find in Earth's crust do not represent the composition of the entire planet. (2) Earth's crust is rich in uranium and thorium. (3) Just below Earth's surface, however, these two elements are much rarer. (4) In fact, if the core of Earth contained as much uranium and thorium as the crust does, Earth would melt from the radioactive heat that would be generated.

1. Which sentence in the passage states a generalization? _____

2. Based on the passage, what can you conclude if the composition of Earth's crust does not represent the makeup of the entire planet?

_____ (1) Different layers of Earth may contain different proportions of an element.

_____ (2) There is no uranium or thorium in Earth's crust.

_____ (3) Only Earth's crust contains uranium and thorium.

_____ (4) Elements are found in roughly the same proportions throughout the different layers of the planet.

Answers are on pages 305–306.

Directions: Choose the <u>one best answer</u> to each question.

Question 1 refers to the following passage.

All car owners are concerned about rust, or iron oxide. Iron oxide is formed when iron and oxygen react with one another. Water and salt speed up this reaction. A protective coating on a metal surface will discourage the formation of iron oxide. The formula for iron oxide is
$4Fe + 3O_2 \rightarrow 2Fe_2O_3$.

1. Where might drivers see little or no rust on their cars?

   (1) in rainy areas
   (2) near the ocean
   (3) in snowy areas
   (4) in desert areas
   (5) high in the mountains

Questions 2 and 3 refer to the following passage.

Oxygen, water, and moderate temperatures are necessary for the survival of living things. If Earth were too close to the Sun, living things could not survive the heat. If Earth were too far from the Sun, living things could not survive the cold.

2. Which of the following is a logical conclusion based on this paragraph?

   (1) Living organisms need only oxygen to survive on Earth.
   (2) There are only two essential factors that are necessary for the survival of life on Earth—water and oxygen.
   (3) Earth accommodates animals and plants by providing adequate amounts of sunlight, oxygen, and water.
   (4) Living organisms on Earth can survive without water.
   (5) Heat is not a critical factor for life on Earth.

3. What is the main idea of the passage above?

   (1) Living things require only sunlight and water.
   (2) Living things require atmosphere for animals.
   (3) Living things require carbon dioxide for plants.
   (4) Living things require rainfall for plants.
   (5) Living things require sunlight, oxygen, and water.

Answers are on page 306.

Comprehending and Applying Science Review

Directions: Choose the <u>one best answer</u> to each question.

Questions 1 and 2 refer to the following passage.

A person can get dizzy from just examining the causes of dizziness! Dizziness can be caused by circulatory system disorders—such as high blood pressure, stroke, anemia, and leukemia. Dizziness is the mildest symptom of a very serious disorder called Ménière's disease. Tumors, hemorrhages, and epilepsy can also cause dizziness. Some infectious diseases can cause temporary dizziness. Less serious causes of dizzy spells include excessive ear wax and new eyeglasses.

1. Which of the following statements about dizziness is true?

   (1) Dizziness is caused by a limited number of factors.
   (2) Dizziness is induced only by blood or vascular problems.
   (3) Dizziness is related to one or two causes.
   (4) Dizziness is caused by any of a broad range of factors.
   (5) Dizziness can be cured by medication.

2. Which of the following are some of the less serious causes of dizziness?

   (1) high blood pressure and strokes
   (2) excessive ear wax and new eyeglasses
   (3) anemia and leukemia
   (4) strokes and leukemia
   (5) tumors, hemorrhages, and epilepsy

Question 3 refers to the following passage.

Gravity is the force that draws all objects toward the center of Earth. For example, gravity causes furniture to remain in place in a room. It keeps your feet on the floor. Airplanes and rockets must overcome the force of gravity to leave the surface of Earth.

3. What can you conclude by using the generalization from this passage?

   (1) Centrifugal force pulls a space capsule toward the center of Earth.
   (2) The law of gravity does not apply to rockets or space capsules.
   (3) Rockets and space capsules are subject to centrifugal forces, not gravitational forces.
   (4) The force of gravity pulls space capsules toward the center of Earth.
   (5) none of the above

Questions 4 and 5 refer to the following passage.

Keeping the proper amount of air pressure in your automobile tires is important. Incorrect tire pressure can cause extra tire wear. It can also cause accidents. Underinflation can cause a tire to heat up, possibly leading to a blowout on the highway. Overinflation prevents tire treads from fully gripping the road, making the car more likely to skid.

4. Which of the following describes an overinflated tire?

   (1) a tire that has uneven tread wear
   (2) a tire that has too little pressure in it
   (3) a tire that is badly worn
   (4) a tire that has too much air in it
   (5) a tire that is likely to cause a blowout

5. Which of the following can you conclude from this passage?

   (1) Having incorrect tire pressure can be dangerous.
   (2) Most people do not inflate their tires properly.
   (3) Cold weather makes tires expand.
   (4) All tires require the same air pressure.
   (5) Only an expert can check tire pressure.

Questions 6 and 7 refer to the following diagram of a thermometer.

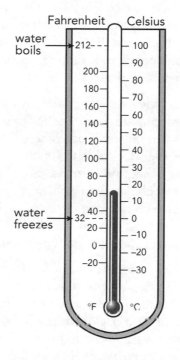

6. To save energy in the winter, you should set the thermostat in your home to a lower temperature. What would be a comfortable setting?

   (1) 4°C
   (2) 11°C
   (3) 20°C
   (4) 25°C
   (5) 32°C

7. Which of the following is closest to normal body temperature (98.6°F)?

   (1) 19°C
   (2) 21°C
   (3) 32°C
   (4) 37°C
   (5) 98.6°C

Questions 8 and 9 refer to the following passage.

One of the most serious medical problems an alcoholic faces is a diseased liver. The liver is the key organ for removing alcohol and other harmful substances from the blood. With excessive and prolonged use of alcohol, liver tissue becomes damaged. The resulting disease is called *cirrhosis*.

In an alcoholic, the liver is scarred. Groups of hard cells replace normal spongy tissue. This prevents the absorption and processing of substances in the blood. Unable to function properly, the liver cannot perform its life-sustaining work. Alcoholics who have liver problems must give up drinking or die of cirrhosis. If liver damage is not yet too severe and if the supply of alcohol stops, a liver can repair itself.

Alcoholics may also suffer from nutritional deficiencies. Since alcohol contains many calories, alcoholics tend to get their calories by drinking instead of eating. Unfortunately, alcohol lacks vitamins, minerals, and other essential nutrients. The lack of nutrients may explain the malnourished condition of so many alcoholics.

8. Which of the following is a consequence of liver damage?

    (1) loss of appetite
    (2) brain damage
    (3) excessive drinking
    (4) insufficient absorption of nutrients
    (5) alcoholism

9. Why may many alcoholics be malnourished?

    (1) Alcohol accounts for much of their caloric intake, but it has few essential nutrients.
    (2) A diseased liver allows only alcohol to enter the bloodstream.
    (3) The hard cells in the liver are replaced by spongy cells.
    (4) Nutrients are absorbed by the blood.
    (5) They have no appetite for food.

Answers are on page 306.

CHAPTER 3

Analyzing and Evaluating Science

Determining the Outcome

Our understanding of the world around us comes through inquiry—asking questions about our world. Scientific inquiry involves gathering, analyzing, and interpreting data. As a student of science, you will analyze science materials. You will look at and ask questions about all the parts to better understand the whole passage or graphic.

On the GED Science Test, some questions may require you to evaluate or make judgments, about scientific findings or experiments or studies. For example, you may have to evaluate whether enough information has been given to draw a conclusion based on the findings.

In your everyday life, you evaluate science materials when you shop at the grocery store, select building materials for home improvements, choose appropriate medications, or think about the best choices for health care. Everyday living requires a series of choices and you prepare for them by reading, by listening to friends, by looking at advertising, and by critical thinking.

Each of us has our own value system, a set of beliefs about what is important and what is right or wrong. We develop this value system as we grow. Our life experiences, what our family communicates to us, and what our culture tells us all shape our value system. We rely on this system to help us make decisions.

Sequence of Events

As you read a description of a scientific process or of a natural occurrence, you may notice that the details are presented in a logical order. For example:

(1) To cure cheese, heat pasteurized milk to 39°C (102°F). (2) Salt the milled curd. (3) Press salted, milled curd into hoops for shaping. (4) After three to four days, drop formed cheese into wax. (5) For milder cheddar, cold-cure at 0°C to 5°C (22°F to 41°F).

As you read the above passage, you probably noticed that each step in the sequence logically followed the one preceding it. The curing process would not make any sense if sentences 2 and 3 were reversed.

Sequence of events may refer to chronological order or logical order. When you determine the **chronological order** of events, you decide which event comes first, second, third, and so on. The events are arranged in the order in which they happen.

When you determine **logical order**, you must decide what step or outcome logically follows the one that comes before it. The passage on the next page gives you further practice in understanding sequence of events.

Thinking About Science

Directions: Read the following passage and answer the questions below.

The incubation period for typhoid fever is from eight to fourteen days. During this time, the typhoid bacilli, or bacteria, travel through the alimentary canal to the small intestine. There they settle in lymphatic tissues known as Peyer's patches. From Peyer's patches, the bacilli enter the lymph system and are transported into the bloodstream. The symptoms of the disease begin as the bacilli enter the bloodstream.

1. Where do the typhoid bacilli lodge as soon as they have passed into the small intestine?

   _____

2. Where are the typhoid bacilli before they enter the small intestine?

   _____

3. Put the following items into order to show the path of a typhoid bacillus when it enters the body.

   _____ (1) lymph system

   _____ (2) Peyer's patches

   _____ (3) alimentary canal

   _____ (4) bloodstream

   _____ (5) small intestine

Answers are on page 306.

Cause-and-Effect Relationships

Certain actions (causes) lead to specific results (effects). For instance, if you push on a wheel, it will roll. The push is the cause; rolling is the effect. These are known as **cause-and-effect relationships**. Often, when a cause produces a certain effect, that effect will become the cause of something else. For example, a lack of B vitamins in the diet may cause eczema. Eczema is the result (effect). Eczema, in turn, becomes the cause of the skin's scaling and itching.

Cause-and-effect relationships often are signaled by words such as *because, since, as a result, led to, therefore, consequently, accordingly, brought about, the outcome was, the end result was, if ... then,* and *was responsible for.*

Thinking About Science

Directions: Read the passage below and respond to the statements that follow.

Toxoplasmosis, an infectious disease of animals and people, is caused by a parasitic protozoan. The disease is commonly transmitted by house cats. The disease is difficult to recognize. Toxoplasmosis usually appears with no symptoms. At times, it may produce mild symptoms that resemble those of mononucleosis or a cold.

1. Write *E* for *effect* in front of each phrase that describes a symptom of toxoplasmosis.

    _____ (1) a common cold

    _____ (2) none

    _____ (3) mild symptoms

    _____ (4) a parasitic protozoan

    _____ (5) mononucleosis

2. Put a check mark in front of the direct cause of toxoplasmosis.

    _____ (1) house cats

    _____ (2) an infection

    _____ (3) a protozoan

    _____ (4) humans

Answers are on page 306.

Drawing Conclusions

You will not always find the answer to a question stated directly in the reading passage. Sometimes what you already know plus the information given in a passage will enable you to predict an outcome or to draw a reasonable conclusion. For example, you know that water conducts electricity and that electricity is harmful—if not deadly—to a human being. These facts should lead you to conclude that operating an electrical appliance with wet hands or leaving an electrical appliance near a bathtub is dangerous.

 **Thinking About Science**

Directions: Read the passage below and put a check in front of the correct answer to the question that follows.

Paleontologists learn many interesting things from fossils. They can determine the age of rocks by examining the fossils in them. They can also tell whether the rocks were formed on the land or under the ocean. Most rocks that contain animal or plant fossils formed on land. Those that contain marine shell fossils formed in the ocean.

What can you conclude about the study of fossils by paleontologists?

_____ (1) It gives the exact location of deep ocean trenches.

_____ (2) It provides the ability to date plant fossils more accurately than animal fossils.

_____ (3) It gives information about the kinds of life that existed during different periods of Earth's history.

_____ (4) It gives many kinds of information, but nothing that tells them the ages of rocks.

_____ (5) It gives the information they need to explain the origin of Earth.

Answers are on page 306.

Directions: Choose the <u>one best answer</u> to each question.

Questions 1 and 2 refer to the following passage.

In nature, the animal population is limited by certain factors. Two important factors are the presence of predators—organisms that prey upon others—and the amount of available food. Disease-causing organisms also limit population growth.

Although most species of animals produce large numbers of offspring, relatively few reach adulthood. As a result, plant and animal populations tend to be stable from year to year.

1. What would be the effect of an unusually large increase in the number of predators or disease-causing organisms?

   (1) The prey animal population would grow.
   (2) More than enough food would be available for the population.
   (3) The prey animal population would decrease.
   (4) The prey animal population would not be affected.
   (5) Large numbers of offspring would reach adulthood.

2. If humans eliminated the predators, how would this initially affect the number of prey animals?

   (1) The number would remain constant.
   (2) The number would slowly decrease.
   (3) The number would rapidly decrease.
   (4) The number would increase.
   (5) The number would be subject to minor fluctuations.

Questions 3 and 4 refer to the following passage.

When an egg is fertilized, it undergoes cell division to form an embryo. How that embryo is protected varies from species to species. In plants, the fertilized ovule develops into a seed that contains an embryo, a store of food, and a protective covering. In most lower-level animals, the embryo is encased in a protective shell. The shell is discharged from the female's body. Some animals, such as birds, lay their eggs before their young are fully developed. Others hatch the eggs within the mother's body. In higher-level animals, the embryo grows in the uterus and is nourished by the mother until it is developed sufficiently for birth.

3. How would an organism that nurtures its embryo in the uterus until the embryo is mature enough for birth be classified?

   (1) bird
   (2) plant
   (3) lower-level animal
   (4) higher-level animal
   (5) none of the above

4. What could result from an injury to the covering of the embryo?

   (1) fertilization
   (2) nourishment
   (3) a speeding up of birth
   (4) damage to the embryo
   (5) damage to the mother

Answers are on pages 306–307.

Evaluating the Relevance of Information

When you must make a decision about something, your first consideration is getting the information that you need. Unfortunately, the information does not usually come in neat packages. You have to sort through **relevant information,** which includes any facts that directly affect your decision. You also have to rule out **irrelevant information,** which includes any facts that do not affect your decision and are not relevant to your needs.

For example, you may have heard about something called *lake-effect snow*. If you were trying to decide whether to live near a lake, you might consider information about lake-effect snow. The diagram below describes what happens when there is lake-effect snow.

LAKE-EFFECT SNOW

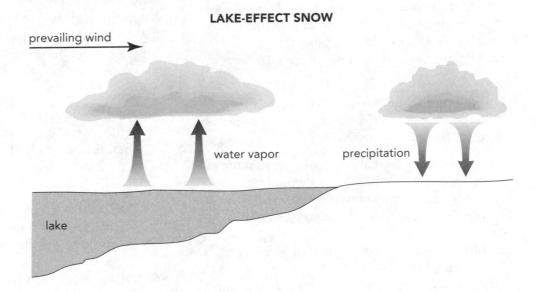

Check only those factors that would be relevant to deciding if lake-effect snow could be a problem.

_____ **1.** the direction of the prevailing wind above the lake

_____ **2.** the side of the lake that your house would be on

_____ **3.** information from people who live on the lake

_____ **4.** the average water temperature of the lake

_____ **5.** the speed of evaporation from the lake

In deciding about the potential for snowfall in the lake area, the most relevant piece of information would most likely be item 3. Also important would be the answers to items 1 and 2, since the lake-effect snow would be more pronounced on the side of the lake that gets the wind. The answers to items 4 and 5 are not particularly relevant to deciding to what degree the lake-effect snow is likely to be a problem.

 **Thinking About Science**

Directions: Read the passage below and answer the question that follows.

As you read the news, listen to TV, and hear comments from "the man on the street," it appears more and more that the word *chemical* is a dirty word. You hear of chemicals in foods as though they were poisons. Drinking chemically treated water doesn't sound appealing, but you would get quite sick if water were not treated.

Check only the statements that would be relevant to your deciding whether the word *chemical* should be considered negative or not.

_____ (1) Without chemical preservatives, most of the food that you purchase would be spoiled before you get it.

_____ (2) Aspirin is a chemical.

_____ (3) Carbon tetrachloride is a chemical.

_____ (4) The best and the worst bottled water is a chemical.

_____ (5) The molecules that make up the human body are chemicals.

_____ (6) Battery acid is a chemical.

Answers are on page 307.

PRE-GED PRACTICE

Directions: Choose the <u>one best answer</u> to each question.

Question 1 refers to the information on page 58 and the following passage.

Suppose that you are considering whether to buy an asbestos-shingled house. You have heard about the hazards of asbestos as a cancer-causing material.

1. Which of the following facts is probably <u>not</u> related to your decision about buying a house?

    (1) The house was built three years ago.
    (2) Asbestos shingles pose no danger if they are intact and in good shape.
    (3) The shingles on the house are broken in places.
    (4) Shingles in poor condition do not have to be removed, as new siding can be installed over them.
    (5) Asbestos shingles pose no threat unless sanded or abraded.

Answers are on page 307.

Judging the Adequacy of Information

Just as important as deciding if information is relevant or irrelevant is the question of deciding if you have enough, or adequate, information to support a conclusion.

For example, suppose you go home for lunch and find that the digital clock in your kitchen is flashing on 12:00. This alerts you that your power has gone out, at least in the kitchen. Until you investigate further, you won't know if the power is out in your whole house or in just this room. You also won't know without further investigation whether the power in only your house went out or whether the power in the whole neighborhood went out. You also need to investigate and ask questions until you get adequate information about what caused the power outage.

Read the passage below and answer the following question.

> If you take a metal wire and hold it in the flame of a gas burner, the wire will glow and become red-hot. As you continue to hold the wire in the flame, the glow of the wire will turn orange, then yellow, and finally white.

Why does the wire turn colors in that particular order?

Check the item of information you would need to know to answer this question.

_____ **1.** the size of the flame on the gas burner

_____ **2.** the amount of radiant heat given off as the temperature increases

_____ **3.** the size of the metal wire held in the flame

You would have to know item 2, how much radiant energy is given off as the temperature increases. Knowing this would help explain why the wire turns various colors as you continue to hold it in the flame. Knowing the size of the flame or of the metal wire would not give you adequate information about why the colors change.

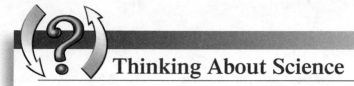

Thinking About Science

Directions: Read the passage and study the diagram below. Then answer the questions that follow.

Many regions of the country have water with relatively high levels of calcium (Ca), magnesium (Mg), and/or iron (Fe). This water is called hard water and can be a nuisance because it shortens the life of appliances that use water, such as water heaters and washing machines. Hard water is also responsible for bathtub ring as well as water that does not lather easily. Many homeowners install water softeners to remedy the problems of hard water.

A diagram of a water softener is shown below.

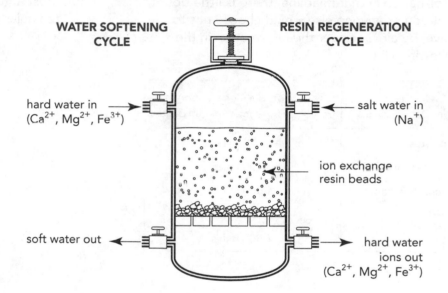

Based on the information above, circle *T* if the statement is true, or *F* if it is false.

T   F   1. The Ca, Mg, and Fe that are the cause of hard water are trapped inside the water softener.

T   F   2. A water softener should not be installed in the home if its occupants have high blood pressure.

T   F   3. The water that is to be treated enters the water softener at the bottom and slowly fills it up.

T   F   4. The sodium (Na^{+1} ion) in salt water, is needed for the softener to work properly.

T   F   5. The water that comes out of the water softener has more sodium in it than it had before treatment.

Answers are on page 307.

Directions: Choose the <u>one best answer</u> to each question.

Question 1 refers to the following passage and chart.

You are planning a cross-country trip. You need to decide whether it would be safer to drive or to fly. You remember a recent headline:

Airplane Crashes Seconds After Takeoff No Survivors

If the mode of travel were based only on the information in that headline, there is little doubt that you or anyone else would choose not to travel by air. Consider the information in the following chart.

Mode of travel	Distance at which one person in a million will suffer accidental death
bicycle	10 miles
automobile	100 miles
scheduled airline	1,000 miles
train	1,200 miles
bus	2,800 miles

1. Which fact enables you to conclude that there is less chance of being killed in an airplane than in an automobile?

   (1) One in a million people traveling in cars will suffer a fatal accident within 100 miles.
   (2) Alcohol plays a bigger part in auto fatalities than in airline fatalities.
   (3) Air travel is ten times safer than automobile travel.
   (4) There is less risk in traveling by bus than by airplane.
   (5) Most automobile accidents occur within ten miles of home.

   Answers are on page 307.

Recognizing Values

Values are our beliefs that are shaped by family, culture, religion, and individual taste. Values play a part in every decision we make, whether we are aware of them or not.

Sometimes our values conflict with scientific facts. For example, cloning is an issue that is not debated solely on the basis of its scientific and medical aspects. The conflict is caused by a difference in values: Some people believe cloning will help fulfill the need for transplant organs while others believe this practice would violate the rights of the clone.

Values are as important for quality judgments as are scientific facts. Both have their place in the decision-making process. Suppose, for example, that your town uses chemical herbicides (weed killers) along roadsides. Some citizens want to stop this practice because chemicals pollute the environment. Moreover, there have been a few cases in which children and pets exposed to herbicides have become sick. The mayor says that if herbicides can't be used, workers will need to be hired to mow the roadsides, a decision that would result in higher taxes. The mayor says that the town has been using herbicides for years with no known ill effects.

If you were voting on this issue, would you vote for or against the use of herbicides? Here are some questions you might consider in making this decision.

1. Which is more important to you, a cleaner environment or lower taxes?

2. Should everyone have to pay more just because some children may be sensitive to chemicals?

3. Is the mayor right when he says that no one has been hurt, or do you think that a chemical that makes some people really sick might be causing less obvious problems for many people?

Write how you would vote and list your reasons for taking the position you have chosen.

_____

_____

Do you think your answer would be any different if you had a child who was sensitive to herbicides? How about if you were a senior citizen on a fixed income and had trouble paying taxes even without a tax increase? To make a fair decision, you have to examine your personal interests in light of what is best for the community.

Thinking About Science

Directions: Read each situation below. Decide what values are in conflict. Complete each statement in the space provided.

1. An item on the ballot of a city's local election asks voters whether a nuclear power plant should be built in the region. Even though the electricity the plant would generate is needed, because of well-publicized nuclear accidents, Bob is having a hard time deciding to vote for it.

   The conflict is between the safety of a nuclear power plant and the

   _____.

2. The world's population is out of control, but lawmakers are reluctant to pass laws regulating the number of children allowed per family.

   The conflict is between what is good for the country and the protection of people's

   _____.

3. Rico knows that his community could use more jobs, but he is opposed to having a racetrack disrupt the tranquillity in the area in which he lives.

   The conflict is between the need for new jobs and a need to protect the

   _____.

4. Shawna told a lawyer that she could not be an impartial juror in the trial of a doctor accused of mercy killing.

   The conflict is between what is considered merciful treatment and

   _____.

5. Employers should have the right to test prospective employees to find out if they are using drugs.

   The conflict is between an employer's right to guarantee a drug-free workplace and an employee's

   _____.

Answers are on page 307.

Directions: Choose the <u>one best answer</u> to each question.

Question 1 refers to the following passage.

A new treatment on the medical horizon is causing some people to worry. This new approach to healing is called *genetic engineering*. Medical science has progressed to the point that it is now possible to locate the cause of some diseases by pinpointing genes that control specific diseases. There are scientists who are working to treat diseases by altering the DNA of those stricken with specific diseases. While the possibilities are staggering, they are accompanied by ethical dilemmas.

1. Which newspaper headline does <u>not</u> represent a conflict in values over the gene therapy issue?

   (1) "Protestors Picket Gene Therapy Clinic"
   (2) "Religious Leaders Hold Conference on Gene Therapy"
   (3) "Candlelight Vigil over Gene Therapy Held Tonight"
   (4) "Scientists Announce Gene Therapy Breakthrough"
   (5) "Gene Therapy—Tonight's Talk Show Topic"

   Answers are on page 307.

Using the Scientific Method

Scientists use a process called the **scientific method** when they are conducting an experiment or searching for knowledge.

The scientific method has five steps:

1. Identify the problem.

2. Collect information.

3. Make a hypothesis, or guess.

4. Test the hypothesis.

5. Draw conclusions.

If you were trying to decide whether to buy the most expensive gasoline or the cheapest grade at the pump, you would probably experiment using the scientific method. You would try each kind of gasoline and then judge the results.

You might make a hypothesis, or guess, that there will be some noticeable difference with the different grades of gasoline.

Your experiment will involve a variable. A **variable** is a changeable element that affects the quality or reliability of an experiment's outcome, or result. In this case, the variable would be the kind of gasoline, such as "premium," "extra," or "regular."

Successful experimenters make sure there are no unwanted variables. The important thing about variables is not to have too many. With your gasoline experiment, for example, you would have only one variable—the grade of gasoline. If you introduced another variable, such as type of driving—city or highway—this would change the results of your experiment. If you used one type of gasoline for city driving and another kind of gasoline for long-distance highway driving, this additional variable could cloud the picture, changing the results. Your conclusion might result from the grade of gasoline, or it might result from the type of driving you did. Unless you controlled your variables, you wouldn't be sure.

One of the ways you could evaluate the grades of gasoline would be by the mileage that your car gets when using the particular gasoline. The following chart shows the results.

Check only those items that would be accurate conclusions based on information in the chart.

EFFECTS OF GASOLINE ON MILEAGE

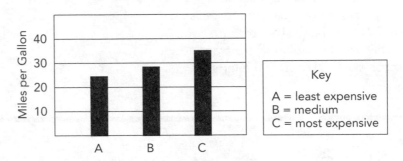

_____ **1.** The higher the grade of gasoline, the greater the gas mileage.

_____ **2.** The improved mileage justifies the added expense.

_____ **3.** The mileage improvement is directly linked to the gasoline's octane rating.

_____ **4.** The gasolines are nearly five miles apart in mileage gains.

_____ **5.** None of the gasolines hits the 40 miles per gallon (mpg) mark.

Conclusions 1, 4, and 5 can be gathered from the graph. There is not adequate information for concluding that items 2 and 3 are correct.

Another key element in experiments is a control. A **control** is a standard against which the effects of an experiment are compared. If you have a very large number of people doing an experiment, a control decreases the chance that something will vary that you are not aware of.

Suppose that you are conducting an experiment about the effects of a particular diet and have not taken the factor of gender into account. If you use a very large number of men and women, then the gender issue will be taken care of by the very large numbers. It is a form of "averaging out."

A third key element in scientific experiments is a placebo. A **placebo** is a "sugar pill," or dosage, that lacks the ingredient being tested in the experiment. For example, in an experiment that studies the effects of vitamin A on inflamed eyelids, an experimenter would give half the test subjects a placebo to take every day while the other half would get vitamin A to take daily. The test subjects would not know who had gotten the placebo or who had gotten the vitamin A. This is done because subjects are not always objective about reporting their experiences.

Thinking About Science

Directions: Suppose that your doctor thinks that you have a food allergy to wheat. Your doctor wants you to experiment with your diet to see if this is true. If you were designing an experiment to find the cause of this allergy, which of the following things would you need?

1. Check only those items that would be relevant to the experiment.

    _____ (1) thermometer

    _____ (2) caloric counter

    _____ (3) ingredients list of your favorite foods

    _____ (4) measuring cup

    _____ (5) scale for measuring your weight

    _____ (6) journal, notebook, or diary

2. Check only those strategies that would introduce additional variables.

    _____ (1) Monitor calorie intake with the intent to lose weight.

    _____ (2) Replace the wheat in the diet with corn and rice.

    _____ (3) Add more fruits and vegetables to the diet.

    _____ (4) Begin an exercise program.

    _____ (5) Get more sleep.

3. Check only those actions that could help you decide whether wheat is causing the allergy.

    _____ (1) Eliminate whole wheat bread from your diet.

    _____ (2) Replace wheat bran with oat bran in your diet.

    _____ (3) Try to time the allergic outbreak with your intake of wheat-based foods.

    _____ (4) Replace white bread with whole wheat bread.

    _____ (5) Increase your daily serving of wheat germ.

Answers are on page 307.

Directions: Choose the <u>one best answer</u> to each question.

Questions 1 and 2 refer to the following passage and illustration.

You have heard that one can of beer will affect your reaction time. Although you do believe that excessive drinking will reduce your reaction time, you find it difficult to believe that just one can of beer could change your ability to react. You decide to test this finding by using the scientific method.

You drink one can of beer. Then you test your reaction time by dropping a pencil from one hand and trying to catch the pencil with the other hand. The drawings below show the results of your experiment.

REACTION RESULTS

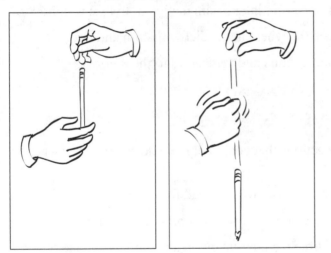

1. Which of the following statements is a hypothesis for your experiment?

   (1) Does excessive drinking reduce my reaction time?
   (2) Does beer affect my reaction time less than wine?
   (3) Does the weight of the pencil affect the speed at which it falls?
   (4) Does my reaction time differ depending on which hand I'm using?
   (5) Does just one can of beer affect my ability to react?

2. From the results of the experiment, which of the following can you most reasonably conclude?

   (1) The blood alcohol level at which most people become impaired varies by a person's size and weight.
   (2) The amount of alcohol in one can of beer is enough to affect reaction time.
   (3) Beer is less detrimental to reaction time than is wine.
   (4) A heavy pencil is more difficult to grasp than is a lightweight pencil.
   (5) If a person tries the experiment using the left hand to catch the pencil, the reaction time will improve.

   Answers are on page 307.

Analyzing and Evaluating Science Review

Directions: Choose the <u>one best answer</u> to each question.

Questions 1–4 are based on the graph and information below.

Tamoxifen is an oral medication used since the early 1970s for the treatment of breast cancer. Breast cancer studies of 30,000 women show a benefit from using tamoxifen. Even though the gain is modest, the large number of women who develop breast cancer means that the number of lives saved is significant. The following graph shows the survival rate of patients who took tamoxifen and those who did not.

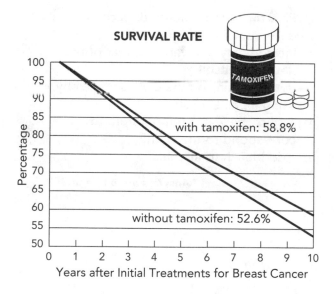

SURVIVAL RATE

with tamoxifen: 58.8%

without tamoxifen: 52.6%

Percentage

Years after Initial Treatments for Breast Cancer

1. Which statement represents the best summary of the graph?

   (1) Breast cancer is a disease with a low survival rate.
   (2) Tamoxifen use makes very little difference in the first five years of treatment.
   (3) Tamoxifen users have an improved breast cancer survival rate.
   4) Tamoxifen is a potent form of chemotherapy.
   (5) Tamoxifen will eventually cure all forms of breast cancer.

2. What control was used in this experiment?

   (1) using a very large number of patients
   (2) administering the same dose of tamoxifen to each patient
   (3) choosing patients with similar lifestyles
   (4) limiting the time period of the study
   (5) monitoring the side effects of the drug

3. Based on the graph, which inference can be made?

   (1) Five years after the beginning of tamoxifen treatment, less than 75 percent of the patients were alive.
   (2) The tamoxifen advantage is more pronounced the longer the patient lives.
   (3) Four years after treatment begins, 90 percent of patients are still alive.
   (4) Patients who are less than 80 years old have the best chance of survival.
   (5) After one year of treatment, all patients take tamoxifen.

4. Which of the following is the conclusion for which you have adequate information?

   (1) Tamoxifen should be taken by women with a family history of breast cancer.
   (2) Patients with breast cancer eventually die of the disease.
   (3) Tamoxifen use improves long-term survival.
   (4) Tamoxifen should be used to prevent heart disease.
   (5) Those who did not take tamoxifen had a better survival rate.

Questions 5–7 are based on the following chart and information.

Suppose that you have decided to conduct your own experiment to find out if high-priced brand-name laundry detergent is worth the expense. You decide to conduct the experiment by taking an old sheet and cutting it into four-inch squares. Each of these squares will be stained with a common stain. One set of squares will be laundered using the high-priced brand of detergent. The other set will be washed using a less-expensive generic detergent.

The graphic shows the stains that will be laundered.

STAIN REMOVAL

Squares to be Treated with Brand-name Detergent

mustard	motor oil	coffee	mud

Squares to be Treated with Generic Detergent

mustard	motor oil	coffee	mud

5. Which of the following would <u>not</u> affect the controlling variables?

   (1) temperatures of wash water
   (2) fabrics for the test samples
   (3) times of day for the two batches
   (4) stains
   (5) size stains

6. Which of the following would be necessary in order for you to draw a valid conclusion about your detergent experiment?

   (1) chemical formulas for the two detergents
   (2) temperature of the water in the washing machine
   (3) size of the spots of stain
   (4) appearance of the stain spots after the laundering
   (5) amount of water used by the washing machine

7. Which of the following is a way to exert experimental control?

   (1) Find the cost per load for each detergent.
   (2) Include only one variable, that of the detergent itself.
   (3) Put the stains on the cloth samples by using a paint brush.
   (4) Adjust the water temperature to correspond to the stain.
   (5) Add bleach to all trials.

Answers are on page 307.

PART TWO

Life Science

- **Plant and Animal Science**
- **Human Biology**

CHAPTER 4

Plant and Animal Science

Life Science (also called biology) is the study of living things. Life scientists study the growth, structure, and classification of all living things. They try to find out how living things are alike and different. They examine how living things, or **organisms,** behave and how they react to one another and to their **environment**, or surroundings. Life scientists have a wide variety of interests. One may record the songs of whales. One might work with farmers to develop better crops. Another might search for the cause of a human disease.

Although life science crosses the borders of many other sciences, it usually is divided into two broad groupings: the study of plants, which is called botany, and the study of animals, known as zoology.

In this chapter you will study:

- Cells, the basic units of life
- Organisms
- Plants and animals
- Ecology
- The history of life on Earth

The Study of Life

The study of living things began early and developed rapidly:

The cave art produced by early humans has convinced scientists that even prehistoric people studied other living things. The ancient Greeks examined the structures of living things and tried to identify the basics of life.

In the seventeenth century, the invention of the microscope revolutionized life science. Using a microscope, Robert Hooke noticed that living tissue was made of small boxes, or cells. Anton van Leeuwenhoek used a microscope and saw the first single-celled organism.

In the eighteenth century, Carolus Linnaeus classified living things. To **classify** means to organize plants and animals into groups based on their structure, growth, and function. Linnaeus's classification system allowed biologists to communicate with one another in spite of language differences.

During the nineteenth century, Gregor Mendel discovered the principles of heredity. Also, Charles Darwin introduced his theory of evolution.

In the twentieth century, scientists discovered the structure of DNA. They also found out how genes and chromosomes work. These successes have led to new frontiers in the life sciences.

Each of these developments in life science has opened a new field for scientists to explore. Some specialties include:

- **Anatomy**—the study of the structure of living things
- **Biochemistry**—the study of the atoms and molecules that form cells
- **Botany**—the study of plants
- **Ecology**—the study of the relationships between living organisms and their environment
- **Genetics**—the study of the inherited characteristics of plants and animals
- **Physiology**—the study of the functions and vital processes of organisms
- **Zoology**—the study of animals

Life Science Today

Scientists continue to learn more about the relationships between the environment and different plants, animals, and other living things. The more scientists learn, the more we all will understand the world we share.

During this century, life scientists will make new discoveries. One finding you can expect: Life is not as simple as we once thought. The differences between plants and animals, the differences between males and females, and even the differences between what is alive and what is not alive are not completely clear.

For example, many small organisms have traits of both animals and plants. Some organisms seem to be only partly alive. As a result, some modern biologists are loosening their ties to traditional specialties, such as botany and zoology. Instead, they are becoming more interested in broad themes.

Themes in Life Science

One major theme of life science is **interdependence**, or the dependence of one living thing on another living thing. Some examples of interdependence are obvious. The lion, for instance, cannot live without eating the grazing animals of Africa's plains. The grazing animals cannot live without eating the grass. Some interdependencies are less obvious. For example, a bone cell from your arm cannot survive without other cells to provide it with nutrients.

A second theme in life science is finding the balance between the continuity and diversity of life. **Continuity** means that life continues as it is. For example, cats have kittens, not puppies. **Diversity** means that living things that look different on the outside often have many similarities on the inside. One result of diversity is that not only do kittens have all the traits of being cats, but so do lions, tigers, and leopards. Life scientists ask questions such as these: Has life always begun simply and become more complex? Are there eras of increased diversity?

Other themes in life science ask basic questions: When exactly is something alive? How can you classify a living thing that is neither plant nor animal? Some of these themes will be explored further in this book.

There are many themes of life science. Being aware of them will help you to organize your knowledge and to increase your understanding of what you read.

Thinking About Science

Part A

Directions: Based on what you have just read, circle *T* for each true statement, or *F* for each false statement.

T   F   **1.** Life science can best be described as the study of diseases.

T   F   **2.** Botany is concerned with animals; zoology is concerned with plants.

T   F   **3.** Genetics is the study of the role of heredity in plants and animals.

T   F   **4.** The theory of evolution is a brand-new idea.

Part B

Directions: Match the people on the left with the subject of their work on the right. Write the correct letter on the line.

_____ **1.** Robert Hooke   (a) DNA

_____ **2.** Charles Darwin   (b) classification

_____ **3.** Twentieth-century   (c) cells
              life scientists

_____ **4.** Gregor Mendel   (d) single-celled organisms

_____ **5.** Carolus Linnaeus   (e) heredity

_____ **6.** Anton van Leeuwenhoek   (f) evolution

Answers are on pages 307–308.

Directions: Choose the <u>one best answer</u> to each question.

Questions 1–3 refer to the following photo and passage.

When *Viking* landed on the surface of Mars, one of its jobs was to look for signs of life. To do this, a special digging arm on *Viking* scooped up a sample of soil. The soil was analyzed in *Viking's* miniature laboratory. Tests were designed to discover if anything in the soil behaved as if it were alive. Did anything in the soil seem to produce food? to consume food? to give off waste? to grow? to die? Was anything in the soil made of the same chemicals that make up living things on Earth?

Scientists were not surprised when the tests neither proved nor disproved the question of life on Mars. It did seem as if something in the Martian soil made "food" out of sunlight and carbon dioxide. Something else in the soil seemed to burn up that "food" and to release waste. Both of these "somethings" were destroyed by heat. However, *Viking* found none of the chemicals on Mars that make up life on Earth. Scientists will need more evidence before they can answer their questions about life on Mars.

1. What were *Viking's* laboratories designed to examine the Martian soil for?

   (1) chemicals that indicate the presence of living things
   (2) anything that produced food
   (3) anything that grew
   (4) anything that died
   (5) all of the above

2. What did *Viking's* test results suggest about something in the soil?

   (1) It was reproducing.
   (2) It was making food.
   (3) It was breathing.
   (4) It was made of organic chemicals.
   (5) all of the above

3. What did the results of the Mars mission indicate?

   (1) The question about life on Mars was inconclusive.
   (2) Life exists on Mars in a different form than on Earth.
   (3) Mars is too cold to support life.
   (4) Mars is too hot to support life.
   (5) Carbon, the element found in all life forms, is absent from Mars.

Answers are on page 308.

The Cell

In the mid-1600s, Robert Hooke was investigating one of the new inventions of his day—the microscope. As he gazed at a thin slice of cork, he noticed that it seemed to be made of "little rooms," which he called **cells**. It was not long before scientists realized that all living things were made of cells. Now we know that cells are the building blocks of life. The presence of cells helps scientists determine if an object is now, or was ever, alive.

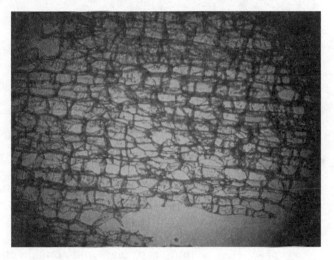

Hooke saw hundreds of cells when he looked at a piece of cork under a microscope.

Cytoplasm

Cells are basic to life, but they are not solid bits of matter. Inside each cell is a jellylike substance known as **cytoplasm**. Some scientists call this the "stuff" of life.

Cytoplasm is hard to describe because it is constantly changing. However, it always contains some of the same ingredients:

- About 70 percent of the cell's interior is made of water.

- Cytoplasm contains about 20 different **amino acids**. These acids combine and recombine to form thousands of different kinds of proteins. Just one cell may contain 2,000 different kinds of proteins. The proteins are used to build and repair the cell.

- **Carbohydrates** provide the cell with energy.

- **Fats** are the cell's storage tanks. Fats contains all the energy the organism did not use immediately.

- **Nucleic acids** control the cell's activities.

Thinking About Science

Directions: Match the words in the column on the left with their description on the right. Write the correct letter on the line.

_____ **1.** water   (a) building blocks of protein

_____ **2.** carbohydrates   (b) the cell's storage tanks

_____ **3.** nucleic acids   (c) 70 percent of the cell's interior

_____ **4.** fats   (d) the cell's energy source

_____ **5.** amino acids   (e) controllers of cell activity

Answers are on page 308.

Cell Structures

Cytoplasm is not just liquid. It contains a variety of structures that help the cell to function. As you read about the structures of the cell, refer to the diagrams of plant and animal cells below.

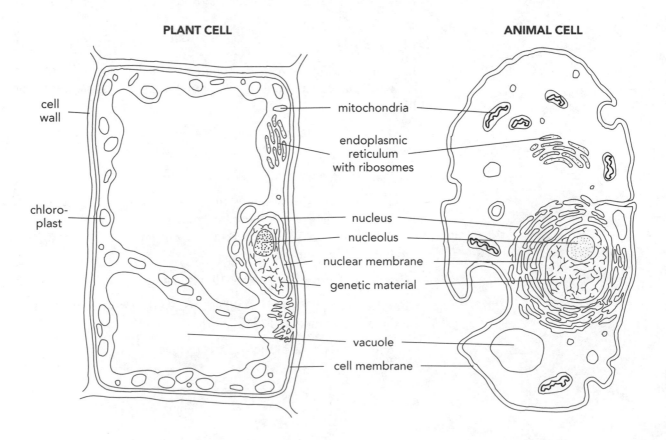

PLANT CELL   ANIMAL CELL

cell wall, chloroplast, mitochondria, endoplasmic reticulum with ribosomes, nucleus, nucleolus, nuclear membrane, genetic material, vacuole, cell membrane

Cell Membrane

Beginning at the outer edge of the cell, notice the **cell membrane**. This structure is soft and flexible, but it holds the cell together. It also serves as a gate. Substances needed by the cell can pass through the membrane and into the cell. Other substances are shut out. Waste products pass out of the cell through this membrane.

Nucleus

The **nucleus** is one of the larger structures of the cell. It controls the activities of the cell. Like the cell, the nucleus is made of a substance much like cytoplasm. It is also surrounded by a membrane. Long, thin strands of genetic material float in the nucleus. Inside the cell is the **nucleolus**, a dense, round body that makes specialized cell structures called ribosomes.

Specialized Cell Structures

Cells may differ in small ways, but all cells contain a membrane, cytoplasm, and nuclear material. In addition, most also contain some specialized structures that help the cell to function. Just a few of these structures are described below.

Most cells contain **mitochondria,** which are shown near the top of the diagram. These sausage-shaped structures trap the energy from food and release it to the cell.

Throughout the cell are canal-like structures known as the **endoplasmic reticulum** (ER). The ER leads from the cell membrane to the nucleus. They transport and store substances needed by the cell.

Ribosomes are the tiny dots seen on the ER. They combine amino acids into proteins.

The **vacuoles** have a variety of functions. Some digest food. Others store or dispose of wastes. In plant cells the vacuole may be filled with water, which helps to support the stem and leaves.

Specialized Cell Structures in Plants

Notice in the diagrams that plant cells have several structures that are not found in animal cells. The **chloroplasts** contain the chlorophyll that plants use to trap energy from the Sun.

The outermost structure just outside the cell membrane is the **cell wall.** This rigid wall provides support for the cell. When Robert Hooke found cells in a slice of cork, he was looking at the cork's cell walls.

Thinking About Science

Directions: Label the structures in the following diagrams by writing the names of the numbered items on the lines below. The first one is done for you.

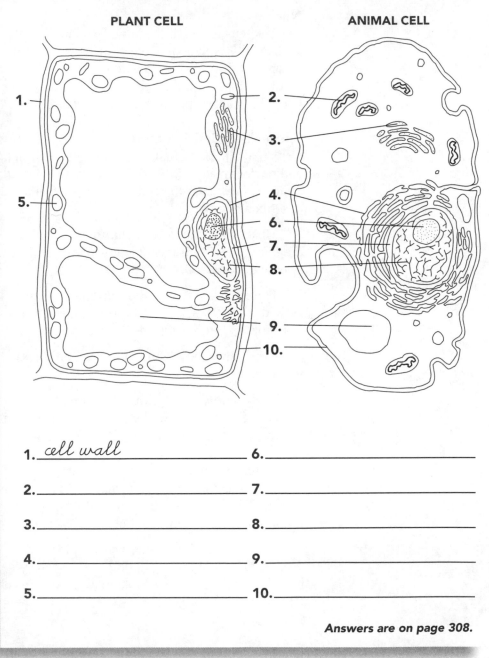

PLANT CELL   ANIMAL CELL

1. _cell wall_ _____   6. _____

2. _____   7. _____

3. _____   8. _____

4. _____   9. _____

5. _____   10. _____

Answers are on page 308.

How a Cell Works

To stay alive, most cells need to take in food, water, and oxygen, and to eliminate wastes. This means cells must let materials pass through the cell membrane without losing their cytoplasm. Transporting materials across the cell membrane takes place one molecule at a time. Like a filter, the cell membrane has tiny holes that allow some small molecules to pass through it. Larger molecules are filtered out.

Diffusion

Materials, such as water or simple carbohydrates, tend to seek a balance on either side of the cell membrane. If more of a specific kind of molecule, such as water, is on the outside of a cell, the tendency is for those molecules to spread into the cell. Scientists describe this process of spreading molecules evenly through an area as **diffusion**. Diffusion moves molecules in and out of cells without using any of the cell's energy.

Active Transport

Cells can also move molecules from less crowded areas outside the cell to more crowded areas inside the cell. This movement against the normal flow of diffusion is called **active transport**. The process uses energy and works something like a revolving door. Special molecules in the cell membrane pick up materials outside the cell. They then turn to the inside of the cell and release the material.

Thinking About Science

Directions: Answer the questions below in the space provided.

1. What are two ways materials can pass in and out of the cell?

   a. _____

   b. _____

2. Each cell membrane has tiny holes that allow small molecules to pass through it. What can a cell membrane be compared to?

   _____ .

3. What is the process of spreading molecules evenly through an area called?

   _____ .

4. What is the process of moving molecules from less crowded areas outside the cell to more crowded areas inside the cell called?

   _____ .

Answers are on page 308.

Directions: Choose the <u>one best answer</u> to each question.

Questions 1–4 refer to the information on pages 77–81.

1. Which of the following is found in plant cells but not in animal cells?

   (1) cell membrane
   (2) chloroplast
   (3) cytoplasm
   (4) genetic material
   (5) nucleus

2. What is the purpose of the cell wall in plant cells?

   (1) to release energy to the cell
   (2) to control the cell's activities
   (3) to trap energy from the Sun
   (4) to separate the cells from the rest of the plant
   (5) to give strength to the cells of the plant

3. Carbon dioxide and waste materials diffuse out of cells. What would happen if a cell did not diffuse these substances?

   (1) The cell would grow bigger and burst.
   (2) The cell would use the substances for nourishment.
   (3) The cell would be poisoned and die.
   (4) The cell would create more carbon dioxide.
   (5) The cell would digest the substances.

4. Sea plants often contain more molecules of iodine than does the seawater around them. Iodine moves from the seawater into the plants. What process is described by this example?

   (1) active transport
   (2) diffusion
   (3) interdependence
   (4) diversity
   (5) continuity

   Answers are on page 308.

Simple Organisms

Years ago, people tried to divide all of Earth's creatures into plants and animals. Scientists were not happy with this classification system because there was always something, such as the mushroom, that just didn't fit. Now scientists are trying new ways of classifying organisms. Most now divide living organisms into five major groups: monerans, protists, fungi, plants, and animals. Two of these groups, the monerans and the protists, consist of just a single cell. For many years, people have called these creatures microbes.

Microbes

A **microbe** is an organism that is too small to see without the help of a microscope. They are almost always made of a single cell. Most microbes are less than 4/1,000 inch (0.1 millimeter) across. Although we cannot see microbes, we do see their effects. Many cause decay and disease. Others are essential ingredients in making alcohol, bread, and cheese. For example, yeast, a microbe, is responsible in the fermentation process for making alcoholic beverages, such as wine and beer. Yeast also is the ingredient that causes bread dough to rise.

Bacteria, another form of microbe, are added to milk to make yogurt. When the bacteria ferment, they multiply and cause the milk to thicken and sour. A third microbe, a certain type of penicillin mold, is added to blue cheese to give it its color and taste. Penicillin is well known as an antibiotic used to fight bacterial infections. **Microbiology** is the study of microbes. **Biotechnology** is the use of microbes to make useful materials for human consumption.

In one-celled organisms, the single cell must perform all the life functions to remain alive. Each structure in the cytoplasm has its function. Examples of single-celled organisms include monerans and protists.

Monerans

The group of organisms known as **monerans** are among the simplest and smallest living things. Bacteria and blue-green algae are the best known monerans. They can live just about anywhere. Bacteria can be found growing under ice, in boiling water, in the air, and even inside your body. They are most commonly found in warm, moist places.

A MONERAN CELL (BACTERIA)

- cell membrane
- cell wall
- genetic material

Some bacteria are essential to the growth of plants. Some are valuable **decomposers**. They break down dead tissue so that dead plants and animals do not litter Earth. As decomposers, the bacteria add nutrients to the soil, which Earth's plant life needs to thrive. They also cause food to spoil. Freezing, boiling, or drying food can slow the spread of bacteria on food. Other bacteria cause diseases, such as strep throat and tuberculosis. Without antibiotics, such as penicillin (itself a bacterium), these diseases could kill many people.

Protists

Like monerans, **protists** are single-celled organisms. Biologists are interested in protists because their development was an important advance in the history of life on Earth. Scientists are also fascinated because some protists have fungus-like traits, some have animallike traits, and some have plantlike traits.

A PROTIST CELL (EUGLENA)

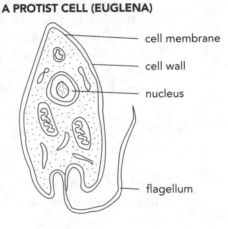

- cell membrane
- cell wall
- nucleus
- flagellum

One protist, the euglena, has traits of both plants and animals. Euglena contain chlorophyll and make their own food. They also swim and have a mouthlike structure.

One fungus-like protist, called a slime mold, exists as a single cell. When food is scarce, the slime mold cells move together into a massive colony. Then they migrate to a new area and reproduce.

A FUNGUS CELL

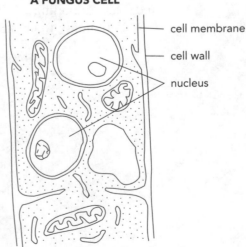

- cell membrane
- cell wall
- nucleus

Viruses

Viruses are microbes but not cells. They are not always included in a life science classification system because many scientists hesitate to describe them as living things. Viruses have no cytoplasm, no nucleus, and no cell membrane. They do, however, have a core of genetic material surrounded by protein.

A VIRUS

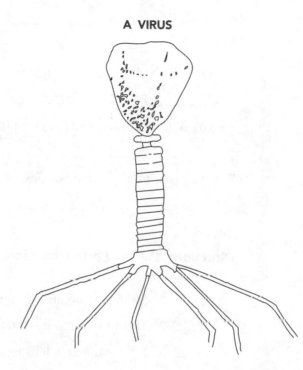

Left to themselves, viruses do not grow or reproduce. Once they invade a living cell, however, they control the cell and use it to produce more viruses. They are responsible for a host of diseases including flu, the common cold, chicken pox, mumps, measles, and AIDS. AIDS is believed to be caused by HIV (Human Immunodeficiency Virus). This virus weakens the body's natural defenses so that other viruses or bacteria can strike. Unable to fend off opportunistic illnesses, the body weakens, and the victim dies.

Thinking About Science

Part A

Directions: Answer the questions below in the space provided.

1. What is a microbe?_____

   _____

2. (a) What traits make the euglena like an animal?_____

   _____

   (b) What trait makes the euglena like a plant?_____

   _____

3. Why don't many scientists describe viruses as living things?

   _____

Part B

Directions: Put an *M* before each moneran trait and a *P* before each
protist trait.

_____ **1.** Strange structures designed for movement

_____ **2.** The simplest and smallest living things

_____ **3.** No separate nucleus in some

_____ **4.** Chloroplasts in some but no cell wall

_____ **5.** A single cell that forms a colony of cells to migrate

Answers are on page 308.

Multicelled Organisms

Although all organisms begin life as a single cell, they don't all stay single-celled. In multicelled organisms, the cells specialize. Each has a function to perform. You can tell from their shapes that they have different functions.

Usually, specialized cells form **tissues**. In animals, several different kinds of tissues may form an **organ**. For example, the heart contains muscle tissue, blood tissue, and nerve tissue.

Groups of organs that work together to perform a life process are known as an **organ system**. For example, the tongue, teeth, stomach, and intestines are all part of the digestive system. They all work together to remove nutrients from food. Examples of simple multicelled organisms include fungi and simple plants, such as algae, mosses, and ferns.

Fungi

Mold, mildew, yeast, and mushrooms are all **fungi**. With the exception of yeast, fungi are multicelled organisms. Fungi are used in the production of penicillin and bread.

FUNGI

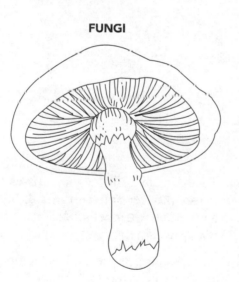

Like plants, fungi are rooted in one place. Their cytoplasm is at least partially enclosed by a rigid cell wall. However, fungi cannot make their own food because they do not contain chlorophyll. They "feed" by releasing a chemical that digests the organic matter around them. Fungi feed on plants and animals that are dead or alive. When fungi attach themselves to living organisms, they can cause a variety of diseases, one of which is athlete's foot.

Some fungi reproduce by growing a new cell, called a bud. Others reproduce by releasing tiny reproductive cells, called spores.

Algae

Algae are the simplest nonflowering plants (a category that also includes mosses and ferns). Although all algae contain chlorophyll, not all algae are green. Some are red or brown. Because algae live in water and absorb their food from the water, they do not need true roots. The water supports the algae, so they do not need true stems. Algae cannot survive out of water.

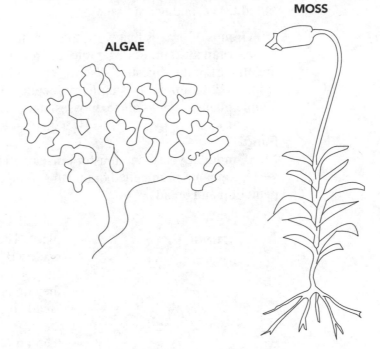

ALGAE

MOSS

Mosses

Mosses live in wet places on land. Like algae, mosses do not have a group of specialized cells to transport water or to carry food. Instead, mosses depend on diffusion to move water into their cells. Because diffusion is a slow process, mosses do not grow large.

Mosses enter two stages in their life cycle. The first stage produces both male and female cells. These cells meet to produce the second stage, a spore-bearing plant. Spores are tiny reproductive cells. Upon ripening, the capsules that contain spores open and scatter the spores. Spores may be scattered by the wind or by animals brushing up against the ripened capsules. If the spores land on fertile ground, they develop into new plants.

Ferns

Some plants have true roots, stems, and leaves but no true seeds. Instead, these plants reproduce by forming spores on the undersides of their leaves. The most familiar plant in this category is the **fern**. Most ferns live in damp, shady places. Instead of stretching up to the Sun, fern stems grow horizontally underground.

FERN

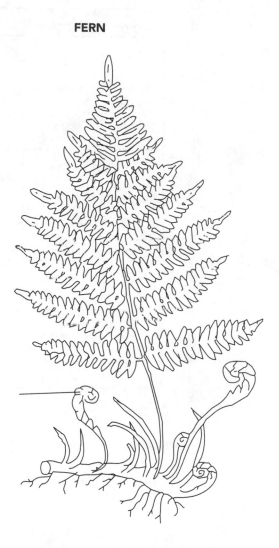

Years ago seedless plants, such as ferns, were abundant. As they died, they were buried and the earth pressed upon them. Today, we dig up this ancient plant matter and burn it as coal.

Thinking About Science

Directions: Complete the following chart by filling in the blanks below with the correct words.

Organism	Structure	Chloroplast	Mobile	Cell Covering	Genetic Material
1. ___	incomplete cell	no	no	none	surrounded by protein
Moneran	single cell	some	no	2. ___	floats in cell
Protist	single cell	some	3. ___	cell wall	in nucleus
Fungus	4. ___	no	no	incomplete cell wall	in several nuclei
Plant	multicell	5. ___	6. ___	cell wall	in nucleus
Animal	multicell	7. ___	yes	cell membrane	8. ___

1. _____   5. _____

2. _____   6. _____

3. _____   7. _____

4. _____   8. _____

Answers are on page 308.

Directions: Choose the <u>one best answer</u> to each question.

Questions 1–3 refer to the chart below.

INFECTIOUS DISEASES THAT OCCUR DURING CHILDHOOD

Disease	Cause	Symptoms	How It's Spread	Prevention/Treatment
mumps	virus	fever; swelling of salivary glands; sometimes a headache and pain when swallowing	air; direct and indirect contact	vaccine
measles (rubeola or red measles)	virus	cough, runny nose, and fever followed by red rash beginning on face	air; direct and indirect contact	vaccine
German measles (rubella or three-day measles)	virus	slight fever and runny nose; red rash beginning on face; swelling of lymph nodes in neck	air; direct and indirect contact	vaccine
chicken pox	virus	slight fever; red bumps beginning on chest and back; severe itching of bumps	air; direct and indirect contact	not currently preventable except with a special vaccine used for children and adults who have certain diseases
cold	virus	runny nose and sneezing; sometimes cough and sore throat; general weakness	air; direct and indirect contact	wash hands and cover mouth and nose; treat the symptoms
influenza	virus	fever; chills; cough and sore throat; general aches and pains and weakness	air; direct and indirect contact	vaccine for older adults and people with certain chronic illnesses
strep throat	bacteria	sore throat; swelling of lymph nodes in neck; sometimes fever and headache	air; direct contact	treated by taking an antibiotic, usually penicillin, for ten days

1. How can most viral diseases of childhood be prevented?

   (1) through vaccination
   (2) by washing hands
   (3) through regular doctor visits
   (4) through antibiotics
   (5) none of the above

2. What might a red rash be a symptom of?

   (1) measles or chicken pox
   (2) flu or a cold
   (3) mumps or measles
   (4) flu or chicken pox
   (5) mumps or cold

3. What is a fever <u>not</u> a symptom of?

   (1) measles
   (2) mumps
   (3) chicken pox
   (4) cold
   (5) flu

Answers are on page 308.

Flowering Plants

Parts of a Flowering Plant

Flowering plants are much more complex than nonflowering plants. There are more than 250,000 species of flowering plants on Earth. When you look at a flower, you see only part of the plant. The other parts are the roots, the stem, and the leaves. Refer to the diagram below as you read about the parts of a flowering plant.

PARTS OF A FLOWERING PLANT

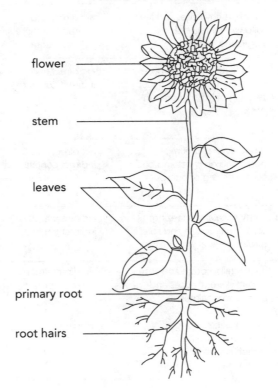

flower

stem

leaves

primary root

root hairs

Roots

After a seed is planted in the ground, the **roots** are the first part of the plant to develop. Roots anchor the plant in the ground. The plant will stay in that spot for its entire life.

The roots also absorb water and food from the soil and transport them to the stem. In some plants, food is stored in the roots. Most roots are covered with threadlike structures called root hairs. These hairs increase the amount of food and water the plant can absorb from the soil.

Not all roots are the same. Some plants, such as grass, have a mass of roots that spread out wide and grow near the surface of the ground. Other plants, such as the dandelion, have one major root that grows deep into the ground. This deep root is called a taproot. Some taproots can grow as deep as twenty feet. Radishes, carrots, and turnips are taproots.

Stems

Stems have two basic functions. They support the plant and they transport food and water throughout the plant. In some parts of the stem, water and nutrients travel up from the roots to the leaves. In other parts of the stem, food manufactured in the leaves moves down to the roots.

Tree trunks are stems that can grow quite tall and strong. Other stems are small and grow close to the ground. Some stems even grow underground. Onions and tulip bulbs are underground stems that also store food.

Leaves

Leaves are green because so many of their cells contain **chlorophyll**, a green pigment that enables plants to make their own food. The chlorophyll reflects the green part of light. It is in these cells, the chloroplasts, that food is made. Leaves also contain tiny openings, called stomates, that allow gases from the air to enter and exit the leaf. Both the chloroplasts and the stomates are essential to life on Earth.

Thinking About Science

Part A

Directions: Label the structures in the diagram shown below by writing the names of the plant parts on the lines that follow.

1. _____

2. _____

3. _____

4. _____

5. _____

Part B

Directions: Check the item below that tells the function of stomates.

_____ **1.** provide an opening for chlorophyll to enter the plant

_____ **2.** provide an opening for light energy to enter the leaf

_____ **3.** provide an opening for gases to enter and exit the leaf

_____ **4.** squeeze excess water out of the leaf

Answers are on pages 308–309.

Photosynthesis

Photosynthesis is the plant's food-manufacturing process. The formulas below will help you to understand the process.

PHOTOSYNTHESIS FORMULA

Sunlight

carbon dioxide + water $\Longrightarrow$ glucose + oxygen

Chlorophyll

$$6CO_2 + 6H_2O \Longrightarrow C_6H_{12}O_6 + 6O_2$$

As the Sun shines on a leaf, chlorophyll absorbs and traps the Sun's light energy. This energy is stored in the chloroplasts of the plant's cells. Meanwhile, water moves up the plant from the roots and is stored in the cells' vacuoles. Carbon dioxide, a gas from the air, enters the plant through the stomates of the leaves.

When the energy stored in the chloroplasts is released, it breaks apart the molecules of carbon dioxide and water. They recombine into a type of sugar known as glucose. Oxygen is left over. A small part of the oxygen is used by the plant during respiration. The rest of the oxygen is released into the air through the stomates. All the animals on Earth use that oxygen to breathe.

We can't see the oxygen released by plants. However, when water plants, such as seaweed or other aquarium plants, carry out photosynthesis, oxygen appears as bubbles on the surface of the plants' leaves.

Reproduction in Flowering Plants

Most people notice and admire the petals of a flower. The petals, however, serve mainly to protect the plant's reproductive structures. In the diagram of the flower, find the stamens that are just inside the petals. **Stamens** are the flower's male reproductive structures. Tiny grains of pollen are produced on the tip of the stamens. **Pollen** is the male reproductive material of flowering plants. These pollen grains hold one half of the plant's genetic information.

REPRODUCTIVE STRUCTURE OF A FLOWER

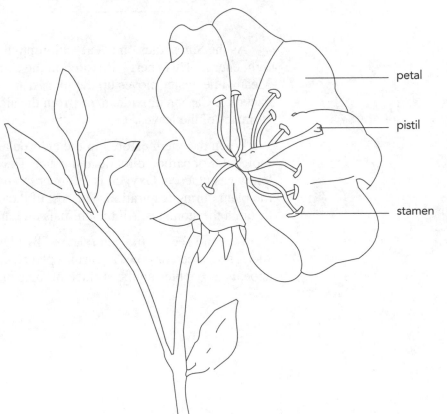

petal

pistil

stamen

The **pistil** is the female reproductive structure of the flower. The pistil is covered with a sticky fluid. When a pollen grain lands on the top of the pistil, a tube grows down to the swollen base of the pistil. The base contains an egg cell, which holds the other half of the plant's genetic information. The pollen grain travels down the tube and fertilizes the egg. Fertilization combines the genetic information from the male and the female cells.

If **pollination**, the process by which plants transfer reproductive materials from one plant to another, succeeds, the egg cell at the base of the pistil develops into a seed. The seed may develop into a fruit. The fruit falls to the ground or is eaten by a bird or an animal. Some seeds, such as dandelion seeds, simply blow away. If the seed lands in a good spot, it will grow into a young plant.

Bees are the major pollinators for most types of plants. Like people, the bees are attracted to the bright colors and sweet smell of the flower. Bees also gather the flower's nectar to make honey. As they explore the flower, they brush up against the stamens. The pollen sticks to the bees' legs. When the bees enter the next flower, the pollen falls onto the pistil.

Other insects, birds, and animals, the wind, and even rain can pollinate flowers. Some types of plants, such as cotton, pea, and tomato plants, can even pollinate themselves.

Thinking About Science

Part A

Directions: Put a check in front of the correct answer to each question.

1. Which of the following is the most likely reason why mature oak trees frequently die four or five years after a building is constructed near them?

   _____ (1) The tree is no longer capable of reproducing.

   _____ (2) The supply of chlorophyll has been reduced.

   _____ (3) The delicate root structures have become severely damaged.

   _____ (4) The trees have grown too tall.

2. What is photosynthesis?

   _____ (1) the reproductive cycle of flowers

   _____ (2) the food-making process in plants

   _____ (3) the growth of young plants

   _____ (4) the manufacture of chlorophyll

Part B

Directions: Complete each sentence in the space provided.

1. According to the diagram of the flower, the flower's female reproductive structure is the _____.

2. Fertilization combines the _____ from the male and female.

Answers are on page 309.

Directions: Choose the <u>one best answer</u> to each question.

Question 1 is based on the information on pages 92–97.

1. The absorption of carbon dioxide and the release of oxygen during photosynthesis permits which of the following processes in a human?

   (1) respiration
   (2) digestion
   (3) circulation
   (4) elimination
   (5) thinking

Questions 2 and 3 refer to the following passage.

Like all living things, plants respond to the world around them. Unlike animals, their responses are often too slow for us to watch.

Instead of moving quickly from one place to another, the plant may respond by growing toward or away from something. Over time, we may notice the change. This response is called *tropism*.

For example, no matter how a seed lands on the ground, the root grows down. The stem grows up. By experimenting, scientists have learned that this happens because the plant responds to Earth's gravity.

Another example you might have noticed is that a plant grows toward light. If the direction of the light changes, the plant's growth pattern will also change. In a few days, the leaves will turn to the light.

Finally, many plants respond to touch. The Venus flytrap uses touch to capture an insect. The pea plant responds to touch when it climbs up a fence.

2. To which sensations do plants respond?

   A. Gravity
   B. Touch
   C. Sight

   (1) A only
   (2) B only
   (3) C only
   (4) both A and B
   (5) both B and C

3. Why do people often not notice a plant's response to the environment?

   (1) It occurs slowly.
   (2) It occurs at night.
   (3) It occurs rarely.
   (4) It happens too quickly.
   (5) People are too busy.

Answers are on page 309.

Animals

The animal kingdom is populated by organisms that are made up of many cells. Animals, unlike plants, live by eating. While most animals are mobile, some animals, such as barnacles, spend all of their adult lives anchored to one place. Also, unlike plants, animal cell structure is different in that animal cells do not have rigid walls.

The millions of species of animals are generally classified as vertebrates or invertebrates. Animals that have backbones are **vertebrates** and include fish, reptiles, birds, amphibians, and mammals. Animals without backbones are called **invertebrates.** This last group includes many familiar creatures, such as sponges, corals, worms, snails, jellyfish, lobsters, spiders, and the group that contains the largest number of species—insects.

Invertebrates

Sponges and Corals

Sponges, the simplest of the invertebrates, have no head, arms, or legs. The adults don't even move from place to place. In fact, for many years, people thought that sponges were plants. A sponge is actually a very simple animal that is shaped like a bag full of holes. Sponges survive because they live in water and food floats right into them. They filter their food from the water. Sponges attach themselves to a convenient spot and stay there for the rest of their lives.

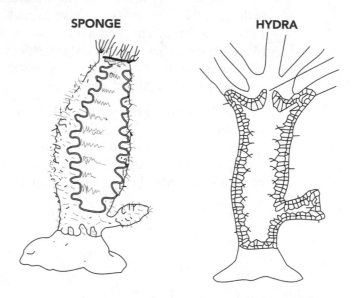

SPONGE　　　　**HYDRA**

The bodies of other such invertebrates as corals, jellyfish, hydras, and their relatives are also rather baglike. But these animals are more complex than the sponges. Around a central cavity, they have long tentacles that can sting or trap prey. The tentacles then push food into the body cavity where it is digested. Most of these creatures, such the corals, spend their lives attached to the seafloor. Some, such as the jellyfish, go through stages of life when they swim freely. Corals join together to form large colonies. The colonies secrete a stony skeleton for the corals to live in. The reefs formed by these skeletons take hundreds of years to build up.

Worms

Worms may look like simple animals, but they are actually more complex than jellyfish. They have head ends and tail ends, tops and bottoms. Except for the parasitic worms, which may attach themselves to other animals, most worms move from place to place. They also have a very simple brainlike structure. Some have a digestive tract.

WORM

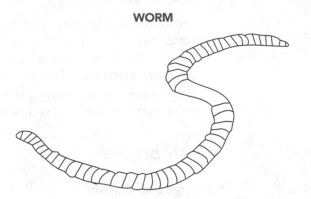

Worms are everywhere. Just one kind of worm, the roundworm, may have as many as half a million species. Many are parasites. Scientists counted 90,000 roundworms in just one rotting apple. An acre of ground may contain 10 million.

Earthworms are among the most advanced worms. They have a body that is divided into sections. They have a mouth at the head end, an anus for waste removal at the tail end, and a digestive tract in between. They have nerves and blood vessels. They also have short, stubby bristles that help them move. Although earthworms have no eyes or ears, they have a nervous system and respond to both light and sound.

Earthworms are unique animals in that they have both male and female reproductive organs. This type of animal is called a **hermaphrodite.** Although these animals do mate in pairs, they exchange sperm so that each individual fertilizes the other's eggs. Sometimes a hermaphrodite can fertilize its own eggs. Other hermaphrodites include snails and their close relatives, slugs.

Mollusks

Shelled animals, such as snails and oysters, belong to a group of animals called **mollusks**. Squids and octopuses also fit into this group, although they don't have shells like the others. Mollusks have no skeletal system, but they have all the other basic organ systems (muscular, digestive, circulatory, nervous, excretory, respiratory, and reproductive). Their bodies are divided into a head, middle, and tail.

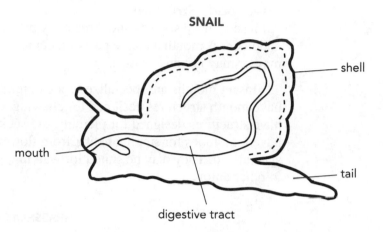

SNAIL

shell

mouth

tail

digestive tract

Arthropods

Arthropods are animals with legs that bend. Spiders, ticks, lobsters, and insects are common arthropods. They also have eyes and antennae for sensing the world around them. They have a hard outer covering known as an **exoskeleton**.

The material that forms the exoskeleton is not living tissue and cannot grow with the rest of the animal. As a result, arthropods must shed their exoskeletons to grow. The process is called **molting.** Before molting, the animal produces a soft, new exoskeleton under the old one. During molting, the old exoskeleton splits open and the animal crawls out. After a short wait, the new exoskeleton swells and hardens into the animal's new size. Although exoskeletons work well for small animals, they would be too heavy for a large animal.

Insects, the largest group of arthropods, not only respond to the world around them, they adapt to it so quickly that they have become among the most successful animals on Earth. This success is related to their ability to live on land, in air, and in water. Scientists have identified more than 700,000 species of insects and no one thinks that list is complete. Insects also reproduce at an amazing rate. A housefly may lay one hundred eggs at a time. The young will hatch, develop, and lay their own eggs in as few as ten days.

Insect Body Structure

All insects have six legs and three body regions—a head, thorax, and abdomen. A mouth and one pair of antennae are located on the head. They may or may not have wings.

Insect mouths are specialized for eating. Some, such as the grasshopper, have mouth structures designed for chewing. Others, such as the mosquito, have structures designed for piercing and sucking. Some, such the butterfly, have long tubes for sipping nectar from flowers. Legs may also be specialized. They may be suited for walking, jumping, swimming, or clinging to other animals.

GRASSHOPPER

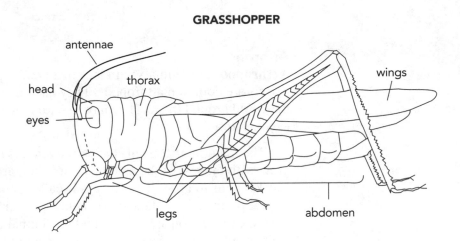

Sense Organs

Insects' eyes may be large or small, depending on how important sight is for the animal. Some insects have tiny eyes, or simple eyes. These insects cannot see very well and make up for it by their sense of touch. Other insects are able to see very well because of their compound eyes, eyes made up of many small parts.

Since insects have no noses, insects smell with their antennae, or feelers.

Insect Life Stages

Like jellyfish and corals, insects live their lives in stages. They go through either three or four distinct stages as they develop. The process is called **metamorphosis**. All insects begin as eggs. Insects that live in four stages hatch into wormlike creatures called larvae. In this stage, the larvae eat constantly and grow quickly. They then go into a resting stage (the pupa), in which they wrap themselves in a cocoon. Inside the cocoon the tissues of the larva change into the tissues of an adult insect. When the insect comes out of the cocoon, it is an adult.

METAMORPHOSIS

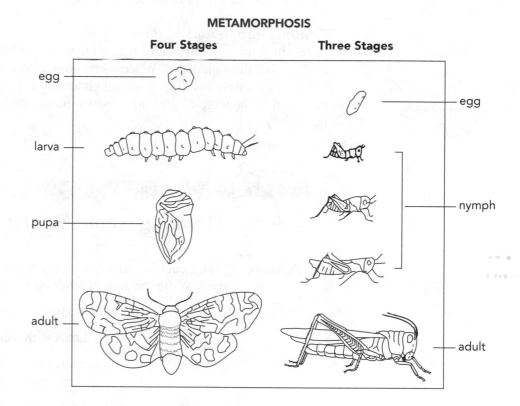

Insects that go through only three stages of metamorphosis skip both the larva and pupa stages. Instead they hatch into nymphs. The nymphs are much smaller than the adults. They have no wings, and their reproductive structures are incomplete. With each molting, however, a nymph is more and more like an adult.

Insect Behavior

Most insects are solitary creatures that meet others of their kind only to mate. Some, however, live in large, organized colonies with an obvious division of labor. Termites, wasps, ants, and bees are among these social insects. Bees, for example, live in large hives. Each nest has one queen bee that spends its entire life laying eggs. Drone bees have but one job—to mate with the queen. They can do little else and cannot even feed themselves. Most of the bees in the nest are worker bees. As the name suggests, they do all the work in the colony. They build and clean the hive, collect food, care for the young, guard the nest, and feed the queen and the drones.

Communication Among Bees

In recent years, scientists have learned that worker bees communicate with one another through dance. When a bee finds a good source of nectar, it returns to the nest and does a special abdomen wiggling dance. The speed and direction of the wiggles give other bees information about the location of the nectar.

Thinking About Science

Directions: Match each invertebrate on the left with its description on the right. Write the correct letter on the line.

_____ **1.** Sponges   (a) animals with shells

_____ **2.** Corals   (b) animals with jointed legs

_____ **3.** Worms   (c) animals having heads, tails, tops, and bottoms, but not feet

_____ **4.** Mollusks   (d) animals shaped like a bag full of holes

_____ **5.** Arthropods   (e) animals that spend their lives on the sea floor

Answers are on page 309.

Vertebrates

Having an internal skeleton makes a major difference among animals. Unlike the exoskeleton, the internal skeleton is made of living material. It grows as the animal grows. Most creatures with internal skeletons have two pairs of limbs that may be specialized as legs, arms, wings, fins, or flippers. Vertebrates have a backbone, an efficient circulatory system, and a well-developed nervous system. They respond to the world around them. Most can learn to change their behavior to suit their environment.

Vertebrates have two ways of responding to the environment. Some behaviors, such as reflexes and instincts, are inherited from the parents. For example, moving your finger close to your eye will cause a reflex. Your eye closes. Reflexes protect the animal from harm. Instincts are more complicated. The way a bird builds a nest or follows its mother, for example, is considered to be an instinct. The animal acts without having to be taught how to do it.

Self-preservation is instinctive for just about every animal. In times of danger, an animal will try to escape. If escape is impossible, it will fight. For example, a rabbit will run from a dog, but if the rabbit is trapped, it will turn and fight. Species preservation is also an instinct. It is this instinct that causes the mother cat to feed and defend her kittens. It causes salmon to swim upriver to reproduce even though the fish may die from exhaustion.

Most vertebrates can also learn a new behavior. If you repeatedly place food in one spot of an aquarium, a fish will look there for its dinner. A parrot learns to imitate certain words. A horse soon learns just how high to jump to clear a hurdle. A human will learn to read and spell.

Intelligent behavior, such as problem-solving and decision-making abilities, is more complex. Birds and mammals are more likely to show intelligent behavior than do other vertebrates.

Cold-blooded Animals

Cold-blooded animals do not necessarily have blood that feels cool. They do, however, have a body temperature that changes with their surroundings. In a cold environment, the animal becomes cool; in a warm environment, the animal's body temperature rises.

Fish

There are three main groups of **fish**. Those that have skeletons made up of cartilage, a tough, elastic tissue, belong to the cartilaginous group. Sharks are members of this group.

The largest group of fish are the bony fish, fish that have bony skeletons. Trout and many others belong to this group.

A third group is composed of jawless fish, a group that includes lampreys and eels.

In addition to the internal skeleton, fish have a tough outer covering of scales.

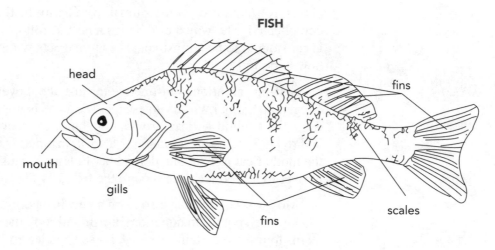

FISH

All fish live in water. Their bodies are suited to a watery environment. They have fins and a tail for swimming and gills that allow them to obtain oxygen from the water.

Fish reproduce by laying eggs in water. The males spread sperm over the eggs. What happens next varies. Most fish leave their eggs, and the young hatch on their own. Some fish guard the eggs until they hatch. A few fish protect the young until they grow to a certain size. An interesting exception to this method of reproduction occurs with the seahorse, a bony fish. The female of this species lays a small number of eggs in a special pouch on the male's abdomen. The male seahorse takes care of the eggs until they hatch and continues to look after the baby seahorses.

Amphibians

The most familiar **amphibians** are frogs and salamanders. Like insects, amphibians undergo metamorphosis as they develop. After hatching from eggs, the fishlike tadpoles live in water. Like fish, young amphibians breathe with gills. During metamorphosis, most amphibians develop lungs for breathing air and legs for moving on land. As adults, amphibians live on land. When they are ready to reproduce, they return to the water to lay their eggs.

METAMORPHOSIS IN THE FROG

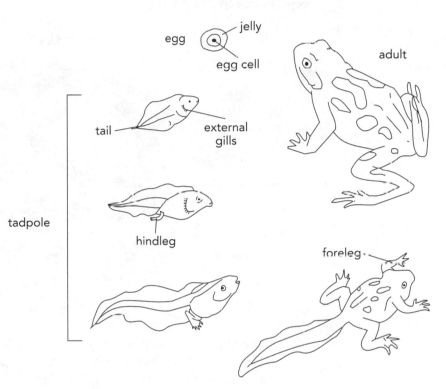

Because they are cold-blooded, the activity level of some amphibians decreases when the temperature drops. In cold areas, they may bury themselves in mud and hibernate. While amphibians are inactive, they live off body fat until they can feed again in the spring. Some amphibians also bury themselves during very hot, dry weather and become inactive.

Reptiles

Most people are familiar with **reptiles**, such as snakes, turtles, alligators and lizards, because of their relationship to the dinosaurs that once roamed Earth. No one knows for sure why the dinosaurs became extinct, but many scientists believe that the process began when a huge asteroid hit Earth.

The bodies of modern reptiles are dry and covered with scales. The scales are made of a hard material that is similar to human fingernails. The scales help to protect the animal from enemies and from drying out. As a result, reptiles can live in dry places.

REPTILE EGG

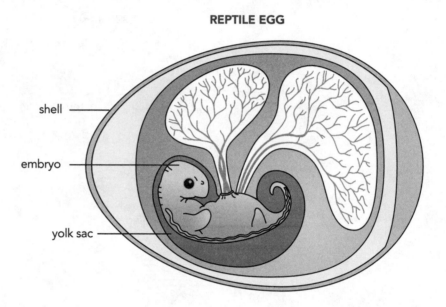

Unlike amphibians, reptiles do not have a tadpole stage. Young reptiles are small versions of the adults. Reptiles do not even need water to lay their eggs. Instead, the eggs have a shell that keeps the moisture inside the egg. The male sperm must reach the egg before the shell forms, so reptile fertilization is internal. A few reptiles give birth to live young.

Warm-blooded Animals

The internal temperature of warm-blooded animals does not depend on the weather outside. These animals use the energy released from food to keep their bodies warm. Feathers and fur trap air, which provides insulation from the cold. As a result, the body temperature of birds and mammals remains almost constant.

Birds

Because they fly, **birds** seem quite different from other vertebrates, but there are more similarities than differences. The wings are specialized front limbs. Feathers are modified versions of the reptile's scales. The feathers keep the animal warm and help provide the lift when a bird takes off. The bones of birds are hollow, which greatly reduces the weight of the animal. With larger, solid bones, birds probably would be unable to fly. In fact, the world's largest bird, the ostrich, cannot fly. Other birds, such as the penguin, use their wings as swim fins.

BIRD

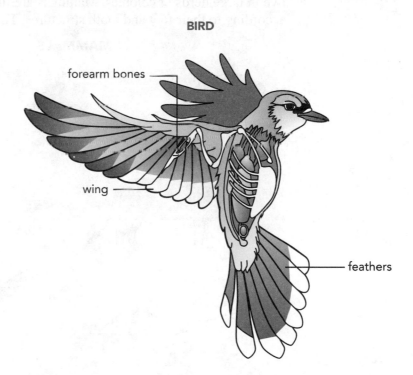

forearm bones

wing

feathers

As with the reptiles, bird fertilization is internal. Their eggs are protected by shells and laid on land. Birds, however, cannot leave their eggs. They must keep them warm until they hatch. Some young birds are quite independent when they hatch. Others must be fed and protected by their parents until they can fly.

Mammals

About 200 million years ago, the first **mammal**, a small shrewlike creature, appeared in the fossil record. It probably ate insects and parts of plants. Because of its warm blood and large eyes, scientists think the creature was active in the cool of the night when the great dinosaurs were resting. As the dinosaurs died out, the mammals spread throughout the world. Some mammals, such as bats, fly. Some, such as moles and shrews, live underground. Whales and dolphins live in the ocean. Hundreds of species of mammals share the land.

Instead of scales or feathers, mammals have hair. The young are fed by the mother from special glands that produce milk. Although there are mammals that lay eggs (the platypus), most young mammals are born alive. Some mammals, such as kangaroos and opposums, nourish their live-born young in pouches. These animals are called **marsupials**. Some mammals get together only for mating. Others live in pairs or family groups. Still others live in large herds or colonies. Mammals are further divided into groups according to their foot and tooth structures. These groups vary enormously.

MAMMALS

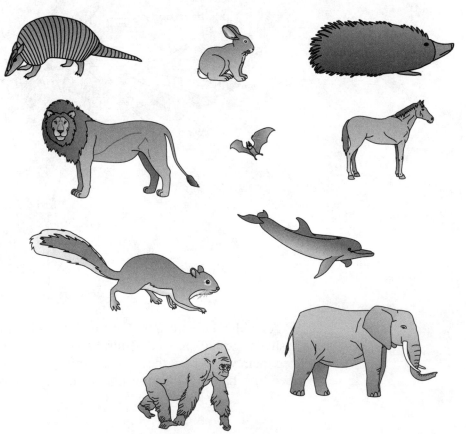

As a group, mammals are the most intelligent creatures on Earth. Their ability to adapt to new situations, to learn from past experience, and to communicate with one another has enabled them to thrive in many habitats. Many mammals use tools and build simple shelters. They live in complex social groups that require cooperation and communication.

Thinking About Science

Directions: Answer the questions below in the space provided.

1. What are the three major groups of cold-blooded animals?

   a. _____

   b. _____

   c. _____

2. What do insects and amphibians have in common?

   _____

3. What are the three major categories of fish?

   a. _____

   b. _____

   c. _____

4. What happens to the body temperature of cold-blooded animals?

   _____

5. What are the two major groups of warm-blooded animals?

   a. _____

   b. _____

6. Why is the body temperature of warm-blooded animals kept constant?

   _____

Answers are on page 309.

Directions: Choose the one best answer to each question.

Questions 1 and 2 refer to the following passage.

Penny: WHAT DID YOU DO TO PENNY?

Koko: BITE.

Penny: YOU ADMIT IT?

Koko: SORRY BITE SCRATCH. WRONG BITE.

Penny: WHY BITE?

Koko: BECAUSE MAD.

Penny: WHY MAD?

Koko: DON'T KNOW.

The conversation printed above may seem odd. Part of the oddity may be that the speakers were using sign language and that Koko is a gorilla.

Koko is the subject of a scientific experiment conducted by Penny Patterson, a university student. She taught Koko ASL—the hand sign language used by deaf people. Penny estimates that Koko has learned 1,000 signs, but uses only about 500 in everyday conversation. Koko talks about being happy, sad, or angry. She talks about things she did in the past and sometimes lies to avoid getting into trouble. She asks people for hugs and makes up insults about those she doesn't like. Although Koko can't read, she loves to look at picture books and signs to herself when she recognizes a picture.

One Christmas, Koko signed that she wanted a cat for a present. Her teachers gave her a stuffed cat. Koko responded angrily to the stuffed cat and covered it with a blanket. Finally, the scientists realized that Koko wanted a real cat. Six months later, they brought her a real kitten. At first sight, she signed, "Love that," and she did.

Now Koko lives with a male gorilla, Michael, who has also learned sign language. Koko and Michael often sign to one another. Scientists are wondering if Koko and Michael will raise babies that use sign language.

Because their vocal cords do not allow speech like ours, scientists look for other ways to communicate with primates. In addition to sign-language methods, primates have learned to use elaborate computer programs to imitate language. The chimpanzee Kanzi responds immediately to spoken language. When the teacher says, "I hid the surprise by my foot," Kanzi lifts up the teacher's foot to look for the prize.

1. Why do scientists need to find alternate ways to communicate with primates?

   (1) Primates are too intelligent to speak to humans.
   (2) The vocal cords of primates are not designed for speech.
   (3) Primates respond only to voice commands.
   (4) Primates are not smart enough to remember words.
   (5) The tongues of primates cannot shape the sounds of speech.

2. What can you infer from Koko's use of language?

   A. Primates are capable of thinking.
   B. Primates are capable of planning.
   C. Primates have emotions.

   (1) A only
   (2) B only
   (3) C only
   (4) A and B only
   (5) A, B, and C

Answers are on page 309.

Communities of Living Things

No organisms live alone. Every living thing depends on other living and nonliving things. The part of Earth in which life exists is termed the **biosphere**. The biosphere covers the entire surface of Earth and includes the atmosphere. Scientists call the system of interacting organisms and their environment an **ecosystem**. A healthy ecosystem must stay in balance. However, change in an ecosystem is constant. Most of these changes are small and help to keep the ecosystem in balance.

Many people have become concerned about human impact on ecosystems. Humans depend on the environment to supply everything they need to stay alive. Unfortunately, people have not always recognized this dependence. Some scientists believe that people have done so much damage to our ecosystem that the entire structure may collapse. The collapse of our ecosystem would mean the end of life as we know it.

Organisms in the Environment

All the organisms—squirrels, birds, trees, humans—in a certain area make a **community**. A **population** is all the organisms of one type. Squirrels and pigeons, for example, may belong to the same community, but not the same population. Within a community, each population has its own place to live— known as its **habitat**. This is sometimes called the population's "address." Trees are an example of a habitat for birds, squirrels, and some insects. When nonliving things, such as air, rocks, and sunlight, are added, the area is termed an **environment**.

Interaction of Organisms

Ecology is the study of how organisms interact with one another and with the world around them. Within a given community, many of the organisms interact. Each organism has a role to play within the community. The predator-prey relationship is the best known. **Predators** hunt and kill other organisms—the **prey**—for food. Usually, organisms are both predator and prey. The eagle, for example, swoops down on the snake, which has just eaten the frog, which has just eaten the insect, which had before been sucking the sap from a tree.

One community role is more important than all the others. **Producers**, who manufacture food by photosynthesis—directly or indirectly—provide food for all the other organisms. **Decomposers** and scavengers also play an important role. They feed on dead organisms. Without them, there would be no place on Earth for living organisms.

Other roles include **parasitism** and **mutualism**. Ticks, fleas, and lice are parasites. They live on other creatures and usually harm the organism on which they live. The remora fish that swim with sharks are an example of mutualism. The fish clean parasites off the shark. The shark protects the remora fish by keeping predators away.

Energy Cycles

Energy from the Sun is the source of almost all life on Earth. Green plants (the producers) trap energy during photosynthesis and convert it into glucose. Herbivores, such as cows and deer, eat the green plants. Carnivores, such as bears and falcons, eat other organisms. Omnivores, such as humans and raccoons, eat both plants and animals.

The **food chain** is the path that energy follows as it moves through the community. It starts with green plants (the producers) and moves on through herbivores. Large carnivores are usually at the top of the food chain. When an organism dies, decomposers break apart the body, returning the nutrients to the soil. All the many food chains within a community form a **food web**. A change in the population of one organism of the food web will affect every other organism.

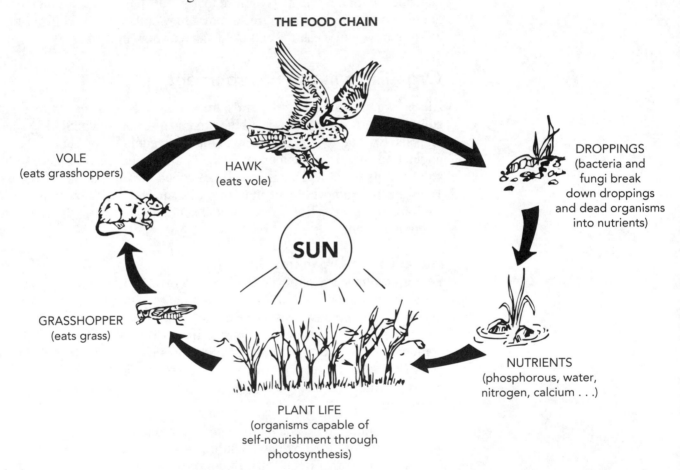

THE FOOD CHAIN

VOLE
(eats grasshoppers)

HAWK
(eats vole)

DROPPINGS
(bacteria and
fungi break
down droppings
and dead organisms
into nutrients)

SUN

GRASSHOPPER
(eats grass)

NUTRIENTS
(phosphorous, water,
nitrogen, calcium . . .)

PLANT LIFE
(organisms capable of
self-nourishment through
photosynthesis)

As demonstrated in the food chain above, each living thing is food for the next; for example, plants become food for grasshoppers, grasshoppers become food for voles, and voles become food for hawks. The hawks' droppings become food for bacteria, which turn it into nutrients for grass.

Thinking About Science

Directions: Answer the questions below in the space provided.

1. What type of organism is the basis of the food chain?

   _____

2. What would happen if there were no decomposers?

   _____

   _____

3. The previous diagram shows one aspect of an ecosystem—the food chain. What would happen if the number of grasshoppers decreased?

   _____

Answers are on page 309.

Biomes

A large group of ecosystems with similar climates and communities is known as a **biome.** Scientists disagree about exactly where one biome ends and another begins. Most agree, however, that there are at least six distinct biomes throughout the world. These are deserts, grasslands, tropical rain forests, temperate forests, tundras, and oceans.

Deserts

Lack of rainfall is the major characteristic of a desert biome. Most of the southwestern United States is a desert biome. Deserts tend to be hot during the day. At night, however, surface heat is rapidly lost. The desert at night can become quite cool.

Desert plants and animals are adapted to harsh, dry conditions. They have adapted to survive with very little water. Most desert animals are active at night when the temperature is cooler. Many of the plants, such as the cactus, store large amounts of water in their roots or stems. Some desert plants have extra deep roots. Other plants have tiny leaves or a waxy covering to reduce water loss from evaporation.

Tundras

If you were to move a desert to an extremely cold area, the result would be a tundra. There are two kinds of tundras: arctic and alpine. The arctic tundra is in the far northern parts of the world. Alpine tundras are at the tops of high mountains.

In many places on the tundra, ice and snow cover the ground for long periods. The soil may never totally thaw. Polar bears, as well as migrating animals, such as birds, reindeer, and caribou, live in the tundra. Small plants, such as lichens and mosses, grow close to the ground where strong, icy winds will not damage them.

Grasslands

Grasslands get more rainfall than deserts, but not enough to support large trees. They have long, hot summers, cold winters, and high winds. The soil is generally fertile. The dominant plants are a wide variety of grasses. Animals tend to be small, but some large grazing animals are also common.

America's prairie is made up of grasslands that once were home to huge herds of bison. Today, there are cattle ranches on these grasslands. This area is also known as "the world's breadbasket" because of the huge quantity of grain produced from it.

Forests

Each year, huge tracts of forest land are cut for timber or fuel or cleared for farming or ranching. Once the trees are cut, the topsoil erodes quickly. Since the world's supply of oxygen is mainly produced by these large expanses of forest, cutting the trees is a threat to our existence.

Tropical Forests

In a tropical rain forest, the weather is mild all the time. Both sunlight and rain are abundant. Surprisingly, the soil is not very fertile. Because of the abundance of sunlight, moisture, and minerals from decomposing plant matter, however, trees grow tall. Vines and other plants grow in the trees. Huge varieties of insects, snails, birds, snakes, frogs, and small mammals are at home in the tropical rain forest.

Temperate Forests

Temperate forests have distinct seasons. Temperature and rainfall vary with the seasons. Trees that lose their leaves in the fall are most common in southern temperate forests. Farther north, evergreens are the most common trees. Birds and mammals are abundant throughout the forest, but because so much has been cut to make room for farms and homes, the number of animals has greatly decreased. Much of the United States is now—or once was—temperate forest.

Oceans

The ocean biome covers two-thirds of Earth's surface. Climates vary, depending on location. Most of the plants and animals, such as algae, plankton, fish, and whales, live near the surface of the ocean where sunlight reaches.

Some organisms exist deep below the ocean surface where sunlight cannot penetrate. Most of these animals scour the ocean bottom for organic matter that sinks. Some, however, live near hot vents in volcanic areas. Rather than converting the Sun's energy to produce food, these creatures produce food by converting the energy in chemicals that rise from beneath the ocean floor.

Freshwater Areas

Lakes, ponds, streams, and rivers are home to plants, insects, amphibians, and fish. Fast-moving water allows for only limited numbers of organisms. As the water slows, plants take root and provide food and shelter for other organisms. Freshwater areas are usually incorporated into other biomes.

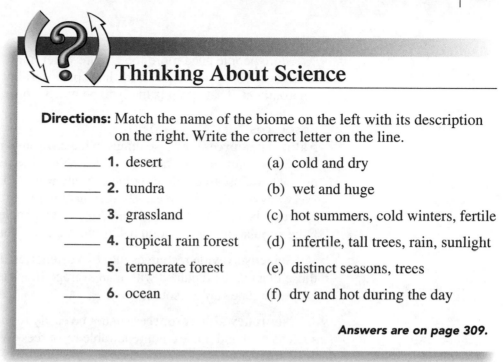

Thinking About Science

Directions: Match the name of the biome on the left with its description on the right. Write the correct letter on the line.

_____ **1.** desert   (a) cold and dry

_____ **2.** tundra   (b) wet and huge

_____ **3.** grassland   (c) hot summers, cold winters, fertile

_____ **4.** tropical rain forest   (d) infertile, tall trees, rain, sunlight

_____ **5.** temperate forest   (e) distinct seasons, trees

_____ **6.** ocean   (f) dry and hot during the day

Answers are on page 309.

Environmental Problems

At the time of the Roman Empire, there were only about 250 million people living on Earth. Now there are that many just in the United States. The world population is over 6 billion.

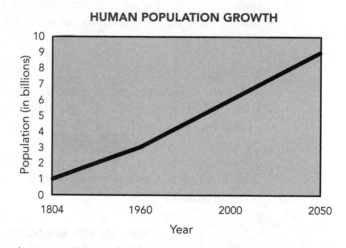

HUMAN POPULATION GROWTH

Notice that between 1804 and 1960, a period of nearly 150 years, the world population tripled. Between 1960 and 2050, a period of only 90 years, the world population is expected to more than triple. Unless the growth rate slows, the population may triple again by 2060!

In times past, war, famine, or disease killed people at an early age. Many children died young. The death rate was high, and the birthrate was low. Now health care, improved nutrition, and a more peaceful environment have slowed the death rate and increased the birthrate. The result has been an enormous increase in population.

More people need more food, more water, more space to live in, and more resources. These increased needs have put a serious strain on our environment. That strain is likely to be much worse for coming generations.

Resources

Natural resources are those things in the environment that we use to survive. The air we breathe, the water we drink, the food we eat are resources. The products we use to build our homes, to stay warm, to make all the things we use every day are also resources. All these natural resources are in limited supply and must be used by everyone on Earth. Many people fear that because of our large population and wasteful habits, we are using Earth's resources too quickly.

Scientists divide resources into two categories. **Renewable resources** are those that can be replaced within an average lifetime. Trees, animals, and crops are renewable resources.

Nonrenewable resources cannot be easily replaced. Topsoil and fuels, such as coal and oil, are nonrenewable resources. When they are gone, they're gone forever.

Conservation is a method of using nonrenewable resources in a way that does not waste them. Forests, water, soil, and any other resource can be conserved.

Pollution

Human activities do not just use up our natural resources. They also pollute, or contaminate, the environment. **Pollution** takes many forms. Solutions can be as simple as picking up the litter or as complex as reducing the output of fluorocarbons.

Garbage

Solid waste is all the garbage that comes from homes, businesses, mines, farms, and even schools and hospitals. The chart below shows that the amount of trash we produce has greatly increased. In the 1960s, we produced trash at the rate of about 2 1/2 pounds of trash per person each day. Now we produce about 4 pounds of waste per person per day. Most of that waste ends up in landfills. Some waste is burned. More and more waste is now recycled into other products.

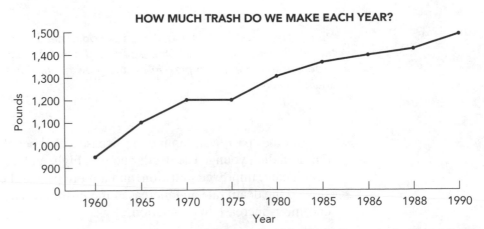

HOW MUCH TRASH DO WE MAKE EACH YEAR?

Each year, we make more and more trash. Trash production in the United States has nearly doubled since 1960, from 2.66 pounds per person per day to 4 pounds.

Hazardous wastes come from the hundreds of chemicals that we produce and use in the United States. These chemicals include house paints, automotive oils and fluids, as well as many poisons used by farmers. Safely disposing of these wastes is an enormous problem. More and more states are trying to control how these hazardous wastes are handled.

Air

Air pollution can be as ugly as the smog that hangs over major cities and industrial areas. It can also be an invisible threat. CFC pollution (pollution from chlorofluorocarbons), for example, cannot be seen. It is an invisible threat to the ozone layer that blocks harmful radiation from the Sun.

Burning fuels, such as coal, oil, and gas, can produce smog. The air looks and smells bad. It can also be deadly. Many years ago, twenty citizens of a town in Pennsylvania died from smog-related problems. More than 14 thousand others complained of headaches, dizziness, vomiting, and diarrhea. Studies showed that the air was poisonous.

Now the government tries to limit the amount of pollutants released into the air. Cars must have devices to reduce the poison carbon monoxide. The smokestacks of many factories have been fitted with scrubbers that can actually remove pollutants from the air. Although air quality is improving, there is more to do. In recent years, we have released 2 1/2 billion pounds of toxic chemicals into the air.

Water

The water on Earth today is the same water that was present billions of years ago when Earth first formed. Water evaporates from the oceans and rises into the sky as clouds. There water condenses and falls to the ground as rain or snow. The water then trickles down through the earth or rushes into streams. Eventually it returns to the oceans, and the cycle begins again.

WATER CYCLE

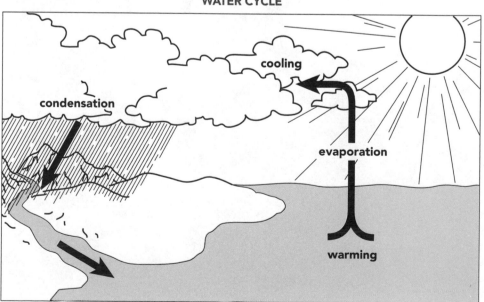

The water that your great-great-grandchildren will drink may contain the same water molecules that you use today to wash your hands. Pollution does not reduce our supply of water, but it does make it unsafe.

Many pollutants, such as fertilizers from farms and chemicals from mines and factories, pollute water. As rain forms, it picks up pollutants in the air and becomes acidic. This acid rain then falls onto trees, buildings, the soil, lakes, and streams. The result is dead and dying trees, crumbling buildings, poisonous soil, and lakes with no plant or animal life.

Thinking About Science

Directions: Answer the questions below in the space provided.

1. How does a larger population affect the environment?

   _____

   _____

2. Trees are mentioned as a renewable resource and yet environmentalists worry about the destruction of old-growth forests. Why do you think cutting a tree from an old-growth forest is different from cutting a tree at a tree farm?

   _____

   _____

Answers are on page 309.

Directions: Choose the <u>one best answer</u> to each question.

Questions 1–3 refer to the following passage.

For years, scientists have known that energy cycles through an ecosystem. Now we are learning that pollutants also cycle through the ecosystem. Stuart Slorach and Reggie Vaz are two scientists who have studied how pollutants may travel from mother to child during breast-feeding.

The scientists took samples of breast milk from mothers in China, Mexico, the United States, West Germany, Japan, and India. They looked for traces of several dangerous chemicals that have been used to grow food. The chemicals in the study— DDT, HCH, and PCB—are all lipophilic, which means "fat-seeking." They stay in the body's fat cells and are seldom shed. The exception is nursing mothers who shed fat cells in their breast milk. Women who were exposed to any of these chemicals at their jobs were not included in the study. This exclusion allowed scientists to assume that most of the chemical contamination occurred when women ate food that had been grown using these chemicals.

Slorach and Vaz found that breast-feeding mothers in developing countries, such as China, India, and Mexico, may pass on DDT, DDE, and HCH to their babies. In developed countries, such as West Germany, the United States, and Japan, nursing mothers pass on PCBs.

Although the study shows that these toxic chemicals are passed from mother to child, the scientists do not want to discourage breast-feeding. They say that the infant's exposure exceeds daily intake guidelines. However, the exposure is only for a short time and the daily intakes are still within acceptable limits for a lifetime.

1. How do DDT and HCH enter the environment?

    (1) They are used by farmers to grow food.
    (2) Women use them to prevent nausea while pregnant.
    (3) They are by-products of the petrochemical industry.
    (4) Farmers use them to store their crops.
    (5) They are car emissions.

2. Why were women who may have been exposed to DDT and HCH on their jobs excluded from this study?

    (1) They could have been exposed to DDT and HCH at their jobs rather than through food sources.
    (2) They were so weak from the high concentrations of DDT and HCH that the tests might have killed them.
    (3) Their food sources had DDT and HCH levels higher than the accepted daily intake.
    (4) They were not old enough to have the levels of DDT and HCH that the researchers were looking for.
    (5) The levels of HCH and DDT in their breast milk would have been too high to measure.

3. Why were PCB levels higher in the breast milk of mothers from the United States and Japan than it was in the milk of mothers from China and India?

    (1) Mothers in underdeveloped nations breast-feed more often than mothers in industrialized countries.
    (2) PCBs have been used more in the underdeveloped nations.
    (3) PCBs were used only in meat production in underdeveloped countries, and these women probably could not afford meat.
    (4) There was so much DDT and HCH that their level of PCBs could not be measured.
    (5) The use of PCBs is much more widespread in developed countries.

Answers are on page 309.

The History of Life

People have talked about evolution ever since Charles Darwin wrote *The Origin of Species* in 1859. Darwin was not the only naturalist to recognize the connection between ancient and modern organisms. It was Darwin's theory, however, that sparked widespread controversy and debate. Since Darwin's time scientists have discovered an overwhelming amount of evidence for the idea of **evolution**, the theory, or explanation, that complex forms of life develop from simpler forms. Scientists have also suggested an explanation for how evolution occurs.

What Darwin Knew

Darwin traveled the world collecting and observing organisms wherever he went. On the remote Galápagos Islands, he observed many different bird species that intrigued him. Darwin noted that each island had a different species of finch (small seed-eating birds). All the finches had some traits in common. Each species, however, had a unique way of dealing with its surroundings. One major difference among them was the size and shape of their beaks. Each was suited to the kind of food available on its island.

Darwin knew that structural similarities in different animals indicate that these animals might be related. For example, a person's arm, a bat's wing, and a whale's flipper show little resemblance on the outside. Their skeletons, however, are so similar that the same terms can be used to identify the bones. The similarities suggested a common ancestor in the distant past. (With Darwin's help, we now realize that over a long period of time, each of these animals adapted to a different environment—for life on land, in the air, and in the water.)

The similarity of embryos also helped to point Darwin toward the idea of evolution. Early in an organism's development, it is difficult to distinguish a fish embryo from a bird embryo or a human embryo. In fact, at one point, the unborn human has gills and a tail! Even after birth, humans retain the tailbone. Other organisms have equally puzzling structures. Snakes, for example, have tiny, useless leg bones.

Darwin's Theory

Darwin's theory consisted of three major ideas. First, he proposed that all living things—some 2 million different species—developed from just a few primitive, simple organisms. A **species** is the smallest group in the classification system. It contains organisms with similar features. Over a period of 600 million years, gradual changes occurred in these organisms. Sometimes small groups of organisms became isolated from others of their species. In time, some of their offspring differed from their parents. Each succeeding generation was less and less like the original group. Eventually, the offspring differed so markedly that they could no longer interbreed with the original population. It was now a unique species. Through this concept of evolution, Darwin explained how some species of amphibians developed into reptiles and how some species of reptiles developed into birds and mammals.

Second, Darwin had read studies that reported that populations multiply faster than their available food supply. As a result, organisms compete for food. Darwin concluded that nature acts as a selective force in which the least fit die and the most fit survive. Darwin called this idea "survival of the fittest," or **natural selection**.

Finally, Darwin proposed that in a changing environment, some organisms adapt to different conditions. Those that adapt successfully live long enough to reproduce. The offspring of the survivors are better suited to their changing environment and they, too, will survive to reproduce. In this way, the evolution of species is driven by the benefits of adapting to the environment.

What Darwin Didn't Know

It seems amazing that Darwin was able to develop his theory simply from his observations of many species and their structural similarities and differences. In his era, scientists did not know how genes worked. They had not yet unearthed the tremendous fossil record that now helps scientists trace the gradual change of species over the years. Darwin's theory was an incredible burst of understanding.

Since Darwin, scientists have found numerous strong indicators that all life is related. For example, all organisms are composed of similar proportions of carbon, hydrogen, and oxygen. They are all made of one or more cells and use a substance known as ATP to control the storage and release of energy. All known organisms have DNA (or the similar RNA) as their genetic material. The knowledge of how DNA and genes are reproduced and how mutations can produce changes in organisms has greatly strengthened Darwin's theory.

Darwin, Modified

Not all scientists believe that evolution occurred in exactly the way Darwin suggested. Many now feel that evolution is not a slow, smooth march like Darwin suggested. Instead they suggest that the history of life on Earth shows times of stability interrupted by rapid change. This idea, known as **punctuated equilibrium**, suggests that evolution is much like a reading passage. Instead of one long stream of words, history provides sentences that stop and start—and stop and start again. The punctuation can be provided by any event, such as the impact of a comet, that rapidly changes the environment.

Another problem with Darwin's idea of evolution is that it pictured evolution as if all the different species were on one ladder, starting with the simplest organisms on the bottom rung and climbing to humans at the top. Many scientists now suggest that evolution is more like a bush, as shown in the illustration. Some branches have broken off the bush. Other branches have hundreds of twigs. Species at the ends of the branches may be equally complex.

LADDER AND BUSH IMAGES OF EVOLUTION

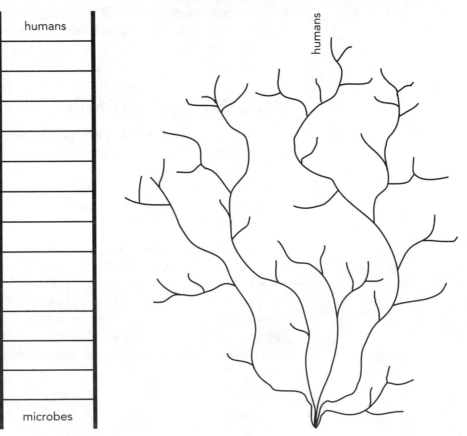

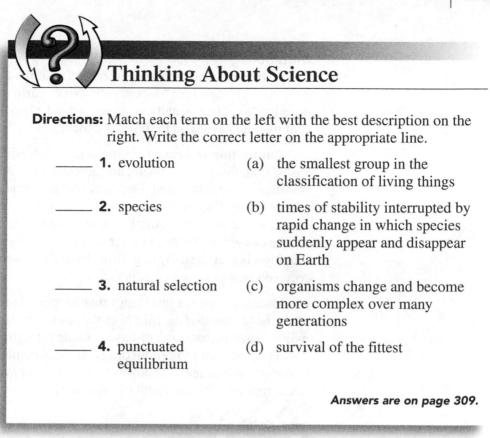

Thinking About Science

Directions: Match each term on the left with the best description on the right. Write the correct letter on the appropriate line.

_____ **1.** evolution

_____ **2.** species

_____ **3.** natural selection

_____ **4.** punctuated equilibrium

(a) the smallest group in the classification of living things

(b) times of stability interrupted by rapid change in which species suddenly appear and disappear on Earth

(c) organisms change and become more complex over many generations

(d) survival of the fittest

Answers are on page 309.

How Evolution Works

Adaptation is a change in a species that improves its chances of survival. For evolution to progress, populations of animals must be able to adapt to their environments. One of the most famous examples of adaptation involves the wing color of moths in England.

About 200 years ago, most of one species of moth living near Manchester, England, had light-colored wings. The light color blended in well with the natural color of the local trees. Predators seldom noticed the light moths and were less likely to eat them. The few moths born with dark wings were not so lucky. They were quickly eaten.

Then coal-burning factories came to Manchester. Soon the tree trunks were dark with soot. Birds that once had trouble spotting the light-colored moths now snapped them up. The few dark-colored moths, however, were hard to see against the soot. Now most of the moths of this area have dark wings. The moth population adapted to the changing environment and survived.

Mutations

Adaptation can occur because of mistakes in the DNA. (See the section on genetics in Chapter 5.) Most genetic errors harm the organism. Others have little impact. Occasionally, a genetic mistake benefits an organism. Then the trait may be passed on to the next generation.

A **mutation** is a change in the genetic information within a cell. In most cases, mutations occur when chromosomes, the structures that contain genetic information, are damaged. Pieces of chromosomes that contain some genes can be lost or find their way into the wrong nucleus. This situation describes a chromosome mutation. Another type of mutation is a gene mutation, which can be caused by X rays, nuclear radiation, or chemicals. The result of gene mutation is that the offspring differ from their parents because the cells have received new genetic instructions.

Mutations are not just things that happened millions of years ago. Scientists know that the microbes that cause diseases sometimes mutate. A major worry is that some disease-causing microbes are mutating and becoming resistant to certain drugs, such as penicillin. Not all modern mutations are dangerous, however. Navel oranges, pink grapefruit, and nectarines are also the result of mutations.

Thinking About Science

Directions: Respond to the statements below in the space provided.

1. Explain why mutations occur to individual organisms, and adaptations occur to populations of organisms.

   _____

   _____

   _____

2. Explain why, although penicillin is effective against many diseases, researchers are working to find a replacement for it.

   _____

   _____

   _____

3. Explain the difference between a chromosomal mutation and a genetic mutation.

   _____

   _____

   _____

Answers are on page 309.

Fossils

A **fossil** is the preserved remains of an organism. It can be anything from a small plant scrap to an entire animal. Fossils form when a dead organism is covered quickly with sand or silt. The covering prevents bacteria and other organisms from beginning the process of decay. If the sand or silt is crushed into rock, the organism's body may be preserved. Scientists have found thousands and thousands of fossils.

Some of the most famous fossils are of insects trapped in tree sap. The sap hardened with the dead animal inside, but still perfectly visible. Another famous fossil is of a dinosaur-age reptile with wings and feathers. Others include a mammoth and a Stone Age human trapped in ice and preserved for centuries. Even the hair and blood are preserved. The mammoth even had food in its mouth!

One of the most exciting discoveries has been the coelacanth—the fossil of a lizardlike fish. The creature had fins that moved like legs and actually allowed the fish to crawl on the beach. The fish also had a bony skeleton and joints in its skull. The fish could even twist its head. Scientists speculated that this creature died out about 70 million years ago.

About 50 years ago, scientists found a live coelacanth off the coast of Africa. Fourteen years later, another was found.

The Ages of Fossils

Scientists use several techniques to determine the age of fossils. One method is to estimate the age of a fossil by determining the age of the rocks in which a fossil is found. Generally, layers of rock deep in Earth are older than layers closer to the surface. A fossil found in a rock layer close to the surface is usually younger than a fossil found in a deeper layer. Scientists can also determine a fossil's age by measuring the amount of a substance known as carbon-14.

Plants and animals have a particular amount of carbon-14 in their tissues. When a plant or animal dies, it stops taking carbon in. As a result, the amount of carbon-14 decreases at a certain rate, known as a half-life. By using the half-life, the age of fossils can be determined by measuring the amount of carbon-14 that is left.

Eras of Life on Earth

By examining fossils of different ages, scientists have pieced together the history of life on Earth. The table below shows the major eras of Earth's history.

THE FOSSIL RECORD

Era	Period	Epoch	Outstanding events	Millions of years ago
Cenozoic	Quaternary	Recent	Major human civilizations	Less than 1
		Pleistocene	Homo sapiens	2?
	Tertiary	Pliocene	Later hominids	6
		Miocene	Increase in mammal populations	22
		Oligocene	Early hominids; grasses, grazing mammals	36
		Eocene	Primitive horses	58
		Paleocene	Mammals, dinosaurs become extinct	63
Mesozoic	Cretaceous		Flowering plants	145
	Jurassic		Birds; dinosaurs climax	210
	Triassic		Early mammals; conifers, cycads, dinosaurs	255
Paleozoic	Permian		Mammal-like reptiles; trilobites extinct	280
	Pennsylvanian		Deserts, coal forests	320
	Mississippian		Club mosses, horsetails	360
	Devonian		Insects, amphibians	415
	Silurian		Land plants and animals	465
	Ordovician		Early fishes	520
	Cambrian		Early trilobites; marine animals	580
Pre-cambrian			Early marine animals	1 billion
			Green algae	2 billion
			Bacteria, blue-green algae	3 billion

Notice in the chart that just as new species have evolved over the years, others have become **extinct**, or disappeared completely. For example, dinosaurs evolved about 225 million years ago and became extinct about 65 million years ago. Many people do not realize that there were other periods of mass extinctions.

One of the most widespread extinctions occurred at the end of the Paleozoic era, about 280 million years ago. Before that time, the world was dominated by small sea creatures called trilobites. They dominated Earth for about 240 million years. The cause of their extinction, like that of the dinosaurs, is a mystery.

Thinking About Science

Directions: Answer the questions below in the space provided.

1. Why doesn't a fossil decay?

   _____

   _____

2. Which species has had a longer history on Earth: humans, dinosaurs, or trilobites?

   _____

3. What organisms were among the first to inhabit Earth?

   _____

4. What are the two methods by which the age of fossils may be determined?

   _____

   _____

5. Which vertebrates have the longest history on Earth?

   _____

Answers are on pages 309–310.

Directions: Choose the <u>one best answer</u> to each question.

Questions 1–4 refer to the information on pages 113–129.

1. Which of the following ideas is <u>not</u> supported by the theory of evolution?

   (1) Human beings and apes descended from the same organism.
   (2) Species have not changed over time.
   (3) Complex forms of life have evolved from simpler forms.
   (4) Populations of organisms adapt to different conditions.
   (5) Some offspring could no longer interbreed with the original population.

2. On what knowledge did Darwin base his idea of the "survival of the fittest"?

   (1) On the Galápagos Islands, only finches with large beaks could fit the seeds in their mouths.
   (2) Populations multiply faster than the food supply.
   (3) Populations multiply at the same rate as food supplies.
   (4) Different species can interbreed.
   (5) Organisms share food with other species.

3. According to recent ideas, when might evolution occur?

   (1) in slow, smooth stages
   (2) only during cataclysmic events
   (3) after long periods of stability
   (4) when the environment is stable
   (5) when DNA structures change

4. Which of the following facts does <u>not</u> suggest that all life is related?

   (1) All organisms have ATP to control the storage and release of energy.
   (2) All organisms are made up of carbon, hydrogen, and oxygen.
   (3) All organisms descended from a common ancestor.
   (4) All organisms are made of one or more cells.
   (5) All organisms have DNA or RNA as their genetic material.

Answers are on page 310.

Plant and Animal Science Review

Directions: Choose the <u>one best answer</u> for each question.

Questions 1–12 refer to the information on pages 73–129.

1. Which of the following is a major theme in life science?

    (1) whether or not humans could live another 50 years
    (2) the interdependence of living things
    (3) the simplicity of life
    (4) how objects move
    (5) how Earth was formed

2. What are cells?

    (1) solid bits of matter
    (2) constantly changing
    (3) the building blocks of life
    (4) soft and flexible
    (5) mostly air

3. What are the major groupings of living organisms?

    (1) plants and animals
    (2) bacteria and viruses
    (3) protists, monerans, fungi, plants, and animals
    (4) flowers and mammals
    (5) insects, fish, reptiles, and mammals

4. Which of the following is a key difference between a plant and animal cell?

    (1) A plant cell has a cell wall; an animal cell doesn't.
    (2) An animal cell has a cell wall; a plant cell doesn't.
    (3) A plant cell has a cell membrane; an animal cell doesn't.
    (4) An animal cell has a chloroplast; a plant cell doesn't.
    (5) A plant cell is smaller than an animal cell.

5. Microbes are used in the production of which of the following foods?

    (1) milk
    (2) sausage
    (3) pasta
    (4) yogurt
    (5) crackers

6. Plants make food through what process?

    (1) respiration
    (2) evolution
    (3) active transport
    (4) photosynthesis
    (5) chlorophyll

7. Which of the following describes a warm-blooded animal?

(1) Its body temperature changes with the surroundings.
(2) Its blood feels cool, but its skin feels warm.
(3) It must use the energy in food to keep warm.
(4) It should not be in the hot sun on a warm day.
(5) Its body temperature will never drop below 98.6°F.

8. Viruses are known to cause which of the following?

(1) strep throat
(2) tuberculosis
(3) food poisoning
(4) measles
(5) asthma

9. Which of the following is not true of fungi?

(1) They cannot make their own food.
(2) They feed on other plants and animals that are dead or alive.
(3) They contain no chlorophyll.
(4) They cause athlete's foot.
(5) They have no beneficial uses for humans.

10. Which of the following is released at the end of the process of photosynthesis?

(1) hydrogen
(2) carbon dioxide
(3) oxygen
(4) carbon monoxide
(5) water

11. Which of the following undergoes incomplete metamorphosis?

(1) a butterfly
(2) a moth
(3) a frog
(4) a grasshopper
(5) a toad

12. What is evolution?

(1) the theory that humans developed from monkeys
(2) the idea that dinosaurs are extinct because of an asteroid hitting Earth
(3) the theory that complex forms of life develop from simpler forms
(4) the idea that only the strongest survive
(5) the drive for species to reproduce

Questions 13–15 refer to the following passage.

The discovery of microbes was a new beginning for scientists who were searching for the causes of disease. Louis Pasteur, a French chemist, was one of those scientists. In the mid-nineteenth century, he began to explore the idea that some diseases might be caused by microbes.

Pasteur discovered how to grow bacteria in the laboratory. He then experimented with several different bacteria. He found that different types of bacteria cause different diseases. One bacteria—*bacillus*—caused a deadly sheep disease, called *anthrax*. Pasteur discovered that he could make sheep immune from this disease by giving them a very weak form of the *bacillus* bacteria. His method was the first vaccine. The vaccination protected the sheep because their bodies developed antibodies to fight off the weak *bacillus*. When the stronger *bacillus* invaded, the antibodies were ready to destroy them.

Although viruses were too small for him to see, Pasteur applied this knowledge of immunity from microbes to develop the first effective vaccine against rabies.

Pasteur discovered that foods spoiled because of the presence of microbes. He developed a process for protecting perishable foods, such as milk, from bacteria. His process, called pasteurization in his honor, destroys harmful microbes with controlled heat.

13. What can you infer about the work of scientists before the microscope was invented?

   (1) It would have been impossible for scientists to treat any illness.
   (2) Scientists knew that milk would not sour because it contained no microbes.
   (3) Scientists were not interested in finding the causes of diseases.
   (4) There was no laboratory work at all.
   (5) It would have been difficult for scientists to discover the relationship between microbes and disease.

14. What are rabies shots for dogs?

   (1) an experimentation
   (2) a sanitation
   (3) an immunization
   (4) a pasteurization
   (5) a sterilization

15. What is the process of applying controlled heat to perishable food to control the spread of bacteria?

   (1) immunization
   (2) sanitation
   (3) pasteurization
   (4) vaccination
   (5) classification

Questions 16–18 refer to the following passage.

Hardly anyone in Minamata, Japan, noticed when fish were found floating in the water and shellfish frequently died. Two years later, seagulls began dropping out of the sky. Then several cats danced convulsively until they dropped dead. Soon there were no cats left. Eventually, dogs and pigs also went mad and died.

The fishermen continued to fish. People continued to eat the fish. Then a six-year-old girl was admitted to the hospital with brain damage. Her younger sister and four members of a neighboring family had similar symptoms. Within a year, fifty-two people were affected. Twenty-one died.

Before long, 103 people from Minamata had died, and 700 more had been seriously and permanently damaged. Severe mental retardation, tremors, and limb deformities were among the symptoms. The local plastics factory did an environmental study. The results were never released.

This disturbing description is not from a science fiction novel. It is the true story of mercury poisoning through man-made environmental pollution. Mercury in industrial wastes was dumped into the ocean and thus polluted the feeding grounds of shellfish and fish. The poisoned fish were eaten by animals and humans.

Mercury must accumulate in cells before there is enough to become toxic. As a result, smaller animals were affected first. (They weighed less, so they needed less mercury to display the symptoms.) Eventually, enough mercury accumulated in the brain cells of humans to cause damage. The symptoms of this tragedy were first noticed among small children.

Although Minamata is across the ocean, our country, too, has had problems with industrial wastes. Love Canal, New York, and Times Beach, Missouri, are two notable examples. In each place, humans seeking progress and economic growth disrupted the ecosystem. People were slow to realize the extent of the damage. Many years later, we are still paying the consequences for our disregard of the ecosystem.

16. What caused the tragedy in Minamata?

   (1) poisoned fish
   (2) mercury poisoning
   (3) plastics
   (4) convulsive dancing disease
   (5) mental retardation

17. What is the result when enough Mercury accumulates in cells to become toxic?

   (1) Only small organisms are harmed.
   (2) Small organisms are the first to display symptoms of mercury poisoning.
   (3) Small organisms become slightly ill, but large organisms die.
   (4) Large organisms rarely become ill.
   (5) Large organisms become ill, but rarely die.

18. Which of the following is a good title for this passage?

   (1) "Mercury Monsters"
   (2) "Dancing Death"
   (3) "An Early Warning Ignored"
   (4) "Mercury Poisoning in America"
   (5) "Love Canal Revisited"

Questions 19–22 refer to the following passage.

Orangutans are the most intelligent of all land animals (other than humans). The Malay words *orang hutan* mean "man of the forest." The two Indonesian islands of Borneo and Sumatra are the only places where these "forest men" live.

The adult males of Borneo roam freely and do not seem to belong to a family unit. A few miles away on Sumatra, however, an adult male orangutan stays close to his mate and offspring. British zoologist John MacKinnon wondered what could account for this difference in the father's behavior.

On the island of Borneo, nothing ties males to the family unit. They wander freely through the feeding ranges occupied by the females and their young. The older, dominant males mate with any fertile, receptive female. Younger males, whose advances are often rejected by the females, sometimes resort to rape.

Yet on Borneo, if a large male stayed within the family feeding range, he would compete for food and decrease his offspring's chance of survival.

On Sumatra, however, females have good reasons for keeping a strong male nearby. Leopards on Sumatra prey on female and infant orangutans. The orangutans also must compete with siamangs, another ape species, for food.

MacKinnon reports that male orangutans on Sumatra stay close to the family unit. Pairs mate without regard to the female's fertile period. MacKinnon thinks that this sexual behavior keeps the strong males nearby where they are available to defend their offspring and drive away competitors. Family life and non-reproductive sex—once thought to be uniquely human activities—seem to be a survival advantage for Sumatran orangutans.

19. What threats do orangutans face on the island of Sumatra?

    (1) leopards and siamangs
    (2) younger male orangutans
    (3) infertile female orangutans
    (4) inadequate food supplies
    (5) too many offspring

20. What threats do orangutans face on the island of Borneo?

    (1) leopards and siamangs
    (2) younger male orangutans
    (3) infertile female orangutans
    (4) inadequate food supplies
    (5) too many offspring

21. The fact that male orangutans in Borneo and Sumatra show different parenting behaviors is an example of which of the following?

    (1) adaptation
    (2) transmutation
    (3) reproduction
    (4) evolution
    (5) accumulation

22. You can conclude that although the parenting behaviors of the orangutans on Borneo and Sumatra are different, each is suited to which of the following?

    (1) producing the greatest number of surviving offspring
    (2) maintaining cohesive families
    (3) satisfying female orangutans
    (4) competing for food with siamangs
    (5) maintaining more orangutans in Sumatra

    Answers are on page 310.

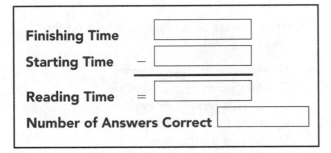

Directions: This activity will help you to improve your reading efficiency. Before you start to read, write the present time at the top of the page. When you have completed the reading and all 5 questions, write your finishing time. Subtract to find out how long you took. Score your answers. Then turn to pages 320–321 to find your E-Factor and to graph your progress.

Finishing Time

Starting Time −

Reading Time =

Number of Answers Correct

Bees

In 1910 Karl von Frisch did a series of experiments with bees. He began by putting out red and blue cardboard squares. He trained the bees to go to the blue square. To do so, he put a little honey on the blue square, but on the red square he put nothing. The bees immediately flew to the blue square. Each time he did the test, the bees flew to the blue square.

Then von Frisch moved the squares around. He didn't put honey on the blue square that time, but the bees still flew directly to it. He tried placing the blue square in different places, but the bees always flew straight to it.

Next von Frisch mixed the blue square in with gray squares that ranged from almost white to almost black. Again the bees flew directly to the blue square. No matter how he arranged the squares, the bees always flew to the blue one.

In other experiments, the bees could not find honey on red cards, but they had no trouble finding it on bluish-red cards. Also, the bees found yellow squares but couldn't easily tell orange or yellow-green from yellow. They could easily tell blue-green squares from blue ones.

1. Which sentence states the hypothesis that von Frisch was testing?

   (1) Bees will fly toward blue cards.
   (2) Bees can see color
   (3) Bees like honey.
   (4) Bees can learn.
   (5) Bees can smell honey.

2. At the beginning of the experiment why didn't von Frisch put honey on both the blue card and the red card?

   (1) He knew that bees liked the color blue.
   (2) The blue card looked more like the gray cards he used later.
   (3) Bees cannot see the color red.
   (4) The bees could see the blue card better.
   (5) He wanted to train the bees to go to only one color.

3. Which color would most likely attract bees?

   (1) red
   (2) orange
   (3) yellow
   (4) gray
   (5) yellow-orange

4. Which conclusion can be made from the results of von Frisch's experiment?

   (1) Bees can see some colors but not others.
   (2) Bees can smell honey.
   (3) Bees like the color blue better than red.
   (4) Bees do not like the color gray.
   (5) Bees only fly to squares with honey.

5. How might the procedure be changed to test whether bees can recognize shapes?

   (1) Mix a square blue card with honey in with round gray cards without honey.
   (2) Place a square gray card with honey among round gray cards without honey.
   (3) Repeat the procedure with all round cards.
   (4) Use round, square, and triangular cards and put honey on one of each.
   (5) Place a square blue card without honey among round gray cards without honey.

Answers are on page 310.

READING EFFICIENCY B

Directions: This activity will help you to improve your reading efficiency. Before you start to read, write the present time at the top of the page. When you have completed the reading and all 5 questions, write your finishing time. Subtract to find out how long you took. Score your answers. Then turn to pages 320–321 to find your E-Factor and to graph your progress.

Finishing Time	
Starting Time −	
Reading Time =	
Number of Answers Correct	

Cells

When Robert Hooke saw the first cells in 1665, he was not aware of how important his discovery was. All living things are made of cells. Cells differ in size, the way they look, and what they do. But all cells have three main parts: a cell membrane, cytoplasm, and a nucleus.

Cytoplasm is a jellylike substance that is made mostly of water. Other important materials are there too. The cytoplasm holds the parts that help the cell function. Most cells have mitochondria. These sausage-shaped structures release energy to the cell. Vacuoles do different tasks in the cell. Some digest food; others store wastes or water. Vacuoles usually are larger in plant cells than in animal cells. Plant cells have chloroplasts, green structures that contain chlorophyll. Plants use chlorophyll when they use sunlight to make sugar.

The nucleus is the "control center" of the cell. It contains DNA, which controls all the activities of the cell.

The cell membrane surrounds the cell and holds it together. It serves as a gate by controlling the kind and amount of substances that enter and exit the cell. To stay alive, a cell must take in the materials it needs—water, oxygen, and nutrients. It must also get rid of wastes. All these materials must pass through the cell membrane.

The illustration below shows one way materials, such as water, move into and out of a cell. If the cell has fewer molecules of water than does the area around it, water will move into the cell. If the cell has more water molecules, water will move out of the cell. This process is called diffusion. Cells do not use energy during diffusion.

DIFFUSION OF WATER INTO A CELL

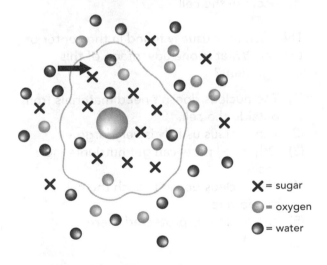

X = sugar
○ = oxygen
● = water

Cells can also move materials from a less crowded area to a more crowded area. This process uses cell energy and is called active transport. Plants use active transport to take in some nutrients through their roots.

1. According to the passage, which statement is <u>not</u> true about cells?

   (1) All living things are made of cells.
   (2) DNA controls all the activities of the cell.
   (3) All cells are exactly alike.
   (4) Cells need water, oxygen, and nutrients.
   (5) All cells have cytoplasm.

2. Which statement describes how materials will move in the illustration above?

   (1) Oxygen will move into the cell.
   (2) Oxygen will move out of the cell.
   (3) Oxygen and simple sugar will move into the cell.
   (4) Oxygen and simple sugar will move out of the cell.
   (5) No movement of oxygen or sugar will occur in the cell.

3. The nucleus is usually found in the center of the cell. What is one advantage of this arrangement?

   (1) The nucleus doesn't need materials from outside the cell.
   (2) The nucleus usually is very large.
   (3) Other cell parts can get nutrients more easily.
   (4) The nucleus doesn't touch the cell membrane.
   (5) The nucleus is protected there.

4. Some cells, such as muscle cells, are more active than others. Which cell part would these cells most likely have more of than less active cells?

   (1) vacuoles
   (2) cell membrane
   (3) mitochondria
   (4) nuclei
   (5) cytoplasm

5. You notice that the soil in the pots of plants you placed in a sunny window dries out quickly and the plants wilt. Plants in shady windows do not wilt as quickly. Which item of information can help you solve the problem?

   (1) The nucleus controls the activities of the cell.
   (2) During active transport cells use energy to move materials into the cell.
   (3) The cell membrane holds the cell together.
   (4) If a cell has more water molecules than the area around it, water will move out of the cell.
   (5) Vacuoles usually are larger in plant cells than in animal cells.

   Answers are on page 310.

CHAPTER 5

Human Biology

Human beings are the most complex and unique members of the animal kingdom. Because the human body has an internal skeleton, humans are classified as vertebrates. Beyond that, humans are grouped as mammals because they are warm-blooded and because females have the ability to nourish their young from special glands that produce milk. Human beings are also placed in a subgroup called primates because of their eyes that face forward, their grasping fingers and thumb, and their ability to walk on two legs. The feature of human beings that sets them apart from other animals, however, is their huge brain that enables them to think, solve problems, and make choices and to live in complex social groups that require cooperation and communication.

Although human beings are different from other organisms, the study of human biology is also about the similarities that are found in all life forms. Such similarities range from the chemical makeup of humans and other animals to their body structures. In this chapter, we will examine the human body structure and the various systems that keep the human body alive.

Human Body Systems

Major systems of human beings include the skeletal, muscular, digestive, excretory, circulatory, respiratory, nervous, endocrine, and reproductive systems. All of these systems interact with one another. A malfunction in one system of the body affects all of the others.

The Skeletal System

The skeletal system is made of bones and cartilage. The skeleton is the support structure of the human body. It protects vital organs. By providing a frame for the muscles, the skeleton allows the body to stand and move. An illustration of the human skeletal system is on page 140.

Human bones are not solid. They are more like hollow tubes that have been filled with jelly. This jellylike substance is a combination of nerves and blood vessels called **marrow.** New blood cells are produced in the marrow.

How many bones make up the human skeleton? An adult has 206 bones, although some people have an extra rib or extra bones in their fingers. The largest bones are the thigh bones, and the smallest bones are located in the ear. Thigh bones contribute to about a fourth of a skeleton's entire weight.

HUMAN SKELETON

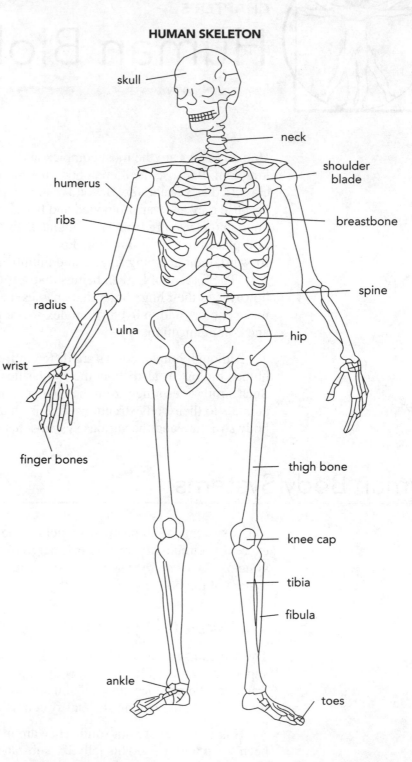

skull

neck

shoulder blade

humerus

ribs

breastbone

radius

spine

ulna

hip

wrist

finger bones

thigh bone

knee cap

tibia

fibula

ankle

toes

As the body grows, the bones grow. The entire skeletal structure grows without ever interfering with other working body systems. With age, however, the bones may harden and become brittle.

Joints

Most bones are connected to one another with tough strands of tissue known as **ligaments.** The points of connection are called joints. Most joints move. Some swing back and forth like a door. These hinged joints are at the elbows, knees, jaw, fingers, and toes. They cannot be twisted without injury.

TYPES OF JOINTS

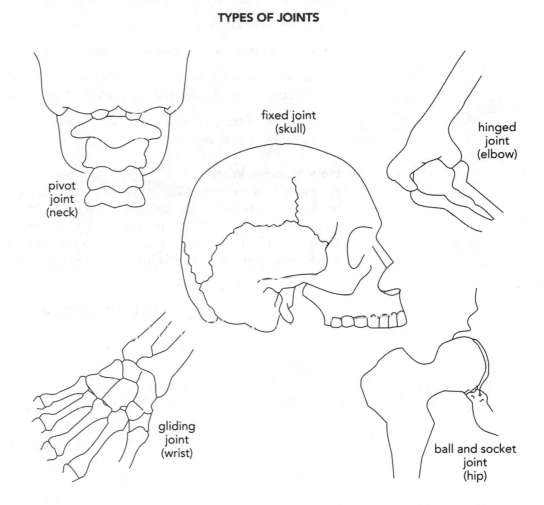

pivot joint (neck)

fixed joint (skull)

hinged joint (elbow)

gliding joint (wrist)

ball and socket joint (hip)

Ball-and-socket joints can be twisted. These joints, found in shoulders and hips, allow flexible movement in many directions. The gliding joints in the ankles, wrists, and the spinal column also allow movement in many directions, but the amount of movement is limited.

Other joints allow only a bit of movement. The ribs, for example are attached to the breastbone. If the ribs did not move, you could not breathe. Skull bones of adults do not move at all.

If bones were allowed to rub together at joints, the ends would be ground away. Instead most bones are padded with **cartilage**. The cartilage acts like a shock absorber for the skeleton.

The Muscular System

The muscular system allows you to walk, breathe, talk, and swallow. Some actions, such as running, are under your control. They are controlled by voluntary muscles. Other actions, such as pumping blood through your body or churning the food in your stomach, are not under your control. These actions are controlled by involuntary muscles.

There are three kinds of muscles in the body:

- **Cardiac muscles,** which are involuntary, control the heartbeat.

- **Smooth muscles,** which are involuntary, are found in the lungs, intestines, and bladder and are controlled by the nervous system.

- **Skeletal muscles,** which are voluntary, allow you to change the position of your body.

How Muscles Work

All muscles work in the same way. They contract. They can only pull—not push—on the bones of the skeleton. Bending a joint, such as the arm, contracts one muscle. If that muscle relaxes, the arm will flop back down. To straighten the joint slowly and smoothly, a second muscle must pull the arm down. Most joints in the body are controlled by pairs of muscles.

MUSCLES IN OPPOSING PAIRS

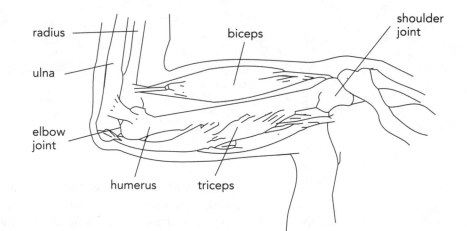

Thinking About Science

Part A

Directions: Fill in the blanks below with the appropriate words.

1. Blood cells are produced in the _____.

2. The two kinds of involuntary muscles are _____
   and _____ .

Part B

Directions: Match the type of joint listed on the left with the correct body
part listed on the right. Write the correct letter on the line.

_____ **1.** hinged joint   (a) shoulder

_____ **2.** ball-and-socket joint   (b) skull

_____ **3.** gliding joints   (c) elbow

_____ **4.** fixed joints   (d) ankle

_____ **5.** limited motion joints   (e) ribs

Answers are on pages 310–311.

The Digestive System

Molecules of food are too large to enter the cells of the body. To make use of the nutrients in food, the body must break the food molecules down. This process occurs in the digestive system. When food is chewed, the teeth grind and tear the food into small bits. Saliva not only keeps the food moist, it also begins to digest the largest molecules.

The Stomach

When you swallow, the food goes down the esophagus and into the stomach. There, smooth muscles repeatedly contract to cause a churning motion that stirs the food. Strong acids begin to break the molecules apart. The food is like a thin soup by the time it leaves the stomach.

HUMAN DIGESTIVE SYSTEM

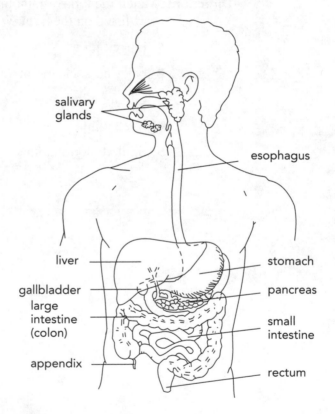

The Intestines

In the small intestine, nutrients are diffused into the blood vessels. The blood carries nutrients throughout the body. The undigested food passes into the large intestine, where much of the water in the waste is absorbed into the body. The remaining solids, called feces, leave the body through the anus.

The Excretory System

Like all cells, human body cells produce wastes. The lungs and skin excrete some waste from the body, but most waste is removed from the blood as it passes through the kidneys. Inside the kidneys are millions of tiny filters that remove waste, water, glucose, and minerals from the blood. The water, glucose, and minerals are returned to the blood, leaving behind only the wastes. The waste, called urine, passes through a tube and into the bladder for storage. When it is full, the bladder contracts, pushing urine out of the body.

HUMAN EXCRETORY SYSTEM

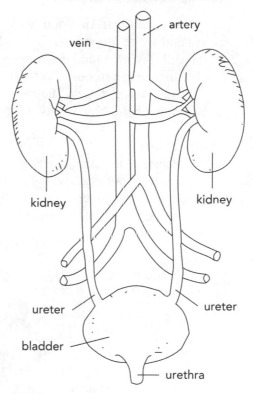

The liver is another organ that filters harmful substances out of the blood. Before nutrient-rich blood moves throughout the body, the liver removes extra sugar. Excess sugar that is not needed by the body is changed to glycogen, a carbohydrate, and stored.

The Circulatory System

Food and oxygen must reach every cell in the body. Waste from every cell must be removed. In times of infection and disease, antibodies must be rushed to the infected site. The job of transporting nutrients, oxygen, antibodies, and waste belongs to the circulatory system.

Blood

Blood is a tissue that is part liquid and part solid. About half of the blood is **plasma**, a light-colored watery liquid. Plasma contains some proteins, minerals, vitamins, sugars, and chemicals. Plasma transports nutrients, vitamins, minerals, and oxygen throughout the body.

The solid part of blood, which is suspended in the plasma, contains the red and white blood cells. The red blood cells carry oxygen from the lungs to the cells. White blood cells are much larger than red blood cells, but they are able to squeeze through body tissue to reach an infection. The white blood cells attack and destroy the invading cells. **Platelets** are tiny particles in the blood that form blood clots. Without platelets, a person could bleed to death.

The Heart

The center of the circulatory system is the heart. The heart is a fist-sized muscle divided into four chambers. The two upper chambers, called atria, collect the blood returning to the heart through the veins. The two lower chambers, called ventricles, pump blood away from the heart through the arteries.

THE HUMAN HEART

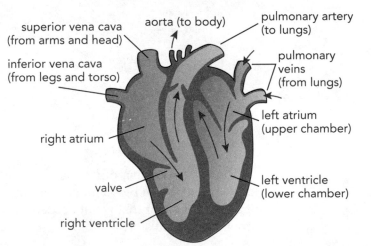

The two sides of the heart work like separate pumps. The right atrium receives blood from the body. This blood has little oxygen in it. The right atrium pumps the blood down into the right ventricle. From there the blood is pumped through an artery to the lungs, where the blood releases its carbon dioxide and picks up oxygen. This oxygen-rich blood flows through veins to the left atrium of the heart. The left atrium pumps the blood down into the left ventricle. From there the oxygen-rich blood is pumped through arteries to all parts of the body, except the lungs. The arteries branch off to smaller and smaller arteries called arterioles and capillaries. In this way oxygen reaches every cell in the body. The cells release carbon dioxide into the blood and absorb oxygen.

The Respiratory System

The body can survive only a short time without oxygen. Cells use oxygen to burn food and release the energy in the nutrients. The waste product of this activity is carbon dioxide. The function of the respiratory system is to supply oxygen and remove carbon dioxide.

HUMAN RESPIRATORY SYSTEM

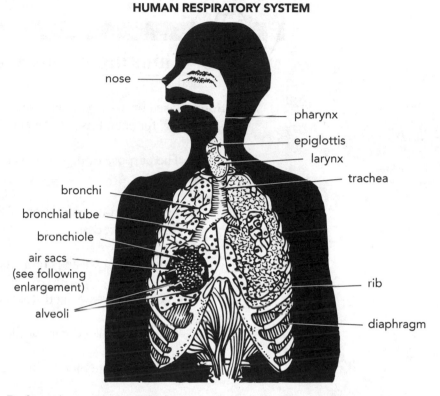

Before air enters the lungs, it must be warmed, moistened, and cleaned of dust and dirt. The hairs and the mucous lining of the nose perform that job. The air enters a cavity at the rear of the mouth and then goes down the windpipe (called the trachea), through the bronchial tubes, and into the lungs

In the lungs are millions of tiny air sacs. Each sac is surrounded by a network of capillaries. It is here that oxygen diffuses into the blood vessels and carbon dioxide diffuses out of the blood vessels. The oxygen-rich blood heads straight for the heart, where it is pumped throughout the body. The carbon dioxide leaves the body when you exhale.

ENLARGEMENT OF AIR SACS

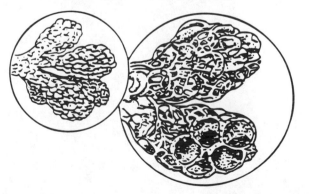

Speech

The air that we breathe in and out also allows us to speak. At the top of the windpipe is the larynx, or voice box. Two ligaments in the larynx (known as the vocal cords) vibrate when air passes over them. When we speak, we control those vibrations and shape them into the sounds of our language.

Thinking About Science

Directions: Based on what you have read, circle *T* for each true statement or *F* for each false statement.

T   F   **1.** The purpose of digestion is to break apart large molecules of food.

T   F   **2.** The up-and-down motion of the intestines completes the digestive process.

T   F   **3.** Most human waste is removed by the kidneys.

T   F   **4.** The liver converts and stores extra sugar from the blood.

T   F   **5.** About half the content of blood is tiny platelets.

T   F   **6.** Red and white blood cells are about the same size.

T   F   **7.** Blood is pure and contains no waste.

T   F   **8.** Before circulating throughout the body, blood enters the lungs where it absorbs oxygen and releases carbon dioxide.

T   F   **9.** The waste product of respiration is oxygen.

T   F   **10.** When you speak, air passes over your vocal cords.

Answers are on page 311.

The Nervous System

The nervous system enables us to sense, analyze, and respond to changes inside and outside the body. The central nervous system is made up of the brain and spinal cord. Sensations enter the body through the major sense organs—eyes, ears, nose, mouth, and skin. Tiny nerve cells in the sense organs react to changes in the environment. The information is converted to electrical and chemical signals that travel quickly along the thin nerve cells to the brain or spinal cord.

Nerve Cells

Notice the shape of the nerve cell in the diagram below. The shape helps the cell to function. Dendrites spread out, ready to pick up information. The axon provides a quick path to the next nerve cell. The synapse is the small gap between cells. There the electrical message changes into a chemical message and flows to the next nerve cell.

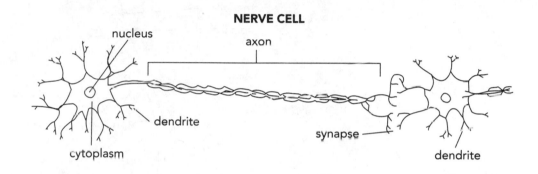

NERVE CELL

Reflexes

Sometimes nerve cells react to changes in the environment faster than we can think. This type of reaction is called a **reflex.** For example, suppose your finger brushes against a hot stove. Dendrites pick up the "hot" signal and immediately transmit it to the spinal cord and the brain. The spinal cord gets the message before the brain does. The spinal cord sends a message back to the muscle of your hand to contract. Before your brain ever has a chance to tell you that something is hot, your reflexes have already caused you to pull your hand away from danger.

Peripheral Nervous System

The peripheral nervous system connects the central nervous system with all parts of the body. It is made up of the cranial nerves (found inside the skull), which branch from the brain, and the spinal nerves, which branch from the spinal column. The **autonomic nervous system** makes up a third part of the peripheral nervous system. The autonomic system works automatically. It enables the body to perform actions involuntarily, such as the heart's pumping and the movement of digested food through the intestines.

The Brain

The brain is the most complex part of the nervous system. It contains 90 percent of the body's nerve cells. Every action except for reflex actions is controlled by the brain. The upper portion of the brain, called the **cerebrum,** looks like a large wrinkled prune. It receives, stores, and recalls all the information picked up through the senses. It is also the processing center for memory, decision-making, thinking, speech, smell, taste, touch, vision, and hearing.

HUMAN BRAIN

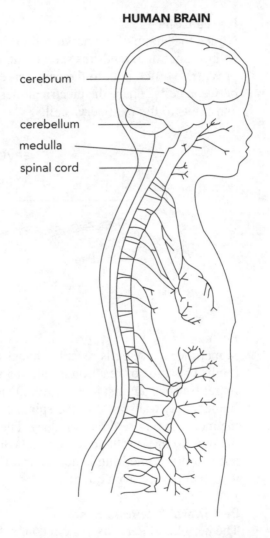

cerebrum

cerebellum

medulla

spinal cord

The cerebrum is divided into two halves. These halves control the opposite sides of the body. (The right cerebrum controls the left side of the body. The left cerebrum controls the right side.) Many scientists think that the left side of the brain controls logic while the right side controls creativity.

Below the cerebrum is the **cerebellum,** which controls muscle coordination and balance. The **medulla** controls involuntary actions such as the heartbeat, breathing, and digestion.

The Endocrine System

Glands are groups of cells that release chemicals into the body. Sweat and salivary glands release the chemicals through tiny tubes. Some glands, however, release chemicals directly into the blood. These are called endocrine glands, and the chemicals they produce are **hormones**.

Hormones control the body's growth, its use of energy, and its ability to reproduce. Adrenalin is a hormone released into the body in times of danger. Some hormones control the levels of sugar or calcium in the blood. Others control the sexual maturation process of men and women.

Thinking About Science

Directions: Fill in the blanks below with the appropriate word(s).

1. The five major sense organs are the

   a. _____

   b. _____

   c. _____

   d. _____

   e. _____

2. A _____ moves your body without your having to think about it.

3. The left side of the brain controls the _____ side of the body.

4. Glands release _____ directly into

   the _____.

Answers are on page 311.

The Reproductive System

The diagram of the male reproductive system has three main parts. The testes produce the male sex cells, which are stored in the scrotum. The sperm leave the body through the penis. Millions of sperm are produced every day. The process is controlled by hormones.

MALE REPRODUCTIVE SYSTEM

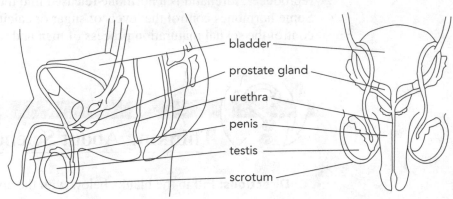

- bladder
- prostate gland
- urethra
- penis
- testis
- scrotum

FEMALE REPRODUCTIVE SYSTEM

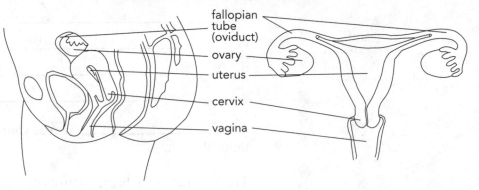

- fallopian tube (oviduct)
- ovary
- uterus
- cervix
- vagina

The female reproductive system is also controlled by hormones. Female sex cells, the eggs, are produced in the ovaries. Usually, one egg matures at a time. When the egg matures, it is released into the uterus. If it is fertilized, it attaches to the wall of the uterus. If not, it passes out of the body through the vagina.

Menstrual Cycle

The growth and release of a mature egg is called the **menstrual cycle.** The cycle starts when an egg begins to mature. The lining of the uterus thickens. In about two weeks, the egg is ready to be released into the uterus. If the egg is not fertilized, the lining of the uterus breaks down and is shed through the vagina as menstrual blood. The cycle, which takes about 28 days, then begins again. If a mature egg and sperm unite, pregnancy results, and the menstrual cycle stops.

Growth of the Fetus

As soon as an egg is fertilized, it connects itself to the uterus through a membrane called the **placenta.** There it begins to divide and grow. The rapidly developing organism is called an **embryo.** During the first three months of pregnancy, the head and brain grow quickly, but body growth is slow. The heart forms and begins to beat. Although all the body systems are present, most of them cannot yet function. During this period, the embryo is very sensitive. Nicotine, alcohol, and drugs can do serious damage to it.

At the end of two months, the embryo begins to look somewhat human. At that stage it is called a **fetus.** During the next three months, the body begins to catch up with the head. Skin develops, and the mother may feel the fetus kick. During the last three months, the fetus gains a great deal of weight. Soon it can no longer move freely in the uterus. Bones, blood, and nerves develop rapidly. At this time, good nutrition—especially the addition of calcium, iron, and protein to the diet—is essential.

Birth

At the end of about nine months, the mother's body produces hormones that control the baby's birth. The smooth muscles of the uterus begin to contract and relax. This movement, called **labor,** pushes the baby down the birth canal and into the world. The umbilical cord that joined the baby to the mother is cut. After a few more contractions, the placenta is forced out of the mother's body.

Thinking About Science

Directions: Respond to the statements below.

1. Male sex cells are produced in the _____. The female

   sex cell is produced in the _____.

2. An egg is released about _____ after the start of the menstrual cycle.

3. When do the baby's head and brain grow most quickly?

   _____

4. When can the embryo first be recognized as human?

   _____

5. The contractions of the uterus during birth are called _____.

Answers are on page 311.

Directions: Choose the <u>one best answer</u> to each question.

Questions 1–4 refer to the information on pages 139–153.

1. Which of the following is <u>not</u> a function of the skeleton?

   (1) provides support for the body
   (2) protects soft organs of the body
   (3) gives the body its basic shape
   (4) provides nourishment for the body
   (5) allows for body movement

2. Which of the following is the best example of the use of voluntary muscles?

   (1) jumping
   (2) eye blinking
   (3) sneezing
   (4) shivering
   (5) blood flowing

3. Which of the following phrases best sums up the function of the digestive system?

   (1) support structure
   (2) waste elimination
   (3) food transportation
   (4) oxygen and carbon dioxide exchanger
   (5) food processing

4. Which of the following organs is <u>not</u> involved in excretion?

   (1) skin
   (2) lungs
   (3) heart
   (4) kidneys
   (5) bladder

Answers are on page 311.

Human Genetics

People often comment on how much some children look like their parents. Remarks such as, "He has his mother's eyes" or "He's tall like his dad," remind us that certain characteristics—or **traits**—are passed on from parents to children. The study of genetics concerns how traits are passed on and how they are expressed in an organism.

Chromosomes and DNA

The nucleus of every living cell carries genetic material—the **chromosomes**—that determines the traits of that organism. Chromosomes are made of many different proteins and a substance called deoxyribonucleic acid, or **DNA**. Each molecule of DNA consists of thousands of atoms linked together into a chain. The chain resembles a twisted ladder. Each small section of DNA, which we call a **gene**, forms part of the rung and rail of that ladder.

The gene is like an instruction manual for assembling specific molecules of the body. Some genes determine eye color. Some determine the shape of blood cells. Others control whether the right or left side of the brain is dominant. Scientists are exploring whether genes may even determine what jokes a person finds funny, whether or not a child chews his fingernails, and what subjects a student prefers.

How Genes Are Expressed

The way we look, act, and perhaps even feel can be traced to the genes we inherit from our parents. We each have two genes for every human trait—from the shape of our ears to the ease with which we fight off certain diseases. Sometimes, the mother's gene and the father's gene is the same. Both parents, for example, may have brown eyes. In that case, the child will almost always have brown eyes.

Usually when genes are not the same, the traits of only one of the genes will appear in the offspring. The trait that is expressed is called the **dominant** gene. The other gene, termed **recessive,** is still present in the body, but it is not expressed. For example, the gene for brown eyes is dominant. A blue-eyed mother and a brown-eyed father will usually have brown-eyed children. However, the children still carry one gene for blue eyes and one gene for brown eyes. In the next generation, the blue-eyed trait may be expressed, as shown in the chart below.

POSSIBLE OFFSPRING OF TWO BROWN-EYED PARENTS WITH RECESSIVE GENE FOR BLUE EYES

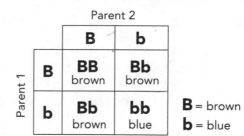

Genetic Reproduction

In most body cells, chromosomes come in pairs. When the cell reproduces, the DNA molecule "unzips," as shown below. Each half of the molecule serves as the pattern for a new DNA molecule. The result is two DNA molecules that are exactly alike.

DNA "UNZIPPING"

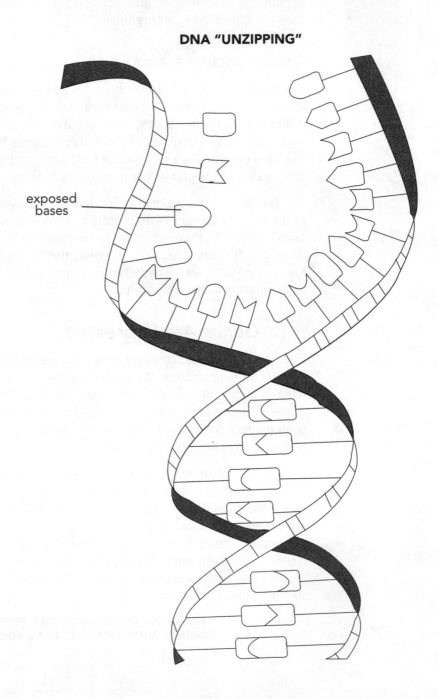

exposed bases

Sex cells, however, contain only half of a chromosome pair. When the sperm and egg unite, the two halves combine to make a new, unique whole. Half of the DNA will be from the mother. Half will be from the father. The new individual will have traits of both the mother and the father but will not be exactly like either of them.

After the egg cell is fertilized, it begins dividing until all of the trillions of cells that make up the human body have been produced. During each cell division, the chromosomes duplicate themselves. Each new cell contains chromosomes that are identical to those of the original cell.

Genetic Errors

Usually, the reassembly of DNA is perfect, and two identical chromosomes result. Sometimes, however, a mistake in the instructions occurs. We say the gene has **mutated**—or changed its instructions. This change can affect the way the organism develops. If the organism survives the mutation, that mutated gene may be inherited by future generations. Many inherited mutations are harmful. Some inherited conditions are:

- muscular dystrophy—a disease characterized by the progressive wasting of the muscles

- hemophilia—a condition in which the blood fails to clot normally

- sickle-cell anemia—a condition in which the shape of the red blood cells is altered to the point that the cells cannot carry enough oxygen throughout the body

Thinking About Science

Directions: Circle *T* for each true statement or *F* for each false statement.

T F **1.** Except for sperm and egg cells, every new human cell has chromosomes identical to the ones in the original cell.

T F **2.** Chromosomes are found in egg and sperm cells only.

T F **3.** Genes can be dominant or recessive.

T F **4.** A recessive gene will never be expressed in an organism or its offspring.

T F **5.** A mutation is a mistake in a gene that cannot be passed on to the next generation.

Answers are on page 311.

Directions: Choose the <u>one best answer</u> to each question.

Questions 1 and 2 refer to the diagram below.

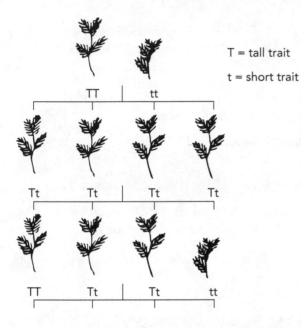

T = tall trait

t = short trait

1. The diagram shows a cross between a tall plant and a short plant. Each row shows a possible generation. What can you conclude about the trait for short size (t)?

   (1) It is dominant.
   (2) It is recessive.
   (3) It is a mutation
   (4) It is a blend.
   (5) It is harmful to the plant.

2. If tall size (T) is dominant, the next generation would be

   (1) all short
   (2) all tall
   (3) mostly medium
   (4) mostly tall
   (5) mostly short

Questions 3 and 4 refer to the following passage.

Scientists have discovered thousands of human diseases that have a genetic link. One such disease is PKU, or phenylketonuria. Most people have a dominant gene (type PP or Pp) that provides the code for the body to produce a special enzyme. This enzyme changes a harmful acid in milk into a harmless acid that humans can digest.

A child with two recessive PKU genes (type pp) cannot make this acid-changing enzyme. If a PKU child drinks milk, the harmful acids will build up and damage various body organs—especially the brain.

Hospitals now test all newborns for PKU. Those with the recessive trait are given special diets that prevent the buildup of harmful acids. These children will not get sick from PKU. They still carry the recessive gene, however, and pass it on to their offspring.

3. What is the cause of PKU?

   (1) an enzyme that makes a harmful acid in milk digestible
   (2) a recessive gene that prevents the body from making an important enzyme
   (3) a special enzyme
   (4) a damaged brain
   (5) the chemical phenylketonuria

4. Why do hospitals now test all newborns for PKU?

   (1) PKU is highly contagious.
   (2) PKU children need a special diet.
   (3) PKU children will be mentally disabled.
   (4) The gene can be fixed.
   (5) The gene must be replaced.

Answers are on page 311.

Health and Disease

Good health habits include a balanced diet, adequate amounts of sleep and exercise, cleanliness, and a positive mental attitude. Maintaining these habits can help people avoid many health problems. However, very few people go through life without getting some type of disease.

Some diseases are more common in young people than in any other age group. Most of these diseases, such as measles, mumps, and polio, are easily avoided by having children vaccinated by a doctor. The chart on this page shows symptoms and treatment for several common adult diseases.

Diseases of Adults

Although adults certainly can and do get the diseases children get, they are less likely to do so. Part of the reason is that they develop **immunities** that protect them. Adults have also had time to learn better hygiene habits. As a result, they avoid many germs.

STDs

Some diseases, however, are more common to adults than to children. An obvious example is an STD—or sexually transmitted disease. The chart below shows symptoms, diagnosis, and treatment of the most common STDs. Unlike STDs, most adult diseases are not contagious. Many, however, are fatal.

ADULT DISEASES

Disease	Symptoms	Treatment
AIDS	First stage: fever, fatigue, weakness, diarrhea, weight loss, swollen lymph nodes, skin infections Later stage: many infections, especially pneumonia, meningitis, rare tumors, and skin cancer	some limited treatment but no cure
Gonorrhea	Females: slight discharge from reproductive organs and mild burning sensation; often no symptoms Males: burning pain during urination and discharge from reproductive organ; often mild symptoms	penicillin and other antibiotics
Syphilis	First stage: sore appears at area of contact Second stage: rash anywhere on body; sometimes fever, headache, sore throat, and swollen joints Final stage: no symptoms for years but eventually damages body—may cause blindness, crippling, heart disease, mental illness, and even death	penicillin and other antibiotics
Herpes II	cluster of small blisters on the reproductive organs; blisters break open to form red, painful sores	treatment for pain but no cure

Cardiovascular Disease

Cardiovascular diseases affect the heart and the blood vessels. One such disease is atherosclerosis. With this disease, fatty deposits build up inside the blood vessels. If the buildup occurs in the arteries that supply the heart, a heart attack may occur. If the buildup occurs in the arteries that supply the brain, a stroke may result.

Another type of cardiovascular disease is hypertension, or high blood pressure. This disease strains the walls of the arteries, which increases the risk of heart attack or stroke.

Smoking, obesity, stress, lack of exercise, and a high-fat diet can increase the risk of cardiovascular disease. A high-salt diet makes high blood pressure worse.

Cancer

Cancer is the uncontrolled growth and spread of abnormal cells in the body. Cancer may appear in the breasts, lungs, brain, bones, skin, or other organs. The seven warning signs of cancer, shown in the chart below, have saved many lives. Some doctors add rapid weight loss and extreme fatigue to those warning signs.

EARLY WARNING SIGNS FOR CANCER
• unusual bleeding or discharge
• a lump or thickening in the breast or elsewhere
• a sore that does not heal
• a change in bowel or bladder habits
• hoarseness or cough that continues
• indigestion or difficulty in swallowing
• a change in size or color of wart or mole

Researchers are learning more and more about cancer. Many cancers can now be treated successfully if they are found and treated in the early stages. Surgery to remove tumors is now routine. Radiation and a variety of chemicals are used to destroy cancerous cells that cannot be removed surgically.

Diabetes

Diabetes is a disease in which the body does not produce enough insulin. The result is that the person with diabetes cannot use or store the sugar glucose properly. Frequent urination and extreme thirst and fatigue are symptoms of diabetes. Uncontrolled diabetes can lead to blindness, amputation of the legs and arms, and, ultimately, death.

Many people inherit a tendency to develop diabetes. Being overweight and not getting enough exercise greatly increase the risk of diabetes. The disease can be controlled through diet and exercise and/or regular injections of insulin.

Cirrhosis

In cirrhosis, the cells of the liver are replaced by scar tissue. The result is that the liver can no longer function properly. People with the disease may bruise easily, have nose bleeds, and vomit blood.

Alcoholism and poor nutrition are the major risk factors for cirrhosis. Correcting the diet and avoiding alcohol can stop the disease, but the liver cannot be repaired. Without treatment, people with cirrhosis die.

Arthritis

As people age, many get arthritis. They have some pain or difficulty with their joints. When the joints become swollen and stiff, the pain can be quite severe. Bony deposits may develop over the joints, locking them in place. Knees, hips, fingers, and toes are common sites for arthritis.

Heredity and obesity contribute to the disease. Although there is no cure for arthritis, the pain can be reduced with medicine, special exercises, and the application of heat.

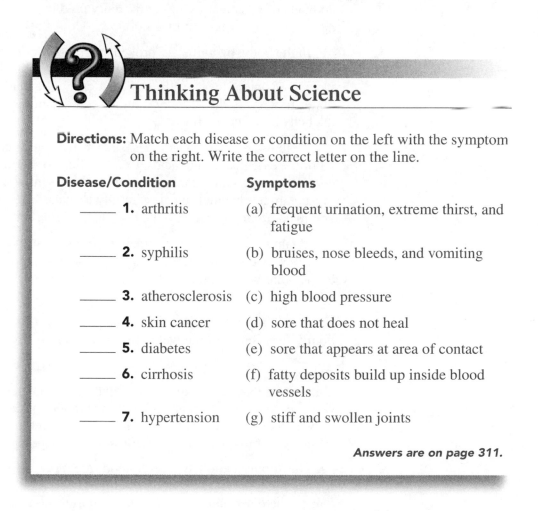

Thinking About Science

Directions: Match each disease or condition on the left with the symptom on the right. Write the correct letter on the line.

Disease/Condition

_____ **1.** arthritis

_____ **2.** syphilis

_____ **3.** atherosclerosis

_____ **4.** skin cancer

_____ **5.** diabetes

_____ **6.** cirrhosis

_____ **7.** hypertension

Symptoms

(a) frequent urination, extreme thirst, and fatigue

(b) bruises, nose bleeds, and vomiting blood

(c) high blood pressure

(d) sore that does not heal

(e) sore that appears at area of contact

(f) fatty deposits build up inside blood vessels

(g) stiff and swollen joints

Answers are on page 311.

Nutrition and Diet

The body needs nutrients to carry out the functions of maintenance, growth, repair, and reproduction. As a result, a well-balanced diet is essential. **Nutritionists** study foods that the body needs to stay healthy. Six types of nutrients are vital to life. They are carbohydrates, fats, proteins, vitamins, minerals, and water.

Good nutrition means eating the right foods in the proper proportions. A meal should include a range of different foods that provide a balance of carbohydrates, proteins, vitamins, and minerals. Every packaged food sold in the United States is required by the Food and Drug Administration to bear a nutrition facts label that lists the percentage of nutrients contained in it.

Vital Nutrients

Carbohydrates are the starches and sugars that are the main energy source for the body. They are supplied in large amounts in grains, fruits, and vegetables.

Like carbohydrates, **fats** provide a concentrated dose of energy. Large amounts of fats are present in oils, dairy products, nuts, and meats. The body needs only very small amounts of fat.

In the body, **proteins** are broken apart into amino acids. The body can manufacture most of the amino acids it needs to make new cells and to repair old cells. Nine of these acids, however, cannot be made and must be supplied in our food every day. To work, these essential amino acids must be present in the body at the same time.

Proteins from animal sources, such as fish, eggs, cheese, and meat contain all of the essential amino acids. Combinations of certain vegetables, such as corn and beans, can combine to provide the essential amino acids. Vegetarians must learn to plan their meals carefully to make sure that all the essential amino acids are available to the body at the same time.

Vitamins and minerals in small amounts are needed to regulate the body's activities. Each has a specific function. Some break down fats into proteins. Some build bones. Others allow nerves to carry messages or muscles to contract.

Water is the body's most important nutrient. It is used for almost every bodily function. Without water, people can survive for only a few days.

Calories

Calories are a measure of energy value. Everyone needs calories for energy. Not everyone, however, needs the same number of calories. People who are very active need more calories than those who get little exercise. Younger people generally need more calories than older people.

Nutritionists know that some foods are more valuable than others. Milk, for example, provides just a bit of almost everything the body needs. A candy bar, on the other hand, provides only calories, no nutrients. Nutritionists call these "empty" calories. They may provide energy but are of no lasting benefit to the body.

A Balanced Diet

The body needs nutrients to carry out the functions of maintenance, growth, repair, and reproduction.

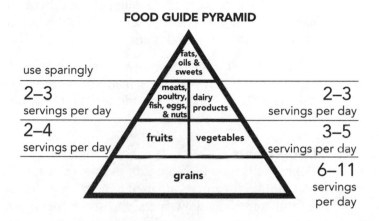

FOOD GUIDE PYRAMID

use sparingly

2–3
servings per day

2–4
servings per day

2–3
servings per day

3–5
servings per day

6–11
servings
per day

The USDA has replaced its four basic food groups chart that stressed eating a variety of foods from each group. It now advises that some foods are better for you than others. It shows you the types and amounts of foods to eat in a pyramid-shaped chart.

For a well-balanced diet, nutritionists recommend the pyramid plan shown above. Notice that almost half of the daily calories should come from grains. About a third should come from fruits and vegetables. The remainder should be supplied by meats and dairy products. Fats and sweets should be taken only in very small amounts.

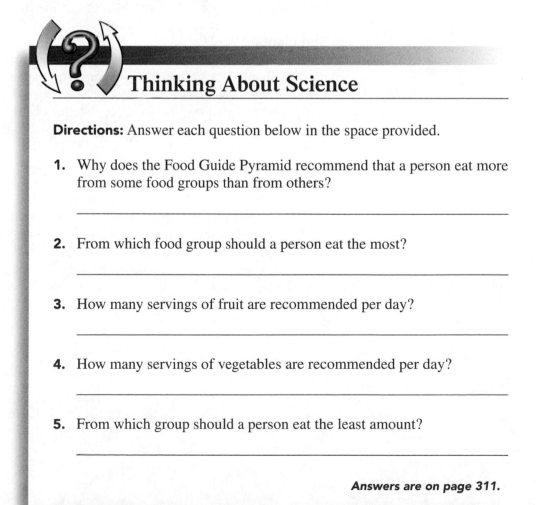

Thinking About Science

Directions: Answer each question below in the space provided.

1. Why does the Food Guide Pyramid recommend that a person eat more from some food groups than from others?

   _____

2. From which food group should a person eat the most?

   _____

3. How many servings of fruit are recommended per day?

   _____

4. How many servings of vegetables are recommended per day?

   _____

5. From which group should a person eat the least amount?

   _____

Answers are on page 311.

Drugs

Drugs are any kinds of chemicals that affect the body, mind, or behavior. Most drugs are carefully regulated by the medical community and used to improve health. Some drugs, such as the caffeine in coffee, tea, and chocolate, have uses that are beneficial. Others, such as heroin can be addictive and may cause physical or mental harm.

Any drug can be abused. One common abuse is caused when people share prescriptions. This practice is inadvisable as many drugs are carefully calculated for a person's age and weight. Other people using the drugs may suffer serious side effects.

Depressants

Depressants slow the actions of the central nervous system. Tranquilizers and barbiturates (downers) are used to help people relax and sleep. They also cause mental confusion, drowsiness, and sometimes death. They are especially dangerous when combined with another depressant, such as alcohol.

Narcotics are depressants derived from opium. These include morphine, codeine, and heroin (smack, horse). Medically, narcotics are used to relieve pain. They produce a feeling of well-being. Unfortunately, they also produce both physical and psychological addictions. The addict must keep taking larger doses to produce a drug "high." The addiction is expensive and all-consuming. Death due to overdose often results. Withdrawal from narcotics is severe.

Stimulants

Stimulants speed up the action of the central nervous system. Caffeine and the nicotine in cigarettes are mild stimulants. Amphetamines (pep pills, uppers), methedrine (speed), and cocaine (coke) give people a temporary sense of power and energy. Psychological dependence occurs quickly. Nervousness, depression, sleeplessness, severe fatigue, and malnutrition are common results of stimulant abuse.

Hallucinogens

These drugs alter a person's understanding of what is real and unreal. With use of these drugs, many of the symptoms of psychosis can occur. Users may feel as if they can see sound or hear color. They may also drool, shiver, and feel nauseated. Mood shifts from tremendous joy to unrelenting terror are common. Users may experience frightening flashbacks months after using the drug. During flashbacks users may harm themselves or others. Mescaline and LSD (acid) are common hallucinogens.

Combination Drugs

PCP (angel dust) combines the negatives of a hallucinogenic with a depressant. It is one of the most dangerous drugs because it can produce seizures and slow breathing to the point of inducing a coma or death. Flashbacks and mood alterations can be severe.

Hashish, marijuana, and THC are also hallucinogens and depressants. The drugs slow reaction time but also speed heart rate and raise blood pressure. They affect the brain's ability to interpret what it sees. THC can remain in the body for days and weeks. Scientists do not yet know the long-term effects of marijuana.

Fumes

Some people inhale substances to achieve the same effects as a depressant. Spray paint, cleaning fluids, paint thinner, gasoline, and glues are most frequently abused. The fumes of these substances can seriously damage the lungs, bone marrow, liver, brain, and kidneys. Death is also possible.

Thinking About Science

Directions: Answer the questions below in the space provided.

1. How do depressants affect the central nervous system?

    _____

2. Name three possible results of stimulant abuse.

    _____

3. What mental illness does a hallucinogen mimic?

    _____

4. What makes PCP so dangerous?

    _____

    _____

5. What organs are commonly damaged by inhaling fumes?

    _____

Answers are on page 311.

Directions: Choose the <u>one best answer</u> to each question.

Questions 1 and 2 refer to the information on pages 159–165.

1. Which of the following does <u>not</u> increase the risk of cardiovascular disease?

   (1) stress
   (2) obesity
   (3) low-fat diet
   (4) smoking
   (5) lack of exercise

2. Which of the following foods should be eaten only in very small amounts?

   (1) ice cream
   (2) yogurt
   (3) squash
   (4) bagel
   (5) chicken

   Answers are on page 311.

Human Biology Review

Directions: Choose the <u>one best answer</u> to each question.

Questions 1–8 refer to the information on pages 139–165.

1. Which of the following facts best explains why a fall may result in a broken bone for a senior citizen but not for a younger person?

   (1) The skeletal system is made of bones and cartilage.
   (2) Bones of the skeleton protect vital organs.
   (3) Human bones are not solid.
   (4) An adult has 206 bones.
   (5) Bones harden and become brittle with age.

2. Which of the following best describes what a human body would look like without its skeleton?

   (1) a long-legged figure
   (2) a stunted frame
   (3) a supportive structure
   (4) a shapeless heap
   (5) a lop-sided frame

3. Which organ(s) is <u>not</u> protected by the ribs?

   (1) small intestine
   (2) lungs
   (3) heart
   (4) brain
   (5) both the small intestine and the brain

4. What can you infer is the purpose of ligaments?

   (1) to prevent the bones from rubbing together
   (2) to keep the bones in place
   (3) to allow for circular movement between bones
   (4) to enable bones to move back and forth
   (5) to make new blood cells

5. Which of the following does <u>not</u> describe skeletal muscles?

   (1) make the skeleton move
   (2) vary in size and shape
   (3) attached to bones
   (4) voluntary
   (5) involuntary

6. What is the most likely cause of a stomach ulcer?

   (1) pulled muscles in the stomach
   (2) strong acids that eat a sore in the stomach wall
   (3) not properly chewing food into small bits
   (4) eating too many different types of foods at one time
   (5) absorption of undigested food into the stomach lining

7. Which body system removes wastes from the body?

   (1) circulatory system
   (2) nervous system
   (3) excretory system
   (4) muscular system
   (5) digestive system

8. Adrenaline is released into the body during times of danger. Which of the following actions likely does <u>not</u> result from adrenaline?

   (1) sudden muscle pain
   (2) increased heartbeat
   (3) muscle contraction
   (4) widening of eyes
   (5) release of sugar into the blood

Questions 9–11 are based on the following passage.

A mother's consumption of alcohol can cause great harm to her unborn child. Fetal Alcohol Syndrome (FAS) is the term doctors use to describe children born to mothers who drink. FAS may cause just a slight behavioral problem. More often, unfortunately, mental disabilities or physical deformities may also occur as a result of FAS.

When a pregnant woman drinks, so does her unborn child. The alcohol flows into the baby's bloodstream long before a baby's body system is able to handle alcohol. As a result, the alcohol acts like a poison. Even a mother's social drinking—especially in the first few months of pregnancy—can be enough to damage the baby's developing organs.

The damage done to a FAS baby is not evident until it is born. The FAS baby may show any combination of the following symptoms:

- low birth-weight
- weak heart or kidney problems
- learning difficulties
- slow development

Even when a newborn does not have the characteristics of FAS, the pregnant mother's alcohol consumption may become apparent as the child grows older. Researchers call these less apparent consequences fetal alcohol effects or modified FAS. These include:

- mental retardation
- abnormally high levels of activity
- inability to concentrate
- abnormal sleep patterns

It has been estimated that FAS is the third most common birth defect. The tragedy is that FAS is easily prevented.

9. What should a pregnant mother do to prevent FAS in her unborn child?

   (1) limit alcohol consumption to occasional social drinking
   (2) get lots of sleep
   (3) limit herself to two ounces of alcohol each day
   (4) have a balanced diet
   (5) not consume any alcohol during the pregnancy

10. Which of the following symptoms of FAS becomes evident only as the child grows older?

    (1) mental disabilities
    (2) kidney problems
    (3) failure to develop like other infants
    (4) smaller size than other infants
    (5) heart problems

11. If a woman who is a social drinker discovers she has been pregnant for two months, what should she do?

    (1) maintain her consumption pattern since the damage has already been done
    (2) abstain from alcohol for the duration of the pregnancy
    (3) refrain from alcohol until the second trimester and then resume her drinking
    (4) slowly decrease her alcohol intake
    (5) drink only on a full stomach

Answers are on page 312.

READING EFFICIENCY C

Directions: This activity will help you to improve your reading efficiency. Before you start to read, write the present time at the top of the page. When you have completed the reading and all 5 questions, write your finishing time. Subtract to find out how long you took. Score your answers. Then turn to pages 320–321 to find your E-Factor and to graph your progress.

Finishing Time	
Starting Time −	
Reading Time =	
Number of Answers Correct	

Temperature and the Human Body

Many people do not enjoy being in very hot or very cold temperatures. For some people these extreme temperatures can be serious. But what is extreme to one person might not make as much difference to another.

In extreme weather, the death toll in cities goes up. The temperature at which this happens depends on the city. For example, a temperature of 81°F can cause a big increase in deaths in Los Angeles. In Phoenix, that won't happen until the temperature reaches 112°F. The reason is that the people of Phoenix are used to higher temperatures than the people of Los Angeles are. The same is true for cold weather. People who live in colder temperatures are harmed less by extreme cold than people who live in warmer areas.

TEMPERATURES AT WHICH DEATH RATES INCREASE IN VARIOUS U.S. CITIES	
City	**Temperature**
Atlanta	94°F
Chicago	91°F
Dallas	103°F
Kansas City	99°F
Los Angeles	81°F
Miami	90°F
St. Louis	96°F
Seattle	87°F

Data from *USA Today*

What effect does heat have on the body to cause such harm? The hypothalamus is an area at the base of the brain. It controls body processes, such as breathing, heart rate, and blood pressure. The hypothalamus can sense that the body is too warm. Then it tells the blood vessels to expand and the heart to beat faster. This causes the blood to carry heat from inside the body to the skin's surface. The person sweats, and the sweat evaporates. This process uses heat.

Usually this process works well. But things change during extreme heat. High temperatures often are joined by high humidity. This humidity gets in the way of the body's cooling process. Sweat can't evaporate as quickly, and the body can't cool as fast. The body works harder to make up for the slower heat loss. This puts more stress on the heart and blood vessels. A heart attack or other medical problems can result. Another problem happens when people do not replace water lost by sweating. The chemical reactions in the body take place in water. Without enough water, the body cannot work properly.

READING EFFICIENCY C

1. A temperature drop to 23°F would affect people in which city the most?

   (1) Dallas
   (2) Seattle
   (3) St. Louis
   (4) Chicago
   (5) Kansas City

2. Which statement explains why sweating helps cool the body?

   (1) Heat is used in the process of evaporation.
   (2) The blood vessels expand to carry more blood.
   (3) Sweating uses up water in the body.
   (4) Blood carries heat to the surface of the skin.
   (5) Heart rate increases.

3. Which group of people probably would be more seriously affected by extreme heat?

   (1) people with heart conditions
   (2) people who sweat a lot
   (3) people who exercise regularly outdoors
   (4) people who live near the equator
   (5) people with digestive problems

4. Which of the following actions would not help reduce stress on the body during extremely hot weather?

   (1) drinking plenty of water.
   (2) limiting strenuous activity
   (3) sitting in front of a fan
   (4) wearing clothing that traps moisture
   (5) spraying water on the skin

5. A study was done to test how exercise helps a person deal with heat. Two groups were tested. One exercised for a month and then was tested in extreme heat. The other group did not exercise. Which of the following would not be a necessary part of the study?

   (1) People in both groups should have similar medical histories.
   (2) People in both groups should be young.
   (3) People in both groups should have similar exercise habits before the test begins.
   (4) Both groups should be tested before the study begins to see how their body's response to heat changes.
   (5) People in both groups should be tested at the same temperature for the same amount of time.

Answers are on page 312.

READING EFFICIENCY D

Directions: This activity will help you to improve your reading efficiency. Before you start to read, write the present time at the top of the page. When you have completed the reading and all 5 questions, write your finishing time. Subtract to find out how long you took. Score your answers. Then turn to pages 320-321 to find your E-Factor and to graph your progress.

Finishing Time	
Starting Time −	
Reading Time =	
Number of Answers Correct	

Digestion and Nutrition

All the cells in your body need a constant supply of nutrients to carry on life processes. These nutrients come from the foods you eat. Foods contain six kinds of nutrients: carbohydrates, fats, proteins, vitamins, minerals, and water. Different foods have different nutrients.

Most of the nutrients in food cannot be used directly by the cells. The molecules that make up the foods you eat are too large to pass through cell membranes. Only water and minerals are made of molecules that are small enough to pass through cell membranes. Other nutrients must be broken down into smaller molecules. For example, starch molecules are broken down into simple sugar molecules. That is the job of the digestive system.

During digestion food is broken down two ways—chemically and mechanically. Mechanical digestion takes place when food is chewed and mixed in the mouth or churned in your stomach. Chemical digestion takes place in the mouth, stomach, and small intestine. Chemical digestion breaks down large molecules into smaller molecules.

In order for digested food to get to cells, it must move from the digestive system to the blood. This process happens in the small intestine. There, small nutrient molecules pass into blood vessels in the walls of the small intestine. The walls of the small intestine are not smooth. They have many ridges and folds. Tiny fingerlike structures cover the folds. These structures are called villi. Villi have many blood vessels.

Blood vessels carry nutrient molecules to all the cells in the body. The cells use these nutrients in different ways. Some are used for energy, some to build new cell parts, and some to reproduce.

1. Which type of nutrient does <u>not</u> need to be digested?

   (1) mineral
   (2) vitamin
   (3) fat
   (4) protein
   (5) carbohydrate

2. What might happen if the blood vessels leading to a particular organ were blocked?

   (1) Blood would flow backward.
   (2) Nutrients would pile up in the blood vessels.
   (3) The villi would get larger.
   (4) Digestion would stop.
   (5) The organ's cells would not get the nutrients they need.

3. How do villi help the small intestine absorb nutrients faster?

   (1) They pump nutrients through the blood.
   (2) They catch nutrients as they travel through the small intestine.
   (3) They stir up the nutrients in the small intestine.
   (4) They make more area where nutrients can be absorbed.
   (5) They remove large nutrient molecules from the blood vessels.

4. If a person ate the following foods, which would enter the blood vessels first?

   (1) eggs
   (2) water
   (3) bread
   (4) orange slices
   (5) butter

5. A student wants to loose weight. She thinks that if she eats only one type of food she will loose weight faster. She thinks her body will become better at breaking down that one type of food if it doesn't have to break down other foods at the same time. Why is the student's idea <u>not</u> good for her health?

   (1) Different foods have different nutrients that the body needs.
   (2) The student might get bored if she eats only one food.
   (3) Some foods are absorbed faster than others.
   (4) Some foods can not be chewed.
   (5) Some foods take longer than others to be broken down.

Answers are on page 312.

PART THREE

Physical Science

- Chemistry
- Physics

CHAPTER 6

Chemistry

Chemistry is the study of **matter**. Scientists define matter as anything that has mass and takes up space. A person is matter; so is a desk, water, and air. To learn more about matter, chemists try to break it down into its simplest form. They also examine what happens when different kinds of matter are combined. Through their studies of matter, chemists have made many scientific breakthroughs that affect us all.

More and more of the products we use every day are made of materials developed through chemistry. For example, to prevent breakage, the lenses in eyeglasses are now made of plastic. To prevent wrinkling, a cotton shirt may now contain polyester. To reduce calories, the sugar in food may be replaced with a chemical sweetener. The uses of these products have grown at a phenomenal rate.

Chemistry is also responsible for the development and growth of the pharmaceutical industry. The field of medicine used to rely on simple remedies, such as juices from plants and trees, extractions from the soil, and other products of nature. By studying these home remedies, chemists have isolated the ingredients that were responsible for the healing effects. The new products can be tailored to a specific disease.

Another application of chemistry in everyday life is the cleaning of fabrics. Soap is a chemical agent made of certain salts of sodium, which can break up grease and wash it away. Carbon compounds are the chemical agents used in the dry-cleaning process.

Our study of chemistry in this chapter will involve six major topics:

- Matter
- The atom
- Compounds and molecules
- Chemical reactions
- Solutions
- The chemistry of life

Matter

Two thousand years ago, there were no chemists. Many people, however, were interested in the composition of matter and how it changed. These early researchers were called *alchemists*. The alchemists worked with matter and after many observations suggested that all matter could be divided into earth, water, air, and fire. Notice that from their observations, they chose a solid, a liquid, a gas, and a symbol of energy.

In the early 1900s, Albert Einstein suggested an immensely important idea. He said that matter can be changed into energy and energy can be changed into matter. Einstein's idea was the driving force behind the development of atomic energy and the atomic bomb.

The States of Matter

Scientists define matter as anything that has mass and volume. Matter takes up space. On Earth, most matter exists in one of four states—as a solid, liquid, gas, or plasma.

How the particles of matter are arranged influences whether a substance is a solid, liquid, gas, or plasma. In **solids**, the particles are packed tightly together. They have little room to move. As a result, solids, like a book or a pencil, have a definite shape and volume. In **liquids**, the particles are linked, but loosely. They can slide past one another. Liquids, such as water, have a definite volume, but no definite shape. In **gases**, the particles are free to move about in any direction. As a result, gases have no definite shape and no definite volume. Air is a gas.

Almost 99 percent of the matter in the universe is neither a solid, a liquid, nor a gas. Instead it is a **plasma**—the fourth state of matter. The stars are considered to be plasma.

Scientists describe plasma as a gas that has become so hot that it no longer behaves like a gas. Instead, it conducts electricity. Only small amounts of plasma are found on Earth. The gas inside a fluorescent lightbulb is one example of plasma on Earth.

Plasmas have excited scientists because matter must reach the plasma state if **fusion** is to occur. Fusion occurs when two or more atomic nuclei combine to form a single nucleus and to release energy. Fusion would provide an almost limitless supply of energy. The problem is devising a container for the process. Converting matter to plasma requires a temperature as hot as that of the Sun. As soon as matter touches the walls of the container, it cools below that temperature. Some scientists are now trying to find ways to contain plasmas without using any type of matter at all. One suggestion is to contain plasma with a magnetic force field.

The state of matter—whether it is a solid, liquid, gas, or plasma—depends on temperature. Different types of matter change state (either freeze or boil) at different temperatures. Water, for example, freezes at 0°C (32°F). At 100°C, water boils. Iron melts from a solid to a liquid at 1,535°C.

Properties of Matter

The state of matter—solid, liquid, gas, or plasma—is just one of the physical properties of matter. A stick of butter, for example, might be described by its state (a solid), or by its shape, color, or smell. If you cut the butter, the shape changes, but it is still butter. Even if you melt the butter, it is still butter. **Physical properties** are those that can be examined without changing the identity of the matter. Some other physical properties of matter include hardness, density, and melting and boiling points. Physical changes are changes in which the state of a substance is altered, but not its chemical composition. For example, if you melt butter, it becomes a liquid, but it tastes the same. Its solid state can be restored by cooling it.

Chemical properties are those that describe how a substance reacts with another substance. Chemical changes result in new materials with new properties. For example, a chemical property of wood is that it burns. After the reaction, however, there is no more wood. It has been changed to ash. Most chemical changes can't be reversed; for example, when wood is burned, the resulting ashes can't be turned into wood again.

Some physical changes are easy to confuse with chemical changes. Dissolving salt in water, for example, might seem like a chemical change. The salt no longer exists as tiny grains, but tasting the water will convince you that the salt is still there. In fact, if the water evaporates, the salt will be left behind.

Elements

An **element** is a type of matter that cannot be broken down into a simpler substance. Each different type of matter is made of one or more elements. Some types of matter, such as oxygen, cannot be broken down into a simpler substance. Oxygen is an element. Water, on the other hand, can be broken down into two substances—oxygen and hydrogen. Sugar is made of three elements—oxygen, hydrogen, and carbon.

Thinking About Science

Directions: Answer the questions below in the space provided.

1. What is the difference between a chemical and a physical property of matter?

_____

_____

_____

2. What is an element?_____

Answers are on page 312.

Directions: Choose the <u>one best answer</u> to each question.

Questions 1–6 are based on the information on pages 175–177.

1. What development resulted from Einstein's ideas about matter and energy?

   (1) plasma
   (2) solid-state theory
   (3) the states of matter
   (4) the atomic bomb
   (5) computers

2. Which of the following ideas describes an element?

   A. It can be broken down into simpler substances.
   B. It cannot be broken down into simpler subtances.
   C. It can be combined with other elements.

   (1) A only
   (2) B only
   (3) C only
   (4) both A and B
   (5) both A and C

3. What can you infer to be the largest source of plasma?

   (1) magnetic force fields
   (2) stars
   (3) fusion reactors
   (4) neon lightbulbs
   (5) asteroids

4. What facts about plasma interest scientists?

   (1) That state must be reached for fusion to occur.
   (2) It is the state of matter found in stars.
   (3) It conducts electricity.
   (4) It makes a magnetic force field.
   (5) all of the above

5. Which of the following is an example of a physical change?

   (1) ice melting to water
   (2) a lump of coal turning to ash when burned
   (3) a cake made from flour, sugar, eggs, and butter
   (4) iron rusting when left out in the rain
   (5) the process of photosynthesis by which plants make food

6. Which of the following is an example of a chemical change?

   (1) iron being magnetized
   (2) sodium and chlorine combining to form salt
   (3) brass expanding when heated
   (4) water turning to steam when heated
   (5) a popsicle turning to liquid

7. The Sun is considered to exist in what state of matter?

   (1) solid
   (2) liquid
   (3) gas
   (4) plasma
   (5) none of the above

8. Which of the following is <u>not</u> the result of a chemical change?

   (1) evaporation
   (2) rust
   (3) sour milk
   (4) burnt wood
   (5) bright light from a camera flashbulb

Answers are on page 312.

The Atom

Elements are made up of tiny particles, called **atoms**. If you divided a lump of iron into smaller and smaller pieces until you could divide it no further, you would eventually have a single atom of iron. If you were able to divide the atom of iron, however, it would no longer have the characteristics that make iron.

Atoms are extremely small. They are so small that they cannot be seen—even under a microscope. Scientists, however, have developed several models of the atom. One of the most popular models was developed about 90 years ago by Niels Bohr. Scientists know that Bohr's model is not totally accurate, but it is still very helpful in understanding the atom.

THE BOHR MODEL OF LITHIUM

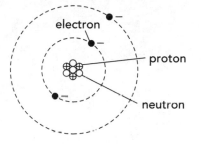

In the early 1900s, scientists had discovered that atoms had tiny particles with electric charges. These particles were named **electrons**. Bohr thought that the atom was made of a central nucleus. He suggested that the electrons circled the atom's nucleus much like the planets orbit the Sun.

The electrons circle the nucleus in paths, or shells, that are like wavy bands of clouds. The electron may be anywhere within that shell. Each shell can hold only a certain number of electrons. The shell closest to the nucleus can hold only 2 electrons. The second shell holds 8, the third 18, and the remaining shells each hold 32 electrons. Each element has a different number of electrons in its shells.

The nucleus of the atom is composed of two types of larger particles: protons and neutrons. Each **proton** has a positive electrical charge, which attracts the negatively charged electrons. **Neutrons** are neutral. They have no electrical charge at all.

Although an atom is made of electrically charged particles, the atom itself is electrically neutral. This means that each atom must have an equal number of protons (positively charged) and electrons (negatively charged).

Atoms may become electrically charged by losing or gaining one or more electrons. An atom then becomes an **ion**, which carries either a positive or negative charge.

THE ATOM WITH ELECTRONS IN A CLOUD PATH

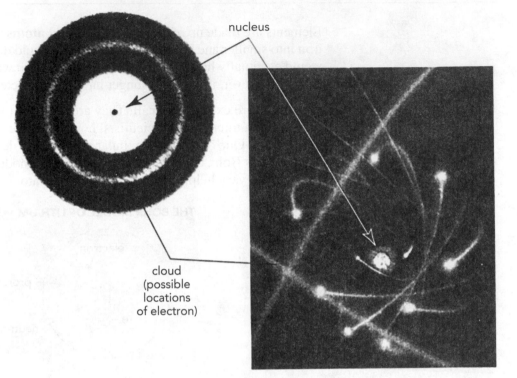

nucleus

cloud
(possible
locations
of electron)

Atomic Number

An element always has the same number of protons and electrons. The gas hydrogen, for example, always has 1 proton and 1 electron. Oxygen has 8 protons and 8 electrons. Scientists have assigned a number to each element. Hydrogen is assigned the atomic number 1. Oxygen is atomic number 8. The atomic number shows how many protons are in each atom.

Atomic Mass

A proton and a neutron in an atom have approximately the same mass. An electron, however, has considerably less mass. For simplicity, scientists assign each proton and neutron a mass of 1. They assign the electron a mass of 0.

Although all atoms of the same element have the same number of protons, they don't each have the same number of neutrons. That means the mass of atoms of the same kind of element may be slightly different. Atoms with different numbers of neutrons are called **isotopes**. Atomic mass is an average of all the isotopes of an element.

Organizing the Elements

During the 1800s, scientists tried to classify the known elements, much as organisms are classified. That attempt failed until the Russian chemist Dmitry Mendeleyev noticed that there was a relationship between the atomic mass of elements and their properties. He listed all the elements known at the time (60), according to their masses. He then put them into columns according to the number of electrons contained in their outermost shells. In some cases, there was no element for a slot in Mendeleyev's table. Mendeleyev left a blank and suggested that such an element might one day be found. Mendeleyev's work resulted in what is called the **periodic table of the elements**.

In the 1900s, scientists determined that an element's properties were more closely related to atomic number than atomic mass. The periodic table was updated and now appears as shown on pages 182 and 183.

MENDELEYEV'S TABLE OF 1872

Group	I	II	III	IV	V	VI	VII	VIII
1	H(1)							
2	Li(7)	Be(9.4)	B(11)	C(12)	N(14)	O(16)	F(19)	
3	Na(23)	Mg(24)	Al(27.3)	Si(28)	P(31)	S(32)	Cl(35.5)	
4	K(39)	Ca(40)	–(44)	Ti(48)	V(51)	Cr(52)	Mn(55)	Fe(56), Co(59), Ni(59), Cu(63)
5	[Cu(63)]	Zn(65)	–(68)	–(72)	As(75)	Se(78)	Br(80)	
6	Rb(85)	Sr(87)	?Yt(88)	Zr(90)	Nb(94)	Mo(96)	–(100)	Ru(104), Rh(104), Pd(106), Ag(108)
7	[Ag(108)]	Cd(112)	In(113)	Sn(118)	Sb(122)	Te(125)	I(127)	
8	Cs(133)	Ba(137)	?Ba(138)	?Ce(140)	——	——	——	
9	——	——	——	——	——	——	——	
10	——	——	?Er(178)	?La(180)	Ta(182)	W(184)	——	Os(195), Ir(197), Pt(198), Au(197)
11	[Au(199)]	Hg(200)	Tl(204)	Pb(207)	Bi(208)	——	——	
12	——	——	——	Th(231)	——	U(240)	——	

(Series)

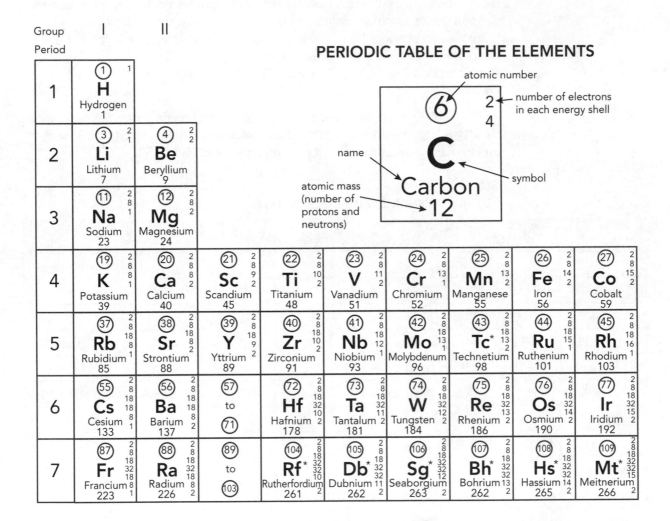

PERIODIC TABLE OF THE ELEMENTS

Rare Earth Elements

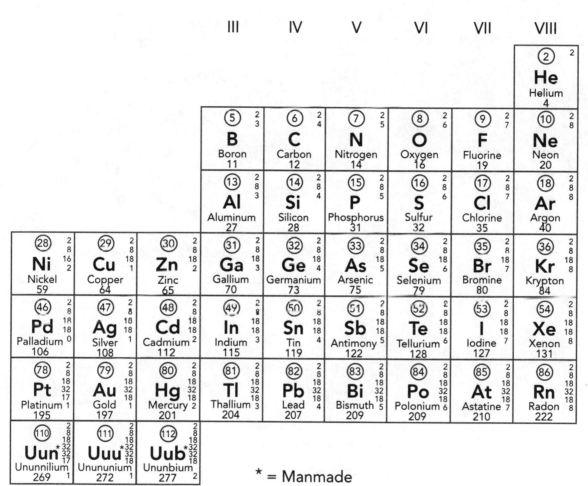

	III	IV	V	VI	VII	VIII
						② 2 **He** Helium 4
	⑤ 2 3 **B** Boron 11	⑥ 2 4 **C** Carbon 12	⑦ 2 5 **N** Nitrogen 14	⑧ 2 6 **O** Oxygen 16	⑨ 2 7 **F** Fluorine 19	⑩ 2 8 **Ne** Neon 20
	⑬ 2 8 3 **Al** Aluminum 27	⑭ 2 8 4 **Si** Silicon 28	⑮ 2 8 5 **P** Phosphorus 31	⑯ 2 8 6 **S** Sulfur 32	⑰ 2 8 7 **Cl** Chlorine 35	⑱ 2 8 8 **Ar** Argon 40
㉘ 2 8 16 2 **Ni** Nickel 59	㉙ 2 8 18 1 **Cu** Copper 64	㉚ 2 8 18 2 **Zn** Zinc 65	㉛ 2 8 18 3 **Ga** Gallium 70	㉜ 2 8 18 4 **Ge** Germanium 73	㉝ 2 8 18 5 **As** Arsenic 75	㉞ 2 8 18 6 **Se** Selenium 79	㉟ 2 8 18 7 **Br** Bromine 80	㊱ 2 8 18 8 **Kr** Krypton 84
㊻ 2 8 18 0 **Pd** Palladium 106	㊼ 2 8 10 18 1 **Ag** Silver 108	㊽ 2 8 18 18 2 **Cd** Cadmium 112	㊾ 2 8 18 18 3 **In** Indium 115	㊿ 2 8 18 18 4 **Sn** Tin 119	51 2 8 18 18 5 **Sb** Antimony 122	52 2 8 18 18 6 **Te** Tellurium 128	53 2 8 18 18 7 **I** Iodine 127	54 2 8 18 18 8 **Xe** Xenon 131
78 2 8 18 32 17 1 **Pt** Platinum 195	79 2 8 18 32 18 1 **Au** Gold 197	80 2 8 18 32 18 2 **Hg** Mercury 201	81 2 8 18 32 18 3 **Tl** Thallium 204	82 2 8 18 32 18 4 **Pb** Lead 207	83 2 8 18 32 18 5 **Bi** Bismuth 209	84 2 8 18 32 18 6 **Po** Polonium 209	85 2 8 18 32 18 7 **At** Astatine 210	86 2 8 18 32 18 8 **Rn** Radon 222
110 2 8 18 32 32 17 1 **Uun*** Ununnilium 269	111 2 8 18 32 32 18 1 **Uuu*** Unununium 272	112 2 8 18 32 32 18 2 **Uub*** Ununbium 277

* = Manmade

63 2 8 18 25 8 **Eu** Europium 2 152	64 2 8 18 25 9 **Gd** Gadolinium 2 157	65 2 8 18 27 8 **Tb** Terbium 2 159	66 2 8 18 28 8 **Dy** Dysprosium 2 163	67 2 8 18 29 8 **Ho** Holmium 2 165	68 2 8 18 30 8 **Er** Erbium 2 167	69 2 8 18 31 8 **Tm** Thulium 2 169	70 2 8 18 32 8 **Yb** Ytterbium 2 173	71 2 8 18 32 9 **Lu** Lutetium 2 175
95 2 8 18 32 25 8 **Am*** Americium 2 243	96 2 8 18 32 25 9 **Cm*** Curium 2 247	97 2 8 18 32 26 9 **Bk*** Berkelium 2 247	98 2 8 18 32 28 8 **Cf*** Californium 2 251	99 2 8 18 32 29 8 **Es*** Einsteinium 2 252	100 2 8 18 32 30 8 **Fm*** Fermium 2 257	101 2 8 18 32 31 8 **Md*** Mendelevium 2 258	102 2 8 18 32 32 8 **No*** Nobelium 2 259	103 2 8 18 32 32 9 **Lr*** Lawrencium 2 260

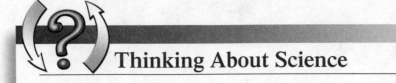

Thinking About Science

Directions: Answer the questions below in the space provided.

1. Can you identify the components in the following diagram of an atom?

THE ATOM

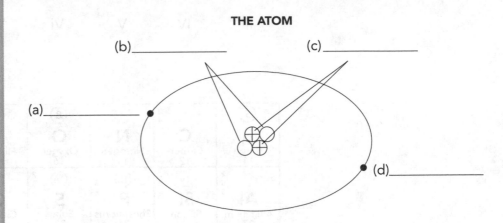

(b)_____   (c)_____

(a)_____

(d)_____

2. How does today's model of an atom differ from the Bohr model?

_____

_____

_____

3. What is the electrical charge of each of the following?

_____ (a) a proton

_____ (b) a neutron

_____ (c) an electron

_____ (d) an atom

_____ (e) an ion

Answers are on pages 312–313.

Directions: Choose the <u>one best answer</u> to each question.

Questions 1–5 are based on the information in pages 179–183.

1. What is the smallest particle of an element that has all the properties of that element?

   (1) electron
   (2) atom
   (3) proton
   (4) nucleus
   (5) particle

2. Which of the following statements is true?

   (1) The atomic number of an atom is equal to the number of protons.
   (2) The weight of an electron is considered to be 1.
   (3) The weight of a proton is about the same as the weight of an electron.
   (4) A proton revolves around the nucleus of an atom.
   (5) The neutron of an atom has no mass.

3. The element helium has two electrons, two protons, and two neutrons. What is its atomic number?

   (1) 6
   (2) 4
   (3) 2
   (4) 0
   (5) 3

4. What is indicated by the design of the periodic table?

   (1) There are 63 elements in the universe.
   (2) Neutrons are the basis upon which elements are grouped.
   (3) All of the elements are found in nature.
   (4) Elements can be grouped according to the number of electrons in their outer shells.
   (5) Each atom of an element must have exactly the same weight.

5. Which of the following statements is <u>not</u> true for an element?

   (1) One or more elements compose all matter.
   (2) An element cannot be broken down into simpler substances.
   (3) An atom is the smallest particle that has properties of an element.
   (4) Gold, lead, aluminum, and carbon dioxide are elements.
   (5) An element's atomic number shows the number of protons in each atom of the element.

Answers are on page 313.

Compounds and Molecules

Atoms are held together partly because the negative electrons are attracted to the positive protons. The protons' attraction extends beyond the outer electrons. The protons of one atom may attract the electrons of another atom. The result is that very few of the elements on the periodic table exist alone. Most combine with two or more other elements to form **compounds**.

As you have read, different elements have different numbers of electrons in their shells. Elements that have eight electrons in their outer shell are very stable. Their atoms may be attracted to one another, but they do not form compounds with other elements. Chemists say they are **inert**. Elements with other than eight electrons in their outer shell are unstable.

Bonding

Bonding, the joining of atoms, can occur either through ionic bonding or covalent bonding. An **ionic bond** is formed when atoms give up or gain electrons. Ionic bonding can be explained by looking at the elements that make up ordinary table salt. In the diagram below, notice that one of the elements of salt—sodium (Na)—has one electron in its outer shell. Chlorine (Cl) has seven electrons in its outer shell.

SODIUM AND CHLORINE ATOMS

(Only the electrons in the outermost energy shells are shown.)

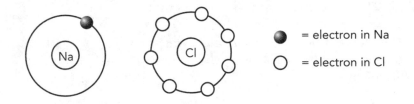

= electron in Na

= electron in Cl

Sodium and chlorine are likely to bond because when they come together, their outer electrons form a stable shell of eight electrons. However, an electron has a negative charge. If a chlorine atom pulls an electron away from another atom, the chlorine atom becomes negatively charged. If a sodium atom loses its outer electron, the sodium atom becomes positively charged. Since opposites attract, the negative chlorine atom bonds with the positive sodium atom, and sodium chloride (NaCl), or salt, is formed.

SODIUM CHLORIDE

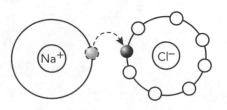

The Na electron has transferred over to the Cl atom.

The new compound may be quite different from the elements that formed it. On its own, sodium is a silvery metal that reacts violently with water. Chlorine is a poisonous gas. The sodium chloride compound is a white, nonpoisonous solid that dissolves in water.

Most ionic compounds are solids at room temperature because the bond between their particles is very strong. As solids, they do not conduct electricity. As liquids, however, they are good electrical conductors. Most have high melting points.

The other process of forming a compound is called **covalent bonding**. In this process, electrons are not transferred from one atom to another. Instead, they are shared. Their electron shells overlap.

Water is an important covalent compound. Notice in the diagram below that each hydrogen atom has two electrons in its shell. The oxygen atom has eight electrons in its outer shell. Together the atoms are more stable than they were alone. This type of formation is called a **molecule**.

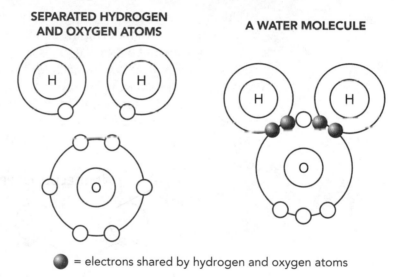

SEPARATED HYDROGEN AND OXYGEN ATOMS

A WATER MOLECULE

⚫ = electrons shared by hydrogen and oxygen atoms

The bonds formed by covalent compounds are weak, which is why so many covalent compounds are gases or liquids. Covalent compounds have low melting and boiling points because little energy is needed to break the bonds between the atoms.

The word *molecule* has two important meanings. One meaning is the joining of two or more atoms of different elements to form a compound, like the water molecule above. The other meaning is the joining of two or more atoms of the same element. This kind of molecule occurs when the atoms of one element stick together in a certain number. A good example is hydrogen, which usually occurs as individual molecules of two atoms each. Because a hydrogen molecule consists of atoms of only one element, it is not considered to be a compound.

Chemical Formulas

Chemists use **formulas** to represent the structure of molecules. These formulas are written in a particular way. For instance, H_2O is the formula for water. The small number 2, a subscript, tells us there are two atoms of hydrogen (H). Since there is no subscript after oxygen, we know the molecule contains only one atom of oxygen (O). The formula for sodium chloride, NaCl, indicates that there is one atom of sodium (Na) and one atom of chlorine (Cl) in each molecule of salt.

If you see the formula H_2O, you can assume that it refers to a single molecule of water. In some chemical equations, there may be a number in front of a formula. If the formula were written $4H_2O$, the formula indicates there are four molecules of water.

One molecule of water (H_2O) has two atoms of hydrogen and one atom of oxygen. Four molecules of water ($4H_2O$) have eight atoms of hydrogen (4 x 2 = 8) and four atoms of oxygen (4 x 1 = 4).

With a molecule such as water, the formula and structure of the molecule is fairly simple. For more complex molecules, a diagram of the structure is helpful to indicate not only what kinds of atoms are present but also how they are connected. For example, propane is a fuel used for heating and in torches. The formula for propane, C_3H_8, shows that a propane molecule has three atoms of carbon and eight atoms of hydrogen. The formula, however, gives no information about how the atoms are arranged. The molecule's structure is shown below.

A MOLECULE OF PROPANE

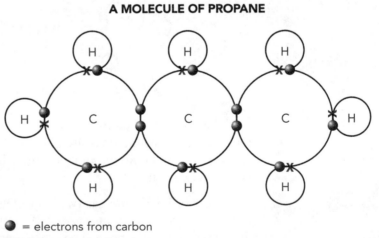

● = electrons from carbon

X = electrons from hydrogen

Thinking About Science

Directions: Circle *T* for each true statement or *F* for each false statement.

T F **1.** Atoms with all 32 electrons in their outer shell are the most stable and rarely combine with other elements.

T F **2.** The positive electric charge of the proton is responsible for the attraction of the negatively charged electron.

T F **3.** The physical and chemical properties of a new compound are almost always very similar to the properties of the elements that formed the compound.

T F **4.** In covalent bonding, electrons are shared.

T F **5.** All molecules consist of two or more different elements.

T F **6.** A formula gives information about what elements are in a compound and how those elements are arranged.

Answers are on page 313.

PRE-GED PRACTICE

Directions: Choose the <u>one best answer</u> to each question.

Question 1 refers to the information on pages 186–188.

1. One molecule of sand contains one atom of silicon (Si) and two atoms of oxygen (O). Which of the following is the correct formula for three molecules of sand?

(1) Si_3O_2
(2) $3SiO_2$
(3) $Si3O_2$
(4) $2Si_3O$
(5) SiO_23

Question 2 refers to the following diagram.

CARBON TETRACHLORIDE

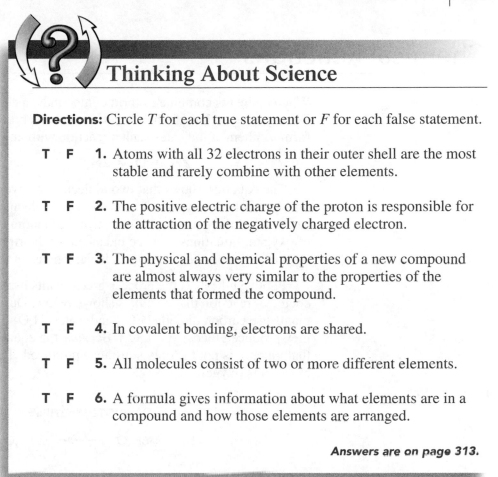

● = electrons from carbon
X = electrons from chlorine

2. The diagram represents the structure of carbon tetrachloride, an industrial cleaner. What is the formula for one molecule of carbon tetrachloride?

(1) C_4Cl
(2) $1C_4Cl$
(3) $4CCl$
(4) CCl_4
(5) C_4Cl_4

Answers are on page 313.

Chemical Reactions

When elements combine to form compounds, a chemical reaction takes place. During the reaction, the bonds between atoms break down and new bonds form. A chemist indicates such a reaction with an **equation**:

$$2H_2 + O_2 = 2H_2O$$

The equation shows that two molecules of hydrogen ($2H_2$) combine with one molecule of oxygen (O_2) to yield two molecules of water. Notice that each side of the equation has four hydrogen atoms. There are also two atoms of oxygen. Equations must be balanced, so the right side of the equation has the same number of atoms of each element as on the left side.

Photosynthesis is the process green plants use to manufacture food. The chemical reaction that occurs is shown below. During the chemical reaction, plants use carbon dioxide (CO_2) and water (H_2O). In the presence of sunlight, they produce glucose ($C_6H_{12}O_6$). Because the equation must balance, we know that glucose is not the only substance produced. The by-product of the reaction is oxygen (O_2).

PHOTOSYNTHESIS

$$6CO_2 + 6H_2O \xrightarrow{\text{light}} C_6H_{12}O_6 + 6O_2$$

carbon dioxide · water · glucose · oxygen

The 6 in front of CO_2 indicates that the process requires six molecules of carbon dioxide. The 6 in front of H_2O shows that six molecules of water are needed during the process.

The Law of Conservation of Matter

You will notice that the same elements are present on both sides of an equation. If there are six atoms of carbon, eighteen atoms of oxygen, and twelve atoms of hydrogen on one side of the equation, there are six carbon, eighteen oxygen, and twelve hydrogen atoms on the other side.

A chemical equation always has the identical number of atoms of each element on each side of the equation. Chemists call this the **law of conservation of matter**. The law states that matter is neither created nor destroyed during chemical reactions. This idea is fundamental to chemistry.

Look at how nitrogen (N) combines with hydrogen (H). The result is ammonia (NH_3). The molecules in this chemical reaction are:

$$N_2 + 3H_2 = 2NH_3$$

Two atoms of nitrogen (N_2) plus six atoms of hydrogen ($3 \times H_2$) yield two molecules of ammonia. If you count the total number of atoms on each side, you will find that they are equal. This is an example of the law of conservation of matter.

Thinking About Science

Directions: Match words on the left with the descriptions on the right. Write the correct letter on the line.

_____ **1.** compound

(a) a bond formed when electrons are exchanged

_____ **2.** ionic bond

(b) two or more elements that are combined chemically to form a single substance

_____ **3.** covalent bond

(c) a bond formed when electrons are shared

_____ **4.** formula

(d) two or more atoms joined through shared electrons

_____ **5.** molecule

(e) a symbolic representation of what types of atoms are in a molecule

_____ **6.** equation

(f) a symbolic representation of a chemical reaction

_____ **7.** chemical reaction

(g) bonds between atoms are broken down and new bonds are formed

Answers are on page 313.

Directions: Choose the <u>one best answer</u> to each question.

Questions 1–4 refer to the information on page 190.

1. Which of the following describes an element with eight electrons in its outer shell?

(1) sodium chloride
(2) inert
(3) a molecule
(4) unstable
(5) a formula

2. Which of the following is true for two atoms that form a covalent bond?

(1) The atoms share electrons.
(2) The atoms give off electrons.
(3) The atoms have opposite charges.
(4) The atoms have more than eight electrons in their outer shells.
(5) The atoms are stable.

3. Carbon dioxide consists of one atom of carbon (C) and two atoms of oxygen (O). What is the formula for a molecule of carbon dioxide is

(1) C_2O
(2) $2CO$
(3) CO
(4) CO_2
(5) $2(CO)$

4. What does the law of conservation of matter state?

(1) Matter is never changed chemically.
(2) An unbalanced equation is an example of chemical change.
(3) Matter can be changed only when an acid is present.
(4) Matter is neither created nor destroyed during chemical reactions.
(5) Only inert matter can be changed.

Answers are on page 313.

Solutions

When salt is placed in water, it seems to disappear. The law of conservation of matter, however, tells us this is not possible. Tasting the water will convince you that the law is correct. The salt is still there. It has merely been broken up, or dissolved, by the water. The resulting salty water is called a **solution**. Sand in water would not be considered a solution because the sand does not dissolve. After a short time, the sand simply settles to the bottom.

Solutions have practical applications. Soaps and detergents, for example, rely on solutions. Water alone cannot dissolve grease or dirt, but soap molecules dissolve in both water and grease. Soap can link together the water and grease molecules. When the grease molecules are linked to water, they can be washed away.

In a solution, the **solute** is the substance that dissolves. The **solvent** is the substance (usually a liquid) in which the solute is dissolved. For example, in a cup of tea, sugar added to it is the solute and the tea itself is the solvent. Gases, liquids, or solids can all be solutes or solvents.

When substances held together by ionic bonds are dissolved, they are broken down into ions. An ion is an atom with either a positive or a negative charge. When salt ($NaCl$) dissolves, it forms positive ions ($Na+$) and negative ions ($Cl-$). The electron does not return to its original atom. The $NaCl$ solution conducts an electric current. A substance that conducts an electric current when dissolved in water (such as salt) is called an **electrolyte**.

Electrolytes can be divided into three types of substances:

- **acids**—An acid in a water solution has a sour taste similar to lemon juice or vinegar. HCl (hydrochloric acid) is a superstrong acid that is often used to clean metal.

- **bases**—A base has a soapy or slippery feel to it. Detergents and lye are bases.

- **salts**—Sodium chloride is a salt. An acid and a base will react to form a salt and water.

Nonliquid Solutions

People commonly think of solutions only as solids dissolved in liquids. Solutions involving other states of matter also exist. For instance, soda pop is a gas dissolved in a liquid. To produce carbonated beverages, carbon dioxide is pumped under pressure into flavored water.

Metal **alloys** are solid solutions that are made by melting different metals together. The result is a new metal. The alloy brass is a solution of copper and zinc. Copper is best known for its ability to conduct electricity. It is also easy to shape. Adding zinc makes the resulting brass stronger and tougher. The metal alloy used to fill cavities is a solution of silver and mercury. Silver does not corrode or decay but is difficult to work with. Mercury is added to make shaping the metal easier.

The air we breathe is a nonliquid solution of oxygen and other gases dissolved in nitrogen.

Thinking About Science

Directions: Fill in the blanks with the apropriate word(s).

1. A solution is _____

   _____.

2. An ion is _____.

3. A base and an acid combine to form a _____.

4. Solid solutions made by melting different metals together are called

   _____.

5. In a solution, the solute is

   _____.

6. In a solution, the solvent is

   _____.

Answers are on page 313.

PRE-GED PRACTICE

Directions: Choose the one best answer to each question.

Questions 1 and 2 refer to the information on page 193.

1. What is the result when one substance is dissolved in another?

   (1) base
   (2) acid
   (3) solution
   (4) salt
   (5) electrolyte

2. According to the passage, when substances with ionic bonds are dissolved in water, the solution can conduct an electric current. Which of the following terms is used to identify these substances?

   (1) molecules
   (2) electrolytes
   (3) neutralizers
   (4) isotopes
   (5) plasmas

Answers are on page 313.

The Chemistry of Life

Carbon is so important to our world that the study of carbon and its compounds is called **organic chemistry**. This branch of chemistry is sometimes called the chemistry of life because all known life forms contain carbon.

Carbon atoms can easily bond covalently with other carbon atoms. These carbon molecules can then bond with more carbon atoms, forming long chains of carbon molecules. Carbon also forms strong bonds with other vital elements, such as hydrogen, oxygen, and nitrogen.

Plants and animals are made of large amounts of carbon. When these organisms die, they decompose. One of two things can happen to the remaining carbon atoms:

1. Some carbon atoms may combine with oxygen in the atmosphere to form carbon dioxide (a key compound in photosynthesis).

2. Other carbon atoms may become trapped under the earth, cut off from oxygen. Over a period of centuries, large deposits of carbon may be transformed into fossil fuels, such as petroleum, natural gas, and coal.

The carbon cycle is as important to life on Earth as the nitrogen cycle and the water cycle. The carbon cycle starts with the circulation of the carbon contained in carbon dioxide (found in the atmosphere), which is then used by plants (by being trapped in carbohydrates through photosynthesis). Animals eat the plants and release carbon dioxide back into the atmosphere through respiration and, when the animals die, their remains decompose, forming carbon-based organic compounds.

Hydrocarbons

Petroleum and coal products that are removed from the earth can be burned or distilled to meet human fuel needs. Coal is heated in the absence of air, leaving coke, which is used to separate metals from ores. Coal tar, which is also produced in this heating process, is an important base for many organic compounds used by industry.

When petroleum is purified through distillation, **hydrocarbons** (compounds of hydrogen and carbon) separate to form different types of fuel. Methane (CH_4) and butane (C_4H_{10}) are important in the production of plastics. Kerosene ($C_{12}H_{26}$) is used in diesel fuel and home heating fuel. The distillation of petroleum also produces the hydrocarbon compounds that make up perfumes, pesticides, preservatives, medicines, and many other items.

When the hydrocarbons in gasoline are burned, such as in the engine of an automobile, they do not just disappear. Instead, they combine with oxygen in the air to form carbon dioxide and water. When there is not enough oxygen available to combine with the carbon, carbon monoxide—a poisonous gas—is formed. Carbon monoxide air pollution occurs most often where traffic is heavy.

Air pollution is not the only hydrocarbon by-product. A majority of the trash that pollutes our land is made of plastics. Scientists have created compounds that can hold up under extreme heat, pressure, and moisture. Examples include plastic bags, cellophane wrapping, six-pack holders, automobile tires, foam rubber, and countless other products. These products are so durable that when we no longer want to use them, they are very difficult to dispose of. We can throw them away, but solid waste dumps are unsanitary and use up valuable land. We can burn them, but burning plastic creates thick black smoke that is another dangerous form of air pollution.

It seems that the law of conservation of matter has a price. We cannot destroy matter. As we consume our natural resources, such as petroleum and coal, we create useful products, but we also create unwanted by-products that do not just disappear.

Thinking About Science

Directions: Answer the questions below in the space provided.

1. Why is carbon considered to be an important element?

   _____

   _____

2. What happens to the hydrocarbons as gasoline is burned?

   _____

   _____

3. Fill in the blanks to complete the carbon cycle.

   Carbon dioxide in the atmosphere is used by

   a. _____ in the food-making process called

   b. _____. Animals eat the plants and release

   c. _____ back into the atmosphere through

   d. _____. When animals die, they decompose

   and release **e.** _____ compounds that

   continue the carbon cycle.

Answers are on page 313.

Directions: Choose the <u>one best answer</u> to each question.

Questions 1–3 refer to the information on pages 195 and 196.

1. Which of the following is a true statement about organic chemistry?

   (1) Organic chemistry is relatively insignificant when compared to other fields of chemistry.
   (2) Organic chemistry is the study of carbon and its compounds.
   (3) The field of organic chemistry got its name because it is the study of human cells.
   (4) The study of organic chemistry is concerned mainly with pollution.
   (5) Organic chemistry is the only really important branch of chemistry.

2. What can you infer from the information on pages 195 and 196?

   (1) organic chemists can play a key role in solving our pollution problems
   (2) the by-products of our chemical advances and discoveries are always beneficial to humans
   (3) plastic refuse will not be a problem in the future because the carbon atoms will decompose into the ground and create new petroleum
   (4) pollution is caused—in part—by our inability to get rid of hydrocarbons
   (5) chemists are totally responsible for our pollution problems

3. Which of the following is a true statement about coal?

   (1) Coal must undergo complicated processing before it can be used to heat homes.
   (2) Coal can be used in place of natural gas to avoid many of the dangers of pollution.
   (3) Coal is formed over a period of thousands of years when carbon is cut off from oxygen under the earth.
   (4) Coal is necessary in the production of plastics.
   (5) Coal can be compressed into oil.

Answers are on page 313.

Chemistry Review

Directions: Choose the one best answer to each question.

Question 1 refers to the following passage.

Many people today are suggesting an odd reason for saving undisturbed tracts of land, such as jungles and forests. They say these areas may hold plants that could be used as medicines. Although this argument may seem ridiculous, it actually shows a good understanding of how new drugs are developed. For instance, an anticancer drug was developed from a tree that grows in the Pacific Northwest.

The most common drug in the world is an example of how some new medicines are developed. For centuries, high fevers were a serious problem. Native Americans, however, used the bark from a type of willow tree as a treatment for fever. When chemists learned that there was an effective native treatment for fever, they began to investigate it. Eventually, they discovered that the chemical that lowered the fever (and reduced pain) was salicylic acid.

Unfortunately, the drug had unpleasant side effects, including a severe irritation of the stomach lining. With further research, chemists were able to reduce this irritation. They added another ingredient. The resulting drug, called acetylsalicylic acid, is what we know today as aspirin.

1. Which of the following statements is true about aspirin?

   (1) It can be dug up from the soil.
   (2) It was accidentally invented by a chemist in his laboratory.
   (3) It is a chemical found in nature and modified by chemists.
   (4) It is called salicylic acid by scientists.
   (5) It can be obtained from any willow tree.

Questions 2 and 3 refer to the following passage.

Ellagic acid is a compound that is found naturally in a variety of sources, including coffee, nuts, and grapes. The acid neutralizes benzopyrene, a cancer-causing environmental pollutant. So far, the neutralizing process has worked only in laboratory tests. Scientists hope, however, that further research may lead to a new kind of anticancer drug.

Benzopyrene forms when fossil fuels burn. It is common in automotive exhaust and industrial smoke. When the chemical enters the human body, enzymes in the body can convert benzopyrene into a potent carcinogen (a cancer-causing agent).

Chemists have found that when ellagic acid is added to a solution of benzopyrene, the two compounds first form an inactive complex. Eventually, the ellagic acid causes the carcinogen to split into noncancer-causing, nonmutagenic components. Scientists are now conducting experiments to find out if ellagic acid can protect animals from getting tumors after they are exposed to benzopyrene.

2. How does ellagic acid neutralize the pollutant called benzopyrene?

   (1) by destroying it
   (2) by combining with it to form noncarcinogens
   (3) by converting automotive exhaust into oxygen
   (4) by emitting the pollutant into the atmosphere
   (5) by converting it to a carcinogen

3. Which of the following is most likely to be a source of ellagic acid?

   (1) almonds
   (2) milk
   (3) fish
   (4) pizza
   (5) bread

Question 4 refers to the following passage.

When your teachers went to school, they probably learned that atoms were made of electrons, protons, and neutrons only. The atom was a tidy package. But then scientists began looking for even smaller particles. So far, they have found a great number.

In 1932, C.D. Anderson found a particle that had the mass of an electron, but also had a positive charge. The particle was promptly called a *positron*. If a positron and electron meet, both particles are destroyed. All their mass is converted to energy. Scientists quickly started looking for more of these antiparticles that were identical to atomic particles but that had an opposite electrical charge. Twenty years later, the antiproton and antineutron were discovered.

By the 1960s, the field of particle physics had exploded. New terms like *muon* and *neutrino*, *photon* and *graviton; baryon, meson,* and *lepton* were introduced. Soon, scientists had found almost as many elementary particles as elements. Obviously, not all these particles were really fundamental to the atom's nucleus.

During a lull in the discovery of new particles, scientists began trying to figure out what all the particles meant. They now believe that protons and neutrons consist of particles called *quarks*. Many scientists think that quarks are the basic building blocks of the nucleus.

4. What does this passage imply about antimatter?

   (1) Antimatter and matter have identical electrical charges.
   (2) Antimatter would totally destroy any matter it encounters.
   (3) Antimatter was thought up by science fiction writers.
   (4) Antimatter does not exist.
   (5) Antimatter exists only on some other planet.

Questions 5 and 6 refer to the following passage.

Water is sometimes called the universal solvent, but it does have some drawbacks. During washing, soap molecules combine water molecules with the grease and dirt in your clothes. To absorb the soap and water, the fibers of the fabric swell. As the fabric dries, some of the fibers shrink down to their original shape and size. Others do not. The result is shrinkage and wrinkling.

Dry cleaners do not use water, but there's nothing dry about the process. It simply uses a different solvent to combat the shrinkage and wrinkling problems. The solvent is tetrachloroethylene (C_2Cl_4). It is a very powerful dissolver of grease and other staining substances. It also has an important advantage over soap and water. C_2Cl_4 evaporates faster than water. The carbon and chloride atoms combine quickly with warm air, leaving the fabric dry in a matter of minutes. The shrinkage and wrinkling that accompany water solvents simply do not occur with dry cleaning.

5. According to this passage, which of the following is the advantage of dry cleaning over washing with water?

   (1) Soap does not build up in the fabric.
   (2) Clothes are much less likely to shrink or wrinkle.
   (3) Tetrachloroethylene is not effective on tough stains.
   (4) Dry cleaning is less expensive because water is not needed.
   (5) The clothing does not need to be pressed.

6. What is one advantage that tetrachloroethylene (C_2Cl_4) has over soap and water?

   (1) It evaporates more quickly than water.
   (2) It causes fibers to swell up, unlike water.
   (3) It is inexpensive compared to detergent.
   (4) It causes the fabric to shrink, unlike water.
   (5) It contains a fabric softener.

Questions 7 and 8 refer to the following passage.

Scientists have long realized that much of our fuel comes from organisms that died and decomposed millions of years ago. To some people, that fact is not just an interesting bit of trivia. It is an alarm. If the supplies were used up, people would not have the luxury of waiting for a million years until more fuel formed in the natural way.

Now scientists have developed a method to use today's plants for today's fuel. The first methods were based on the same process that makes the alcohol for vodka. Although pure alcohol can be used as fuel in specially modified engines, it does not provide as much energy as an equivalent weight of gasoline. Unlike gasoline, which consists entirely of carbon and hydrogen atoms, alcohol also contains oxygen, which lowers its energy level.

Scientists have devised an effective way to take the oxygen out of ethanol and use the remaining atoms to make gasoline. The process involves heating ethanol and water and passing the resulting vapor through a hot bed of mineral called *zeolite*. In a complex chemical reaction started by the zeolite, oxygen in the ethanol combines with hydrogen to form water. The carbon and any remaining hydrogen join to form a hydrocarbon, gasoline. The gas and water then collect in a tank and are separated. Interestingly, a mixture of water and ethanol is exactly what is produced in the process of fermenting grain. Scientists say that someday farmers could make their own gasoline by hooking up an ethanol-to-gas converter to a modern version of the moonshiner's still.

7. According to the passage, how can gasoline be made from alcohol?

   (1) by burning a mixture of alcohol and water
   (2) by using vodka for experimentation and not for drinking
   (3) by using alcohol in farm machinery and other modified engines
   (4) by taking oxygen out of ethanol, leaving behind the necessary hydrogen and carbon
   (5) by waiting for dead organisms to decompose

8. Why is pure alcohol unsuitable as a fuel?

   (1) It is much too expensive.
   (2) It contains too many carbons and not enough hydrogen.
   (3) The zeolite it contains damages the metals in an engine.
   (4) Alcohol contains oxygen, which lowers its energy level.
   (5) It would explode.

Answers are on pages 313–314.

READING EFFICIENCY E

Directions: This activity will help you to improve your reading efficiency. Before you start to read, write the present time at the top of the page. When you have completed the reading and all 5 questions, write your finishing time. Subtract to find out how long you took. Score your answers. Then turn to pages 320–321 to find your E-Factor and to graph your progress.

Finishing Time	
Starting Time −	
Reading Time =	
Number of Answers Correct	

Electrons

The idea of atoms has been around for more than 2,400 years. The Greek philosopher Democritus said that all events in nature could be explained in terms of atoms. These atoms, he said, were small, hard particles. They could be formed into different shapes and sizes.

The ideas of Democritus and other Greeks helped lay the basis for today's ideas about atoms. But it wasn't until much later that experiments showed the structure of atoms. In 1803 John Dalton wrote his atomic theory. It said that all matter is made from atoms. These atoms are small particles that can't be created, divided, or destroyed. In 1897 J. J. Thompson did an experiment and found out that atoms contain small particles. These particles have a negative charge. He called these particles corpuscles. Today we know these particles as electrons.

Scientists have found important uses for electrons. One is the electron microscope. It uses streams of electrons to magnify images. Electron microscopes can magnify images more than 300,000 times. Compound microscopes magnify images much less. The transmission electron microscope (TEM) shoots a beam of electrons through an object. The object must be a thin slice. The electrons hit a sheet of photographic film behind the object. This produces an image.

Objects viewed with a scanning electron microscope (SEM) are coated with a metal. Electrons do not travel through the object. Instead, when electrons hit the surface of the object, they bounce off. A computer changes these reflected electrons into an image.

HELIUM ATOM

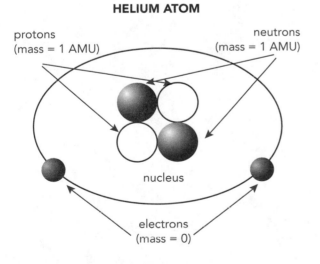

protons
(mass = 1 AMU)

neutrons
(mass = 1 AMU)

nucleus

electrons
(mass = 0)

1. According to the diagram, which of the following statements is true?

   (1) Most of an atom's mass is in the nucleus.
   (2) The charge of a neutron is equal to the charge of an electron.
   (3) An atom has a negative charge.
   (4) The number of neutrons in an atom is equal to the number of electrons.
   (5) The mass of a proton is equal to the mass of an electron.

2. Which of the following atoms would have the most mass?

   (1) an atom with three protons and one neutron
   (2) an atom with two protons and two neutrons
   (3) an atom with one proton and three neutrons
   (4) an atom with one proton and one neutron
   (5) an atom with two protons and three neutrons

3. Which part of Dalton's theory did Thompson's experiment show to be untrue?

   (1) Atoms are very small particles.
   (2) Atoms cannot be created.
   (3) Atoms cannot be divided.
   (4) Atoms cannot be destroyed.
   (5) All substances are made from atoms.

4. Suppose you wanted to see the arrangement of atoms on the surface of a crystal. Which of the following instruments would you use?

   (1) compound microscope
   (2) SEM
   (3) TEM
   (4) hand lens
   (5) all of the above

5. What information in the passage would help explain why a SEM image shows only surface features of an object?

   (1) Electron microscopes use streams of electrons to magnify images.
   (2) Electron microscopes can magnify images more than 300,000 times.
   (3) Electrons have a negative charge.
   (4) In a SEM electrons bounce off the surface of the object being viewed.
   (5) In a SEM a computer uses reflected electrons to make an image.

Answers are on page 314.

READING EFFICIENCY F

Directions: This activity will help you to improve your reading efficiency. Before you start to read, write the present time at the top of the page. When you have completed the reading and all 5 questions, write your finishing time. Subtract to find out how long you took. Score your answers. Then turn to pages 320–321 to find your E-Factor and to graph your progress.

Finishing Time	
Starting Time −	
Reading Time =	
Number of Answers Correct	

Carbon

Carbon is one of the most important elements. All things that are living or have lived contain carbon. It is used to make many products we use every day. Carbon is the main part of fuels, such as coal, petroleum, and natural gas. Most plastics contain carbon. Yet only 0.032 percent of Earth's crust is carbon.

Pure carbon can be found naturally in three forms: diamond, graphite, and fullerines. Each carbon atom in a diamond is tightly bonded to four other carbon atoms. They form a pyramid-shaped pattern. Diamond is the hardest substance found in nature. Diamonds are used in industry to cut and grind hard materials.

Graphite is much less dense than diamond. In graphite the carbon atoms are attached to three other carbon atoms. They form flat layers that are bound loosely. They easily slip over each other. This property makes graphite soft and slippery. One use of graphite is as a lubricant.

The third form of carbon, fullerine, was first made in the laboratory in 1985. The best known fullerine is the buckeyball. It is a molecule that looks like a hollow ball. The molecule has 60 carbon atoms bonded together in the shape of a soccer ball. This form of carbon only occurs naturally in very small amounts. The buckeyball can be used to block a key step in the reproduction of the virus that causes AIDS.

Carbon atoms can combine with as many as four other atoms—not just carbon—to form hundreds of thousands of different compounds. One important compound is carbon dioxide. Plants use carbon dioxide during photosynthesis. Carbon dioxide forms when fuels containing carbon burn. The carbon in the fuel combines with the oxygen in the air to produce the carbon dioxide. Too much carbon dioxide in the air traps heat. This causes the temperature of Earth's atmosphere to rise. This is called the greenhouse effect.

1. Which of the following is <u>not</u> a pure form of carbon?

   (1) graphite
   (2) diamond
   (3) fullerine
   (4) buckeyball
   (5) carbon dioxide

2. Which property of carbon makes it able to form so many different compounds?

   (1) A carbon atom can combine with as many as four other atoms.
   (2) Pure carbon is found in three different forms in nature.
   (3) Carbon combines with oxygen to form carbon dioxide.
   (4) All living things contain carbon.
   (5) Carbon is found in fuels and plastics.

3. Which statement about carbon is <u>not</u> supported by the information in the passage?

   (1) Graphite is found in nature.
   (2) Carbon atoms combine with other kinds of atoms.
   (3) Fullerines did not exist before 1985.
   (4) A diamond can be used to scratch graphite.
   (5) The atoms in diamond are held together more tightly than the atoms in graphite.

4. Which property of carbon makes it a good material for writing?

   (1) Diamonds are the hardest substance found in nature.
   (2) The layers of graphite are loosely bound and slide over each other.
   (3) Carbon atoms can combine with as many as four other atoms to form many compounds.
   (4) A buckeyball molecule is a hollow ball.
   (5) Carbon atoms combine with oxygen to form carbon dioxide.

5. A proposal to reduce the use of fossil fuels has been offered by a group of citizens. Which of the following reasons is <u>not</u> based on scientific information?

   (1) Carbon dioxide traps heat in the air.
   (2) The greenhouse effect causes the temperature of the atmosphere to rise.
   (3) Fossil fuels should be saved for the future.
   (4) When fossil fuels burn, carbon dioxide is produced.
   (5) All fossil fuels contain carbon.

   Answers are on page 314.

CHAPTER 7

Physics

Physics is the study of matter, energy, force, space, and time. This science studies how our world is put together and how it changes. Like all areas of science, physics overlaps the others—geology, astronomy, chemistry, even biology. For example, a physicist who is interested in how objects move might want to know how molecules move through the cell wall, how moons escape their orbits, how earthquakes travel through the crust, or how electrons are transferred during a chemical reaction.

The physics portion of the GED Science Test covers mechanics, optics and waves, and electricity and magnetism. Test questions center around the practical application of physics concepts.

- The science of mechanics examines motion and the application of forces to material objects. The principles of mechanics guide the construction of everything from a simple lever to a high-rise building, a highway, and a spacecraft.

- The study of light and sound are related because both travel as waves. Scientists now know that there are many different types of waves. Ultrasound, for example, is a type of sound wave that cannot be heard by humans. These waves can be bounced off the surface of an object and used to detect the object's shape. Ultrasound is frequently used by doctors to detect tumors in patients or to monitor the growth of the fetus in a pregnant woman. The specialized field of **optics** examines just the behavior of light. This science has led to many improvements in microscopes, telescopes, and cameras.

- Scientists and engineers have built generators for electricity. Electronics has taken us from the study of electrons to the development of silicon chips for personal computers.

Laws of Motion

Sir Isaac Newton (1642–1727) greatly influenced modern physics. He identified three laws that govern the motion of objects. He also suggested that these laws of motion would work best in a vacuum.

Newton pointed out that moving objects collide with millions of tiny air molecules. These molecules drag on the object and slow it down. The laws of motion apply to everyday life, but in a vacuum, objects are not influenced by friction and gravity.

Newton's First Law

The first law of motion states that a body at rest remains at rest and that a body in motion continues to move in a straight line unless some outside force affects it. This property is called **inertia**. Without a force, objects don't move. Without a force, a moving object will not stop.

Understanding the first part of this law is easy. We don't expect things to move unless something moves it. The second part of the law does not seem as reasonable. In our experience, objects do stop moving by themselves. In everyday life, however, the force of friction causes the object to stop. If it were not for inertia, we would not need air bags and seat belts in cars.

Newton's Second Law

The second law of motion states that a change in the motion of an object depends on the mass of that object and the amount of force applied to it. You can separate this law into two parts:

1. An object's speed will increase in proportion to the amount of force applied to it. The stronger the force, the faster the object's speed will increase, or accelerate.

2. This acceleration will also be affected by the mass of the object. The larger the mass, the slower the object will accelerate. The smaller the mass, the faster the acceleration.

To understand the relationship between mass and force, imagine a person struggling to push a piano. Then imagine the person using the same force to push a small book. The piano would barely move, while the book would be moved easily. It is Newton's second law that leads automobile designers to balance the power of the engine with the size of the car.

Many scientists think of Newton's second law in terms of a change in momentum rather than of mass and acceleration. Momentum is related to both speed and mass. A speeding bullet is small, but it has great momentum. A truck—even one that moves slowly—also has great momentum. To change an object's momentum, a force must be applied.

Newton's Third Law

Newton's third law of motion states that for every action, there is an equal and opposite reaction. The recoil, or kick, of a rifle illustrates this law. Gunpowder explodes in a rifle, forcing the bullet through the barrel. At the same time, the explosion pushes the rifle backward against the shooter's shoulder. In the same way, a rocket is pushed up into the air when gas from the engine rushes out of the back. This equal and opposite reaction works equally well in space—even with nothing to push against.

 **Thinking About Science**

Directions: Respond to each statement below in the space provided.

1. Describe how friction affects a moving object.

   _____

   _____

2. Use Newton's first law to explain why people should use seat belts.

   _____

   _____

3. Use Newton's second law to explain why car engineers put more powerful engines in larger cars.

   _____

   _____

4. Use Newton's third law to describe how a rocket thrusts a spacecraft into outer space.

   _____

   _____

Answers are on page 314.

Directions: Choose the <u>one best answer</u> to each question.

Questions 1–5 refer to the information on pages 205–207.

1. Scientists interested in finding out if a new plastic could serve as a replacement for glass in eyeglasses would be most interested in which area of physics?

   (1) optics
   (2) mechanics
   (3) matter and heat
   (4) electronics
   (5) computers

2. Which of the following areas of physics would be most interesting to an engineer designing the body of an airplane?

   (1) mechanics
   (2) ultrasound
   (3) matter and heat
   (4) computers
   (5) optics

3. Which of the following is used as a precaution against inertia?

   (1) child-safety locks
   (2) car headlights
   (3) windshield wipers
   (4) automobile seatbelts
   (5) window defrost

4. Which of the following examples is false?

   (1) A loaded truck has more momentum than an unloaded truck traveling at the same speed.
   (2) A fast-pitched softball has more momentum than a slow-pitched softball.
   (3) A truck has more momentum than a car traveling at the same speed.
   (4) A hard-hit Ping-Pong ball has more momentum than a hard-hit golf ball.
   (5) A quarter tossed in the air has more momentum than a dime tossed in the air.

5. Which of the following statements is true?

   A. The amount of momentum that a refrigerator has depends on its mass.
   B. Momentum is needed to stop a bus.
   C. As you grow, your body gains momentum.

   (1) A and B only
   (2) A and C only
   (3) B and C only
   (4) A only
   (5) B only

Answers are on page 314.

Forces and Machines

Gravity is one of the most basic forces of nature. Gravity is the force of attraction that every object exerts on other objects. The more matter there is in an object, the stronger the force it exerts. Earth's gravity is the force that keeps our feet firmly planted on the ground.

A **force** is defined as anything that can affect the motion of an object. All objects that are not in motion have at least two forces working on them. The first is the downward force of gravity. The second is the upward force of the supporting object. The book you are reading, for example, does not float off into space because of the force of gravity. It does not crash to the floor because of the force supporting it. Airplanes fly because the downward force of gravity is balanced by the upward force of the air pushing against the wings of the plane.

Objects also may have additional forces applied to them. These are push-and-pull forces. If the forces are equal, the object will not move. We say the object is in **equilibrium.** If the forces are not equal, the object will react to the stronger force. A mother with twins understands the idea of equilibrium and force. When two children of about the same mass pull on the same toy, nothing happens. The forces are in equilibrium. If one child lets go, however, the toy will move quickly toward the stronger force.

Force and Work

Most of us think we know what work is. Scientists, however, have a special definition of **work**. Work occurs when a force moves an object in a certain direction.

Work = force x distance

The key is that both force and distance must be present for work to occur. By this definition, the mover that struggles to budge the refrigerator has not done any work at all. Work occurs only when the refrigerator actually moves.

Friction

Friction occurs when two objects rub against each other. This rubbing can slow motion and interfere with work. It also produces heat. Engineers are constantly working to reduce the effects of friction. In some cases, such as a train wheel against a track, the idea is to reduce the amount of rubbing that occurs. In other cases, such as in a car engine, a lubricant (such as oil) is used to lower the heat produced by friction.

Thinking About Science

Directions: Write a definition of each word below in the space provided.

1. gravity_____

_____

2. force_____

_____

3. friction_____

_____

4. equilibrium_____

_____

5. work_____

_____

Answers are on page 314.

Machines

Machines are designed to increase our force to make work easier. Some machines are able to change a small movement into a larger one or change a small force into a larger one. Other machines are able to change the direction or position of a force and put it to bear where the force is needed most.

Machines can be classified as simple or compound. **Simple machines** perform a single function. Examples include levers, pulleys, wheels and axles, and inclined planes. **Compound machines** are made of two or more simple machines. An example is a handheld can opener, which consists of a wedge, a lever, and a wheel and axle.

Levers

One of the simplest machines is the lever. A **lever** is a rod or bar that turns around a point called the **fulcrum**, or pivot, to move a load. There are three kinds of levers, with different arrangements of load, effort, and fulcrum. Some levers increase force, others increase distance. Pliers and nutcrackers increase force. A pair of tongs increases distance.

To build a lever, you need only a long, rigid bar, such as a crowbar or a stick, and a small support, such as a small rock. Pushing or pulling the long arm down is work. The person uses both force and distance. The following diagram shows what happens at the short end of the lever. Notice that the distance is greatly reduced. The work, however, is the same. The result is increased force. A crowbar, shovel, flyswatter, baseball bat, fishing pole, and the oars on a rowboat are all levers.

LEVER

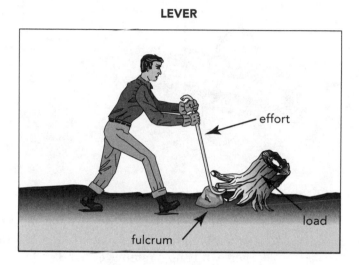

Pulleys

A **pulley** changes the direction of a force. By using a pulley, a person can lift an object by pulling down on it. One end of the rope is attached to the load, and force is applied at the other end to lift the load. Pulleys are used to lift flags on flagpoles and to lift some kinds of windows. Combinations of pulleys can also increase the amount of force.

PULLEY

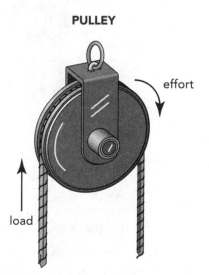

Wheel and Axle

A **wheel and axle** is a simple machine that combines a wheel with the idea of a lever. Screwdrivers and the steering wheel of a car are wheel-and-axle machines. For the screwdriver shown below, the larger the handle (the wheel), the greater the increase in the force of the blade (the axle).

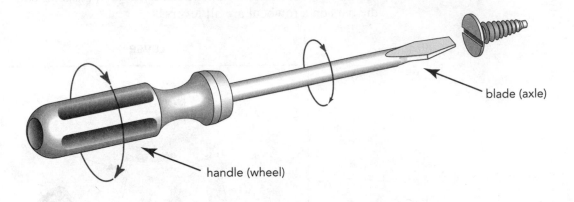

blade (axle)

handle (wheel)

Inclined Plane

An **inclined plane** is simply a flat surface that has one end higher than the other. Inclined planes magnify force. A ramp is an inclined plane. Pushing a heavy box up a ramp is easier than lifting it. Walking up a long gentle slope is easier than climbing up a steep slope. A wedge is also a type of inclined plane.

INCLINED PLANE

Compound Machines

Everyday tools, such as a pair of scissors, a shovel, a bicycle, and an automobile, consist of many different simple machines put together. The pair of scissors, for example, is two levers and two inclined planes. An ax is an inclined plane (the blade) and a lever (the handle).

An eggbeater is a compound machine composed of gears and wheels and axles. The handle turns a wheel which itself turns a smaller wheel. Eggbeaters magnify force.

Gears

Bicycles and automobiles consist of many different types of machines. In these machines, the wheel and axle combination is turned by various sets of gears. **Gears** can change the direction of a force and can either increase the force or change its speed. Automobiles use gears to change the direction of a force (forward or reverse), to move forward slowly with much force (first and second gear), or to move rapidly with little force (third or fourth gear).

GEARS

Engines

Engines are made of many different types of machines, but they add one critical element not seen in a simple machine. That is a source of energy other than human muscle. Some of the earliest engines were windmills and waterwheels. Steam engines followed. James Watt, a Scottish inventor, was the first to popularize the steam engine. In an effort to sell his new, improved steam engine, he compared its power to the power of a horse. We still describe engines by using the term *horsepower*.

Thinking About Science

Directions: Identify the simple machines shown below.

1. _____

2. _____

3. _____   4. _____

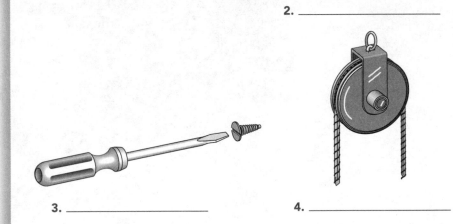

5. _____

Answers are on page 315.

Directions: Choose the <u>one best answer</u> to each question.

Questions 1–7 refer to the information on pages 209–213.

1. Which simple machine can be made with a rigid bar and a small support?

    (1) lever
    (2) axle
    (3) pulley
    (4) compound machine
    (5) wheel

2. Which machine changes the direction of a force?

    (1) lever
    (2) pulley
    (3) wheel and axle
    (4) inclined plane
    (5) axle

3. Which of the following can be changed by gears?

    (1) the direction of the force
    (2) the amount of force
    (3) the speed of the force
    (4) all of the above
    (5) none of the above

4. In which of the following situations is work <u>not</u> done?

    (1) a person pushing lawnmower
    (2) a parent holding a 30-pound child
    (3) the wind pushing a kite into the air
    (4) a child pulling a wagon
    (5) a bulldozer excavating a foundation for a building

5. What may be the most likely result if one of the simple machines in a compound machine breaks?

    (1) The function of the broken simple machine will be taken over by the other simple machines in the compound machine.
    (2) The broken simple machine will be discarded.
    (3) The compound machine will function normally.
    (4) The compound machine will not work.
    (5) The working simple machines will break down as well.

6. When a hockey puck is struck on an ice rink, the puck speeds up, slides across the ice, and gradually slows down and stops. What causes the puck to slow down and stop?

    (1) friction
    (2) momentum
    (3) inertia
    (4) deceleration
    (5) acceleration

7. Which of the following is <u>not</u> a simple machine?

    (1) a clock
    (2) a shovel
    (3) a wedge
    (4) a knife
    (5) a swivel chair

Answers are on page 315.

Energy

There are many different forms of energy. One of the most common is **kinetic energy**, which is the energy an object has when it is in motion. A skater rolling along a street and a hammer swinging down toward a nail have kinetic energy. You can feel the kinetic energy if you try to stop a moving object.

Another form of energy is **potential energy**, the energy an object has because of its position. At the top of a hill, a child on a sled has no kinetic energy because he or she is not moving. But the potential for movement is present because of the sled's position at the top of the hill. Once the sled starts moving, the potential energy changes into kinetic energy.

Conservation of Energy

Like matter, energy does not magically appear and disappear. If you were to add up the energy given off and taken in, the total would always be the same. In the example of the sledder, the amounts of potential energy and kinetic energy should be exactly the same. This idea is known as the **law of conservation of energy**. Unfortunately, real life is not so simple. Friction converts some of the potential energy into heat energy. As a result, the sledder's kinetic energy equals the potential energy minus heat energy lost through friction. Like the sledder, machines and engines encounter friction. The energy put into the engine never quite equals the energy that comes out. Engineers do their best to reduce friction and make engines efficient.

Changing Energy

Both potential and kinetic energy are a type of energy known as **mechanical energy.** This type of energy comes from motion. Because atoms of matter are in motion, every object has a certain amount of mechanical energy. This internal energy is potential energy.

The movement of the electrons of matter has a special name—**electrical energy.** Energy can be stored in matter as **chemical energy**. This, too, is a form of potential energy and depends on how the atoms are arranged.

Splitting or changing the nucleus of the atom results in **nuclear energy**. In this instance, a small amount of the atomic mass is converted to energy. The energy produced by stars is nuclear energy. As the nuclear energy leaves the star and travels through space in waves, it is termed **radiant energy**.

Each of these kinds of energy can change its form. For example, mass is changed into nuclear energy in our stars. The nuclear energy changes to radiant energy that travels through space. Plants use that radiant energy to grow. When the plant dies, the energy trapped within it can eventually be converted to coal, oil, or gas (chemical energy). At the local power plant, the coal may be converted to electrical energy, which in turn may be used to bake a cake. The heat produces chemical changes in the cake batter. If a person eats the cake, the body converts the chemical energy in the cake to mechanical energy (the motion of legs, heart, and so forth). If more than enough cake is eaten, the unused energy is converted back into matter—in this case, fat.

Thinking About Science

Directions: Complete the sentences below by filling in the blanks.

1. _____ energy is the energy an object has when it is in motion.

2. An object's position may give it _____ energy.

3. _____ converts some potential energy into heat energy.

4. The movement of electrons produces _____ energy.

5. Splitting or changing the _____ provides nuclear energy.

Answers are on page 315.

PRE-GED PRACTICE

Directions: Choose the one best answer to each question.

Question 1 refers to the information on page 216.

1. Which of the following is not an example of a form of energy performing work?

    (1) The chemical energy of gasoline being used to drive a car.
    (2) The heat energy from oil being used to drive a ship.
    (3) Electrical energy turning the blades of a ceiling fan.
    (4) The radiant energy of the Sun evaporating water on Earth's surface and forming clouds.
    (5) The nuclear energy found in a radioactive fuel element such as uranium.

2. Which of the following summarizes the law of conservation of energy?

    (1) Energy is needed to do work.
    (2) Kinetic energy is the energy an object has when it is in motion.
    (3) Energy can change forms, but it cannot be created or destroyed under ordinary conditions.
    (4) Potential energy is the energy an object has because of its position.
    (5) Heat is a form of energy.

3. Which of the following describes the change in energy when a log is burned in a fireplace?

    (1) Mechanical energy is changed to chemical energy.
    (2) Chemical energy is changed to heat energy and light energy.
    (3) Mechanical energy is changed to radiant energy and chemical energy.
    (4) Chemical energy is changed to heat energy and electrical energy.
    (5) Radiant energy is changed to chemical energy and heat energy.

Answers are on page 315.

Heat Energy

For many years, scientists struggled to understand heat. Some thought heat was a kind of fluid that flowed through the air. It took several years before scientists realized that heat is a form of energy.

When objects are hot, they increase slightly in size, or **expand**. This occurs because the particles in a hot object move around more and bump each other apart. In cool objects, the movement of the particles slows and the object **contracts**, or gets smaller.

Heat moves from one object to another by one of three processes: conduction, convection, and radiation.

Conduction

In **conduction**, objects must be in direct contact. This is the method that cooks food in a pan. Conduction occurs because the molecules in an object are constantly moving about and bumping into each other. In hot areas, the atoms move faster. They bump more and more molecules.

As matter becomes hotter, the molecules move faster and faster. When they bump into other particles, they transfer heat. Pots and pans are made of metals because metals are good conductors of heat. Pot handles are made of wood because wood (and cloth) are poor conductors of heat. Materials that do not conduct heat quickly are called **insulators**.

Water is a poor conductor, as is plastic. Poor conductors do not feel cold when you touch them. This is because they do not absorb heat from your hand quickly. Cork and fiberglass, because they contain air, are poor conductors. Air is the worst conductor of all known substances.

Convection

Heat can move through the air and water in a process called **convection**. When air is heated, the molecules move faster and bump each other farther apart. With its molecules farther apart, the hot air contains slightly less mass. It rises above the cooler air. The difference in air temperature causes the air to move. In the illustration below, notice that the hot air from the furnace rises into the room. The cool air sinks until it returns to the furnace and is heated again.

CONVECTION

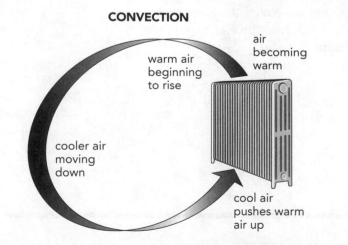

warm air beginning to rise

air becoming warm

cooler air moving down

cool air pushes warm air up

Radiation

The heat from the Sun comes to us in waves of **radiation** (radiant energy). You can feel this energy even through windows that keep out any moving air. On a cool day, the air is cool, and a pane of window glass will feel cool to the touch. If you sit near a sunny window, however, you will soon begin to feel the Sun's warmth. Radiant energy changes to heat energy only when it is absorbed by an object. Clothing and skin absorb radiant energy. Materials with dark, dull surfaces absorb a lot of radiation. Materials with light, shiny surfaces reflect the radiation. Radiant energy passes through clear materials, such as air, glass, and water.

Thinking About Science

Directions: Complete the sentences below by filling in the blanks.

1. Objects _____ when they are hot and
   _____ when they are cold.

2. To transfer heat through _____ _____, objects must be in
   direct contact.

3. Pots and pans are used for cooking because they are good
   _____ of heat.

4. Most home heating systems are based on the principle that warm air
   _____ and cool air _____.

5. _____ colors absorb more radiant energy than
   _____ colors.

Answers are on page 315.

Directions: Choose the <u>one best answer</u> to each question.

Questions 1 and 2 refer to the information on pages 218 and 219.

1. What are materials that transfer heat quickly?

    (1) contractors
    (2) conductors
    (3) insulators
    (4) radiators
    (5) convectors

2. To stay cool in the summer, what type of clothes should you wear?

    A. Clothes that are dark in color.
    B. Clothes that are shiny.
    C. Clothes that are light in color.

    (1) A only
    (2) A only
    (3) A only
    (4) both B and C
    (5) both A and B

    Answers are on page 315.

Wave Theory

Heat is only one type of energy that can move in waves. Almost all of the energy of the universe moves in waves. Like a water wave (which is really energy moving through the water), waves of energy can be described by the size of the crest, trough, wavelength, and **frequency**, or the number of waves that pass a point in a given amount of time. Waves with the greatest frequency carry the most energy. The illustration below shows the kinds of waves that carry energy throughout the universe. This grouping of waves is usually called the **electromagnetic spectrum**. The colors of the rainbow make up the only part of this spectrum that is visible to humans. All the other waves are invisible. Visible light appears in the middle of the spectrum.

ELECTROMAGNETIC SPECTRUM

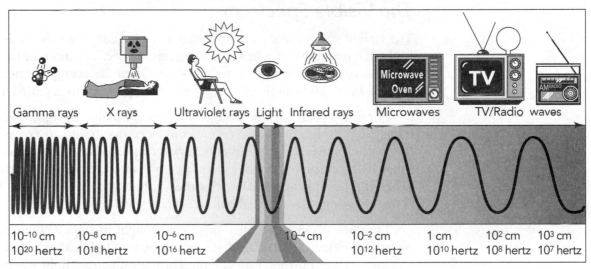

| Gamma rays | X rays | Ultraviolet rays | Light | Infrared rays | Microwaves | TV/Radio waves |

10^{-10} cm 10^{-8} cm 10^{-6} cm 10^{-4} cm 10^{-2} cm 1 cm 10^{2} cm 10^{3} cm

10^{20} hertz 10^{18} hertz 10^{16} hertz 10^{12} hertz 10^{10} hertz 10^{8} hertz 10^{7} hertz

High Energy Waves

The high-energy waves on the left half of the illustration can do the most harm to people. It is necessary to limit human exposure to these waves. Gamma rays penetrate deeply. They have a lot of energy and damage living cells as they pass through. Gamma rays originate from the nuclei of radioactive atoms in nuclear reactions and explosions. Gamma rays, however, are also used to save lives. This is the radiation that is used to kill cancer cells. X rays are frequently used by doctors to take a picture inside the body. X rays can be used to find cavities in teeth, to locate broken bones, and even to find tumors. Sunlight contains ultraviolet (UV) rays. Ultraviolet rays are powerful enough to burn or tan skin. They are also used to kill bacteria.

Low-Energy Waves

The low-energy waves on the right half of the spectrum are very useful. Infrared waves can be used to cook food. Because all warm objects emit infrared rays, they are also used to map Earth from space and to locate people, such as lost children, who cannot be seen in forests or rough terrain. Microwaves have given us a fast new way to cook. They are the shortest of the radio waves and are used in the transmission of radar signals. Since some microwaves have the same frequency as the water molecules contained in food, microwaves are used to cook moist food. As the water molecules in the food vibrate, the energy of the microwaves is converted into heat. Radio waves not only bring us music and news, they also help airplanes and submarines navigate. The length of radio waves ranges from hundreds of feet down to fractions of an inch.

The Visible Spectrum

The visible spectrum is most important to us because we rely on light to see. Light can be produced when an atom gains energy. The atom must release this extra energy and return to its normal state. Often the energy is released in the form of light. The bundle of energy released by the atom is called a **photon**.

For many years, people disagreed about the nature of light. Because it travels in a straight line, many were convinced that light was composed of tiny particles. Several experiments, however, proved that light was a wave. Finally, scientists found that light is a combination of particles and waves. When light is either emitted or absorbed, it behaves like a particle. When light is traveling long distances, it behaves like a wave.

Light travels in waves that move in a straight line. As a result, light cannot go around objects. Materials that block or absorb light cause a shadow. Other objects, such as mirrors, reflect light. During reflection, light waves bounce off an object and change their direction of motion.

Most of us have seen a sunbeam and think of light as white. A rainbow, however, offers proof that what we see as white light is actually a blend of many colors. When light passes through a **prism** (a triangular piece of glass), white light splits into a group of colors that we call the **spectrum**. The diagram of the prism shows the colors of light.

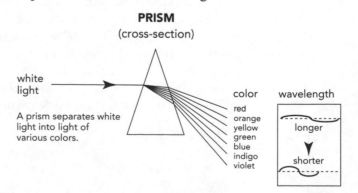

PRISM
(cross-section)

white
light

A prism separates white
light into light of
various colors.

color | wavelength
red
orange
yellow
green
blue
indigo
violet

longer

shorter

Prisms break up the white light because each color of light has a slightly different wavelength. When light passes through an object, it bends. Short wavelengths bend more than long wavelengths.

Thinking About Science

Directions: Complete each statement below by filling in the blanks.

1. High-energy waves include _____,
   _____, and _____.

2. Low-energy waves include _____,
   _____, and _____.

3. Light shows characteristics of both _____ and
   _____.

4. Because light cannot go around an object, it forms a
   _____ when an object blocks its path.

5. White light breaks into various colors as it passes through a prism
   because _____ _____ wavelengths bend more than
   _____ _____ wavelengths.

Answers are on page 315.

PRE-GED PRACTICE

Directions: Choose the <u>one best answer</u> to each question.

Questions 1–3 are based on the information on pages 221 and 222.

1. Why can a glass prism separate white light into its various colors?

   (1) The different particles of light react with the glass.
   (2) The different wavelengths of light bend at different angles as they pass through the glass.
   (3) Certain colors of light do not pass through glass and must bend around it.
   (4) Glass is so dense that it consumes the energy of light.
   (5) Glass contains all the colors of the rainbow.

2. When is light produced?

   (1) when an atom gains energy
   (2) when an atom releases energy
   (3) when an microwave strikes an atom
   (4) when an wave of energy hits the eye
   (5) when an wave of energy penetrates the eye

3. According to the diagram of the prism on page 222, which of the following has the longest wavelength?

   (1) red
   (2) orange
   (3) green
   (4) violet
   (5) yellow

Answers are on page 315.

Sound

Although sound is a wave, it differs slightly from the waves of the electromagnetic spectrum. Sound travels in a special type of wave called a **compression wave**. It is a sound wave of high pressure that vibrates in the wave direction of a line.

Sound begins with a vibration. When an object vibrates, it makes the air around it vibrate, too. These vibrations travel as compression waves through the air to our ears.

The term **pitch** refers to the measure of the frequency at which a note vibrates. A high pitch will have a greater number of vibrations and will create a greater number of sound waves. The loudness of a sound is the strength of the sensation received by the ear.

Sound waves scatter in much the same way that light waves scatter. When light enters a denser material, such as a glass prism, it slows down and bends. In a similar manner, sound travels at different rates in different materials. In air, sound travels at about 1,087 feet per second. In water, it travels at about 4,700 feet per second. In steel, it travels at about 16,000 feet per second.

The waves that create sound and light have similar properties. Just as light is reflected by a mirror, sound can be reflected by a hard surface. **Echoes** are reflected sound waves. The principle of reflected sound has brought us sonar (sound navigation ranging), which has been used to map the ocean floor. Bats and porpoises use sonar to find their way through the dark and to find food. Porpoises even use a high blast of sonar to kill their prey.

 **Thinking About Science**

Directions: Circle *T* for each true statement or *F* for each false statement.

T F **1.** An echo is an example of the refraction of sound.

T F **2.** Sound waves are part of the electromagnetic spectrum.

T F **3.** Sound begins with a vibration.

T F **4.** Porpoises use sound to kill fish.

T F **5.** Like light, the speed of sound depends on the type of material it passes through.

Answers are on page 315.

Directions: Choose the <u>one best answer</u> to each question.

Questions 1 and 2 refer to the information on page 224.

1. What happens when a sound wave is reflected?

    (1) The sound wave changes speed.
    (2) The sound wave changes frequency.
    (3) The sound wave changes pitch.
    (4) The sound wave bounces off an object.
    (5) The sound wave passes through the object.

2. Which is the best explanation of why you may hear voices on the other side of a lake on a summer night but you may not hear voices on the other side of a field on a summer night?

    (1) Sound travels faster in water than in air.
    (2) A field has grass that absorbs sound waves.
    (3) Sound travels faster in a solid than in air.
    (4) A lake is less dense than is air.
    (5) Sound travels slower in water than in air.

    Answers are on page 315.

Electricity and Magnetism

The particles of an atom's nucleus are bound tightly together. They move very little. The electrons, however, are much freer to move from place to place and from atom to atom. When an electron moves from one atom to another, it changes each atom's electrical charge. A positively charged atom pushes away—or repels—another positively charged atom, but it attracts a negatively charged atom. Objects with the same charge repel each other; objects with opposite charges attract each other.

One way to get electrons to move from one atom to another is to rub two neutral objects together. The electrons move from one object to the other. The result is two objects with electrical charges. In a clothes drier, for example, pieces of clothing rub against each other and against the drum of the drier. As they rub, they lose and gain electrons. The result is that some bits of clothing repel each other and some attract each other. In everyday language, we call this static cling.

The same thing happens when a comb is rubbed against hair. Some of the electrons of the hair are rubbed off by the comb. Soon the charge on the comb builds up and attracts the negatively charged hair. That causes hair to stand up. If enough electrical charge builds up on one object, some of that charge may jump to another object. The result is a spark.

Electric Current

One important characteristic of electricity is the way it moves, or flows. This flow is known as electric current. Materials that carry these electric currents easily are known as conductors. Those that do not carry electric current are called insulators. Even the best conductor slows the movement of electrons just a bit. Scientists call this resistance.

Resistance to electric current causes an increase in temperature. If the amount of electric current passing through a wire is more than the wire can carry, the heat from the resistance builds up. Eventually, a fire can start.

Electric current is sometimes compared to a stream of water moving through a hose. The strength of the stream of water depends on how hard it is being pushed through the hose. In electricity, the push that gets the current flowing is measured in volts. The higher the volts, the stronger the push. A typical flashlight battery provides about 1.5 volts.

Circuits

Electric current flows only when it can follow a complete path from starting point back to starting point. This path is called a **circuit**. All circuits have three parts. The first is a source of voltage, such as a battery, to provide the "push" for the electric current. The second is the wires that carry the current. The third is the object that uses the electricity. This object is often a lamp or a motor. If the circuit is broken, electricity will stop flowing through the wires.

A SIMPLE CIRCUIT

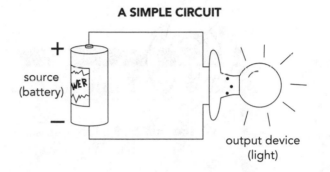

source
(battery)

output device
(light)

Electrical wiring systems in homes and buildings make use of the fact that electricity will stop flowing in broken circuits and thus help prevent fires. When circuits are overloaded and too much resistance builds up, devices called circuit breakers or fuses automatically shut off the current. When that occurs, the overloaded circuit must be found and fixed. Anything done to try to force the wires, fuses, or circuit breakers to carry additional electricity is dangerous.

Magnets

Magnets are objects that attract iron and a few other elements. Magnets are surrounded by a magnetic field that decreases in strength as you move farther from the magnet. All magnets have a south pole and a north pole. Like a giant magnet, Earth turns so that one end of it will always point toward the north. The end of the magnet that points north is called the north pole. The other end is called the south pole. Opposite poles attract each other. Like poles push each other away.

Electricity and magnetism are related. Each can be used to make the other. A coiled wire, for example, will act like a magnet if an electric current passes through it. Such a device is called an **electromagnet**. You use an electromagnet each time you use a hair dryer, doorbell, telephone, or tape player. Electric motors use electromagnets to change electric energy to mechanical energy.

ELECTROMAGNET

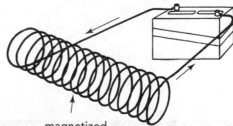

magnetized

Passing a magnet through the coils in the electromagnet shown in the diagram creates an electric current—even without the battery. **Generators** are machines that use the motion of magnets to produce electricity.

Another application of the electromagnetic principle is in the operation of maglev (magnetic levitation) trains. These trains provide a smooth and quiet ride. A current flows through electromagnets installed in the track and on the underside of the train. The magnetism produced lifts the train upward.

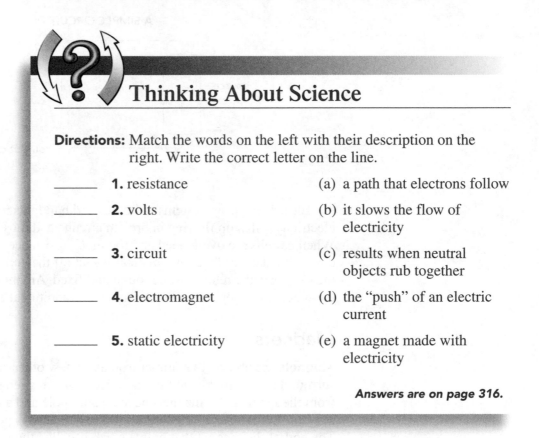

Thinking About Science

Directions: Match the words on the left with their description on the right. Write the correct letter on the line.

_____ **1.** resistance

_____ **2.** volts

_____ **3.** circuit

_____ **4.** electromagnet

_____ **5.** static electricity

(a) a path that electrons follow

(b) it slows the flow of electricity

(c) results when neutral objects rub together

(d) the "push" of an electric current

(e) a magnet made with electricity

Answers are on page 316.

PRE-GED PRACTICE

Directions: Choose the <u>one best answer</u> to each question.

Questions 1 and 2 refer to the information on pages 226–228.

1. Which of the following protects an electric wiring system from overheating?

(1) resistance
(2) circuits
(3) circuit breakers and fuses
(4) insulators
(5) a heat clamp

2. What is the unit of measure for the "push" of electric current?

(1) Ohm
(2) pressure
(3) ampere
(4) volt
(5) watt

Answers are on page 316.

Physics Review

Directions: Choose the one best answer to each question.

Questions 1–3 refer to the following passage and diagram.

One of the most baffling household appliances is the refrigerator. This appliance uses electricity to remove heat from air. The method combines the compression of gases and the process of evaporation.

When a gas is compressed, its temperature rises. When a gas is allowed to expand, or when a liquid evaporates, heat is absorbed by the gas.

**THE COMPRESSION SYSTEM
OF A REFRIGERATOR**

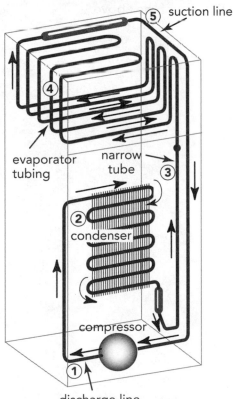

The compressor in a refrigerator pumps a gas, usually freon, through the entire system. The compressor squeezes the freon and pumps it into the discharge line (number 1 on the diagram). As the gas is compressed, its

temperature rises. This heated gas enters the condenser (2), usually on the back or bottom of the refrigerator, where much of the heat is released into the air. As the compressed gas releases its heat, the gas cools and condenses into a liquid

A narrow tube (3) carries the liquid freon from the condenser (2) to the evaporator tubing (4). The evaporator tubing is larger than the tube from the condenser so that as the liquid enters the evaporator tubing, the liquid begins to expand and become a gas.

In the process of passing through the evaporator tubing, the evaporating liquid absorbs the heat inside the refrigerator and cools the contents of the refrigerator. The gas returns to the compressor through the suction line (5), to begin another refrigeration cycle.

1. Which of the following gases is most frequently used in home refrigerators?

   (1) freon
   (2) argon
   (3) ammonia
   (4) helium
   (5) oxygen

2. In a closed system, such as a refrigerator, what happens to liquid that is allowed to evaporate?

   (1) It will be compressed.
   (2) It will remain a liquid.
   (3) It will absorb heat.
   (4) It will release heat.
   (5) It will solidify

3. Which of the following occurs in the condenser?

   (1) Heat is absorbed by the gas.
   (2) The gas is compressed.
   (3) Heat is released by the compressed gas.
   (4) The liquid evaporates into a gas.
   (5) The gases solidify.

Questions 4 and 5 refer to the following passage.

Laser light is very different from the light of a lightbulb. Lightbulbs emit many different wavelengths that move in many different directions. Laser beams are made of a single wavelength. They do not spread, even after traveling for many miles.

At first, lasers were used only for scientific research. One experiment used laser beams to measure the distance from Earth to the Moon to within a half a foot. Using lasers, scientists found that light travels at 186,282 miles per second. Some scientists are attempting to locate intelligent life on other planets by sending messages with lasers.

Lasers have also been used in many practical ways. They are used to weld and cut metals, resulting in stronger welds and cleaner cuts. Lasers are also used to cut fabric for clothing and to drill holes in valves. Cables of glass fibers carry laser beams and are now being used to replace telephone wires. Many weapons, such as the smart bombs that were used in Afghanistan, were guided by lasers.

In medicine, lasers have many applications. Surgeons use laser scalpels to perform delicate surgery. Because lasers cauterize the blood vessels as they cut, laser surgery eliminates much of the bleeding that usually accompanies surgery.

In an effort to prevent the injuries from explosions that occur each Fourth of July, some towns are replacing their annual fireworks display with a laser light show.

4. Which of the following is a characteristic of laser beams?

   (1) Lasers are used only for scientific research.
   (2) Lasers have many different wavelengths.
   (3) Lasers travel long distances without spreading.
   (4) Lasers scatter in many different directions.
   (5) Lasers travel only in bursts of energy.

5. For what purpose have lasers been used?

   (1) to measure the distance to the Moon
   (2) to perform eye surgery
   (3) to guide missiles during wars
   (4) all of the above
   (5) none of the above

Question 6 refers to the following illustration.

TWO BAR MAGNETS

N

S

N

S

6. Which of the following is the most likely reaction when two magnets are placed side by side as shown in the illustration?

   (1) The magnets will move away from each other.
   (2) The magnets will move toward each other.
   (3) Neither magnet will move.
   (4) The poles will reverse themselves.
   (5) The magnets will swing back and forth.

Question 7 refers to the following diagram.

7. Which of the following wires should be removed to turn off only light D?

A SIMPLE CIRCUIT

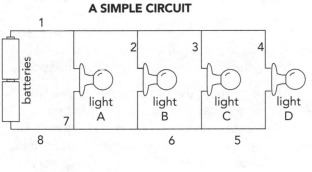

   (1) wires 1 or 2
   (2) wires 3 or 4
   (3) wires 4 or 5
   (4) wires 6 or 7
   (5) wires 7 or 8

Questions 8 and 9 refer to the following passage.

A little more than a hundred years ago, the fastest horses in the country were bought by the Pony Express to carry mail from Missouri to California. The fastest time was an amazingly speedy eight days. Now electronic mail (e-mail) sends letters all over the world in a matter of seconds. The computer has transformed society.

At the heart of every computer is a simple electric circuit that can recognize only two pieces of information: on and off. Thousands of circuits are needed to make the computer work. When computers were first built, even a very simple computer had so many circuits that the machine was as big as a room. Now all those circuits have been made so small that they fit on a tiny chip, called a microprocessor. Most microprocessors are no bigger than a fingernail.

Because of the small size of chips, today's computers can be built to handle vast amounts of information. The newest computers can easily manage entire sets of encyclopedias and a few movies. In fact, most of today's home computers are many times more powerful than the computers used to send the first men to the Moon.

8. What is at the heart of every computer?

   (1) a simple circuit that can manage whole stacks of information
   (2) a simple circuit that can recognize only on and off
   (3) a simple circuit that is far more powerful than old computers
   (4) a simple circuit that is smaller than a fingernail
   (5) a simple circuit that can recognize every letter in the alphabet

9. According to the passage, what are today's home computers powerful enough to do?

   A. contain an entire set of encyclopedias
   B. send a person to the Moon
   C. handle all the e-mail produced in the United States

   (1) A only
   (2) B only
   (3) C only
   (4) both A and B
   (5) both B and C

Answers are on page 316.

READING EFFICIENCY G

Directions: This activity will help you to improve your reading efficiency. Before you start to read, write the present time at the top of the page. When you have completed the reading and all 5 questions, write your finishing time. Subtract to find out how long you took. Score your answers. Then turn to pages 320–321 to find your E-Factor and to graph your progress.

Finishing Time	
Starting Time −	
Reading Time =	
Number of Answers Correct	

Temperature, Heat, and Thermal Energy

All matter is made of particles. These particles never stop moving. Even if the matter is perfectly still, its particles are moving. These moving particles have kinetic energy—the energy of motion. The faster the particles move, the more kinetic energy they have. The particles in a sample of matter aren't all moving at the same speed. Some move faster than others. The faster particles have more kinetic energy.

Temperature is the measure of the average kinetic energy of the particles in a sample of matter. The higher the temperature, the faster the particles are moving. Thermal energy is the total kinetic energy that makes up a substance.

The temperature of a substance changes when thermal energy flows between the substance and another material. This moving of energy between substances is called heat. Heat flows from a warmer substance to a cooler one. It never flows from a cooler material to a warmer one.

The transfer of thermal energy is important for many reasons. It is used to heat homes and to cook. Thermal energy can be a problem when too much enters the environment. For example, electric power plants often are near a body of water, such as a river. When the plant makes electricity, it gives off thermal energy as waste. This waste enters the nearby river as heated water. This thermal pollution can cause damage to organisms in the river. Some power plants use cooling towers to cool the water before it enters the river.

READING EFFICIENCY G

1. What is the meaning of the phrase *thermal pollution* in the last paragraph?

   (1) production of electricity
   (2) energy use
   (3) production of waste
   (4) heating of a body of water
   (5) river water

2. If a man holds an ice cube in his hand, in which direction does thermal energy flow?

   (1) from the ice cube to the surrounding air
   (2) from the hand to the ice cube
   (3) from the ice cube to the hand
   (4) both ways between the ice cube and the hand
   (5) there is no energy

3. Why would a substance have more thermal energy after it is heated than before it is heated?

   (1) It has more kinetic energy after it is heated.
   (2) Its particles slow down after heating.
   (3) It looses particles to the air during heating.
   (4) It looses thermal energy to the air during heating.
   (5) Its particles all move at the same speed after heating.

4. The speed of particles in a substance determines whether it is a solid, liquid, or gas. If heating a solid changes it to a liquid, which statement must be true?

   (1) The particles in the liquid have more thermal energy than the particles in the solid.
   (2) The particles in the liquid move faster than the particles in the solid.
   (3) The thermal energy in the liquid and the solid are the same.
   (4) The particles in a gas would move slower than the particles in a liquid.
   (5) The solid has more kinetic energy than the liquid.

5. A company wants to build a factory next to a river in your town. Some community members are against the factory. Which of the following reasons is based on a value judgment?

   (1) The factory would pollute the air.
   (2) The factory would cause thermal pollution of the river.
   (3) The factory will be unattractive and not blend in to the existing architecture.
   (4) The factory would be built on an existing park.
   (5) The factory would destroy the habitat of a native plant.

Answers are on page 316.

READING EFFICIENCY H

Directions: This activity will help you to improve your reading efficiency. Before you start to read, write the present time at the top of the page. When you have completed the reading and all 5 questions, write your finishing time. Subtract to find out how long you took. Score your answers. Then turn to pages 320–321 to find your E-Factor and to graph your progress.

Finishing Time	
Starting Time −	
Reading Time =	
Number of Answers Correct	

Lasers

Have you ever seen the pencil-thin beams of light that fly across the stage during a rock concert? This same kind of light has many other uses too. The light is laser light. Laser light is so useful because of the way its waves line up.

LIGHT WAVE

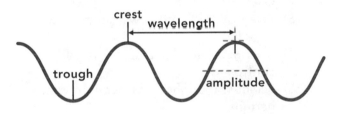

Laser light is made of light waves of one wavelength. The waves travel with their crests and troughs aligned. The waves travel in one direction so they do not spread out like ordinary light. The waves act like a single wave. The result is a straight, strong beam of colored light. The color of the light depends on the wavelength used.

The way lasers make light is simple. In an atom an electron can move from one energy level to another. When an electron moves from a higher energy level to a lower one, the atom releases a photon. A photon is a tiny packet of energy. In a laser, electric current causes electrons in the atoms of the laser material to move to a higher energy level. When the electrons move back to the lower energy level, these atoms give off photons. Mirrors at opposite ends of the laser reflect the photons back and forth many times. The reflected photons cause other atoms to give off identical photons. The photons travel back and forth so many times. Many photons are given off. An area on one of the mirrors allows some waves to escape the laser to form a laser beam.

The first working laser was built in 1960 by Theodore H. Maiman. At first, lasers had few uses. Today lasers are used to measure the distances within an atom or between Earth and the Moon. They can cut through metal. Surgeons use them to do eye surgery. They read bar codes and produce music from CDs. The list of laser uses seems almost endless.

READING EFFICIENCY H

1. What is the highest point of a wave?

   (1) crest
   (2) wavelength
   (3) electromagnetic radiation
   (4) frequency
   (5) trough

2. In which of the following ways would a laser light <u>not</u> be used?

   (1) as a chalkboard pointer
   (2) to light up a room
   (3) to make a light show
   (4) to read prices from packages at the grocery store
   (5) to drill a hole in a steel bar

3. Regular light spreads out in all directions. Which statement tells a reason for this?

   (1) Regular light is made of only one color.
   (2) Light waves in regular light are not aligned.
   (3) Regular light can be made in bursts.
   (4) Regular light is not reflected.
   (5) Light waves in regular light have the same frequency.

4. Which characteristic of laser light makes it useful as a tool to cut through metal?

   (1) A laser gathers energy into a focused beam.
   (2) A laser beam can travel through air.
   (3) Laser light can be made in different colors.
   (4) Laser light can travel long distances.
   (5) Laser light creates a sharp shadow.

5. When Maiman made the first useable laser, many scientists called it an invention with no use. Which statement would be a reason scientists said this?

   (1) At the time scientists knew very little about light.
   (2) Regular light can do the same tasks as laser light.
   (3) Scientists did not know enough about laser light.
   (4) Scientists knew that laser light cannot be controlled.
   (5) Scientist thought that laser light was harmful.

Answers are on page 316.

PART FOUR

Earth and Space Science

- **Earth Science**
- **Space Science**

CHAPTER 8

Earth Science

The earth science passages on the GED Science Test are drawn from the following areas: geology, oceanography, and meteorology. Each of these broad areas contains many topics. You will need to know a little bit about each for the GED Test.

- **Geology** is the study of Earth. It explains how Earth was formed and how it changes. Geologists read Earth's history in its mountains, mineral deposits, rocks, and rock formations.

  Geology has many practical applications. Economic geologists study coal, metals, petroleum, and minerals that are of economic importance. They may search for oil and other energy sources. Environmental geologists use their knowledge to correct the world's environmental problems.

- **Oceanography** is the study of Earth's oceans. Scientists hope that the study of oceanography will help to solve some of the world's problems. The knowledge of sea plants and animals, for example, may increase our food supply. Knowing how pollutants affect sea animals and plants may help us to reduce the effects of pollution. Learning about the seafloor may lead to the discovery of deposits of oil and natural gas.

- **Meteorology** is the study of Earth's atmosphere, which is the blanket of air that covers Earth. Meteorology and oceanography are related because the ocean and the atmosphere affect one another.

  Developments in meteorology have increased our ability to predict the weather. The modern study of the weather actually began in 1593 when Galileo invented the thermometer. With the advent of weather maps in the 1800s, forecasting became possible. Today, weather satellites equipped with cameras have made predicting the weather far more accurate.

Earth's Structure

Most people assume that Earth is solid. They think that since the surface is solid, the interior must also be solid. Actually, Earth is covered by a very thin layer—or **crust**—that is only about twenty miles thick. By studying the patterns of earthquakes, scientists discovered that the earth beneath this crust is divided into three additional layers: the mantle, the outer core, and the inner core.

Below the crust lies the **mantle**, a thick layer of very dense rock. The mantle is about 1,800 miles thick. Near the crust, the mantle reaches temperatures of about 1,600°F. Farther down, temperatures soar to about 4,000°F.

THE STRUCTURE OF EARTH

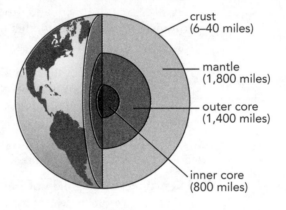

crust
(6–40 miles)

mantle
(1,800 miles)

outer core
(1,400 miles)

inner core
(800 miles)

The **outer core** is about 1,400 miles thick. It is made of melted iron and nickel. Temperatures range from 4,000°F to 9,000°F. The **inner core** extends about 800 more miles to Earth's center. Like the outer core, it is made of iron and nickel. Due to the great pressures, however, the iron and nickel of the inner core are forced into the solid state.

Movement of the Crust

Because of the tremendous forces within Earth, the crust is subject to intense pressure. The result is that the crust has fractured into several pieces, called **crustal plates**. The plates are continuously moving very slowly across the top of the mantle. As they move, they carry the continents with them.

Most scientists believe that until the era of the dinosaurs, the continents were one large land mass, called Pangaea by geologists. Sometime during the Mesozoic era, this large land mass broke apart. The theory that describes the movement of these broken plates is frequently called **continental drift** or **plate tectonics**.

PANGAEA

Mountain Building

Scientists think that many of Earth's most spectacular features have resulted from the motion of the crustal plates. Notice in the illustrations below what happens when crustal plates meet. Some plates meet and push the crust up. The resulting landform is mountains.

FOLD MOUNTAINS

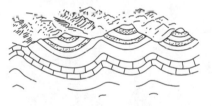

Fold mountains are formed at the edge of a continent by two crustal plates grinding into each other. One of the plates is forced down, and the other crumples and rides up above it. The Appalachians are a product of the crust's gentle folding.

FAULT-BLOCK MOUNTAINS

In other cases, huge blocks of crust are lifted, making high steep mountains, such as those found in east Africa. These are called fault-block mountains. They occur when the crust does not fold but cracks into blocks that move in relation to each other. The cracks are called **faults**. Some of the blocks subside, causing valleys, leaving the blocks that remain standing between them as block mountains.

Not all mountain areas are caused by crustal plates. Some, such as the Catskills in New York or the mesas of the Southwest, were formed by millions of years of erosion.

Volcanoes

Volcanoes frequently occur along the edges of crustal plates. As the plates rub against each other, molten rock heats up. When the pressure builds, the volcano erupts. With each mild eruption, the volcano becomes a bit larger. Sometimes, however, the eruption is huge. Rather than resulting in a bigger volcano, a huge eruption can rip the volcano apart.

The only active volcano in the continental United States is Mount St. Helens in Washington State. Over 25 eruptions have been recorded in the past decade. The last eruption tore the top off the mountain.

Krakatoa, in Indonesia, is perhaps the most famous volcano. An eruption in 1883 wiped out 163 villages, leveled the island, and sounded like the roar of heavy guns almost 3,000 miles away.

Some volcanoes occur in mid-plate regions. Scientists think these volcanoes are caused by hot spots that remain in place while the plate moves across it. The Hawaiian Islands are an example of volcanoes formed as the plate passed over a hot spot. Each volcano is progressively older as the island chain moves away from Mauna Loa, the islands' newest volcano. Mauna Loa still erupts about every 4.5 years.

PATH OF VOLCANIC ISLANDS

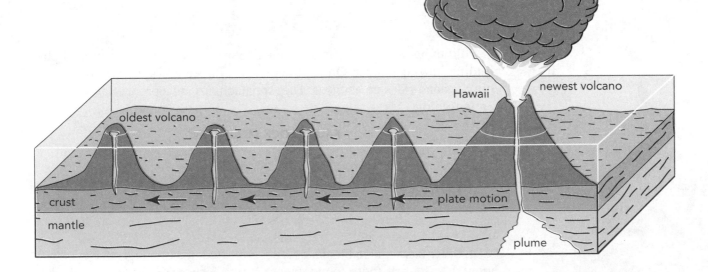

Earthquakes

Where plates meet and slide under or over each other, earthquakes may result. The map below shows the edges of crustal plates as thin black lines. Jagged lines mark areas of frequent earthquake activity.

PLATES AND QUAKES

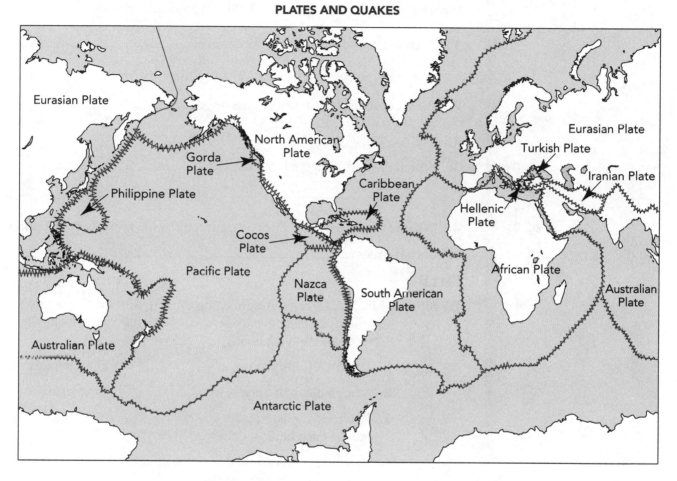

Earthquakes can occur when crustal plates that push against each other suddenly give way. The shaking of an earthquake can be slight, or it can cause considerable damage. Often, the worst damage is not from the shifting ground. Instead, damage may be from other events triggered by earthquakes. For example, underwater earthquakes can cause a deadly wave that can hit land at a height of sixty feet.

Not all quakes occur at plate lines. Like volcanoes, some occur in mid-plate regions. Scientists think that heat and pressure build up under the plate as it is dragged along. The stress may result in an earthquake. Far from any traditional fault lines, New Madrid, Missouri, seems to be a center of mid-plate earthquake activity. Three violent quakes occurred there in the early 1800s and were strong enough to change the course of the Mississippi River.

Thinking About Science

Part A

Directions: Answer the questions below in the space provided.

1. What is the mantle?_____

_____

2. What causes Earth's inner core to be solid?_____

_____

3. Which of Earth's layers is the thickest?_____

_____

4. What is the name of the theory that describes the movement of Earth's

crustal plates?_____

Part B

Directions: Match each cause described on the left with the effect listed
on the right. Effects may be used more than once. Write the
correct letter on the line.

_____ 1. The crust folds gently. (a) earthquake

_____ 2. A large block of crust is lifted. (b) volcano

_____ 3. Two crustal plates pushing (c) mountain
against each other suddenly give way.

_____ 4. Plates drag along, building pressure and stress.

_____ 5. Molten rock heats up when plates rub against each other.

_____ 6. Plates move across a hot spot.

Answers are on page 316.

Types of Rock

Earth's crust contains three different families of rocks: igneous, such as granite; sedimentary, such as sandstone; and metamorphic, such as marble.

Melted rock from deep within Earth pushes up to fill cracks made when the crustal plates move. This type of rock, called **igneous** from the Latin word for "fire," is molten rock that has cooled. The melted rock that spews out of a volcano is in the igneous family.

About 80 percent of the rock that lies under Earth's surface was formed by small particles of mineral or organic matter. Most of the deposits occurred on the ocean floor. As time passed, the loose material was pressed into solid rock, called **sedimentary** rock.

Some types of sedimentary rocks were built up from the shells and skeletons of small sea animals. Other types were formed from the deposits of minerals that were dissolved in water. The third type of sedimentary rock was formed through the erosion of other rocks. Sedimentary rocks usually lie in horizontal layers, but they may fold or undergo other changes if intense pressures are placed on them.

When intense heat and pressure are applied to igneous or sedimentary rock, the structure of the rock changes. These "changed" rocks are termed **metamorphic** rock. There are many different types of metamorphic rock. Marble is the changed form of limestone. Slate is the changed form of shale.

Many of the rocks in Earth's crust are considered valuable. These valuable Earth products are commonly called ores and minerals. Copper and platinum, diamonds and gold, rock salt, sand, and gravel are mined from Earth. Once they are removed and used, they are gone forever.

The Rock Cycle

If metamorphic rock is exposed to more heat and more pressure, the rock may melt. When it cools, it will once again be igneous rock. The igneous rock may weather into sediments that harden into sedimentary rock. The sedimentary rock may change into metamorphic rock. Scientists refer to the changes of rock from one form into another as the rock cycle. It occurs constantly, but very slowly.

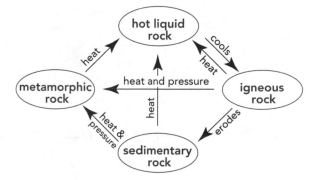

Minerals and Ores

Minerals can be identified by their hardness. A mineral that can scratch another must be harder than the mineral it scratches. The hardness of a mineral is rated according to the Mohs scale of hardness.

The scale ranges from 1 to 10. Talc, from which talcum powder is made, is the softest mineral at number 1; a diamond, the hardest substance known to man, is rated number 10.

Weathering and Soil

"Solid as a rock" is a popular phrase that means something will last forever. Rocks, however, are not solid forever. Weathering breaks them into smaller and smaller pieces. Weathering is a very slow process. It can take 100,000 years or more to convert rock into good top soil. Different types of rock weather into different types of soil. Quartz, for example, becomes sand. Feldspar becomes clay.

In different areas of the world, soil forms in different ways. Some soils are rich in clay. They hold water well but drain poorly. Sandy soils, on the other hand, dry out because water drains away so quickly.

Humus, or decayed plant and animal matter, helps the soil hold water and increases its fertility. Dark soil usually is rich in humus and is excellent for growing crops. Deep red soil, called **laterite**, is very poor for farming because it contains little humus. It is, however, rich in iron and aluminum.

Thinking About Science

Directions: Answer the questions below in the space provided.

1. Label the drawing below to complete the diagram of the rock cycle.

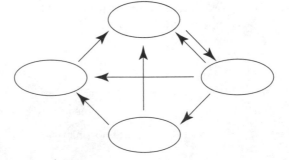

2. How long does it take for rock to weather into soil?

_____

3. What can be added to either clay or sandy soil to increase its fertility?

_____

Answers are on page 316.

Directions: Choose the <u>one best answer</u> to each question.

Questions 1–6 refer to the information on pages 239–346.

1. What part of Earth contains the continents?

    (1) crust
    (2) mantle
    (3) inner core
    (4) outer core
    (5) fault

2. What is the theory that describes the movement of the continents?

    (1) seafloor spreading
    (2) continental drift
    (3) plate drift
    (4) continental tectonics
    (5) crustal spreading

3. Which of the following describes the development of a volcano?

    (1) volcano erupts; crustal plates rub; pressure builds; molten rock heats
    (2) pressure builds; molten rock heats; volcano erupts; crustal plates rub
    (3) molten rock heats; pressure builds; crustal plates rub; volcano erupts
    (4) pressure builds; crustal plates rub; molten rock heats; volcano erupts
    (5) crustal plates rub; molten rock heats; pressure builds; volcano erupts

4. What is the rock cycle?

    (1) the development of mountains and volcanoes on Earth's crust
    (2) the processes by which rocks change from one form to another
    (3) the procedure involving the formation of rock from oxygen and carbon dioxide in Earth's atmosphere
    (4) the series of events that lead to the growth of plants on rock
    (5) the technique in which rocks are pressed together to form coal

5. What transforms sedimentary rock into metamorphic rock?

    (1) erosion
    (2) deposits of sediments
    (3) heat and pressure
    (4) heat from molten rock
    (5) time

6. What can you infer about weathering?

    (1) Weathering helps meteorologists to forecast the weather.
    (2) Weathering changes good topsoil into solid rock.
    (3) Weathering is caused by the action of water, ice, plants, animals, and chemical changes.
    (4) Weathering is the outcome when clay does not hold water well.
    (5) Weathering helps the soil hold water and increases its fertility.

Answers are on pages 316–317.

Earth's Oceans

Oceans cover about 70 percent of Earth's surface. Astronauts report that from space it is easy to see that Earth is mainly water. The Pacific Ocean alone covers almost half the globe. The appearance of Earth as a big blue marble is created by the water together with the effect of the atmosphere. Some people think of the world as one vast sea broken by large islands that we call continents.

Freshwater contains almost no salt. It is the kind of water we need to survive. It is also less than 1 percent of Earth's water supply. The other 99 percent of Earth's water is either saltwater in the oceans or water trapped as ice at the Poles. The freshwater in streams and rivers flows into the sea, where it mixes with the salt of the oceans. The Amazon, the world's largest river, flows into the ocean with such force that the freshwater stretches out of sight of land. Most of our freshwater supply is not in lakes, streams, ponds, and rivers. Instead, it is trapped underground in what we call the water table. It is estimated that 62.5 percent of the world's freshwater is located in groundwater.

The presence of water on Earth makes life itself possible since all life processes involve water. Scientists have theorized that life evolved in the sea about 3.5 billion years ago, and only about a half billion years ago did life move onto land.

Combinations of saltiness, temperature, currents, and other factors determine the extent of life that exists in any ocean region. Most life in the oceans is confined to the surface and only a few hundred meters below it. An interesting fact about the oceans' saltiness is that, if all the salt were removed from the seas, it would cover the land to a depth of 490 feet!

The Ocean Floor

For many years, little was known about the ocean floor. Now research vessels travel to the depths of the ocean. One of the newest discoveries is a mountain range right in the middle of the Atlantic Ocean. The mountains formed when the crustal plates spread apart. Another discovery is a new kind of life form that needs no sunlight. It can manufacture food out of the chemicals that rise up through cracks in the ocean floor.

When we picture the ocean floor, most of us think that the smooth, sandy beaches where we swim just continue at a deeper level. But away from shore, the ocean bottom is anything but flat and smooth. It rolls up huge underwater mountains and down trenches that may be more than six miles deep.

Most of the Pacific Ocean floats on just a single crustal plate. The Atlantic, however, is divided right down the middle. One plate moves east. The other moves west. As the crust pulls apart, the seafloor splits and spreads apart. Ridges of new land are formed by soft, heated rock that rises to fill the opening.

OCEAN FLOOR

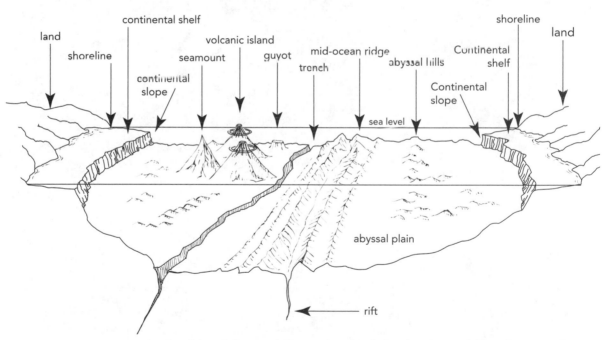

At the side of the world opposite the Atlantic, the moving plates push against each other. Slowly, one plate is ground down under the other. Deep trenches may form as the lower plate is slowly forced back into the mantle.

Currents

As the wind blows across the ocean, it creates surface currents. These currents move like a stream through the world's oceans. When the stream approaches land, it turns and moves along the coast. Most of these streams of currents form huge loops across the oceans, as shown on the map below. The current that loops through the Atlantic Ocean is the Gulf Stream. This stream of warm water travels at about 10 kilometers per hour. Within the loops are quiet areas where the water and wind move slowly.

OCEAN CURRENTS

Circulation Patterns of Surface Currents

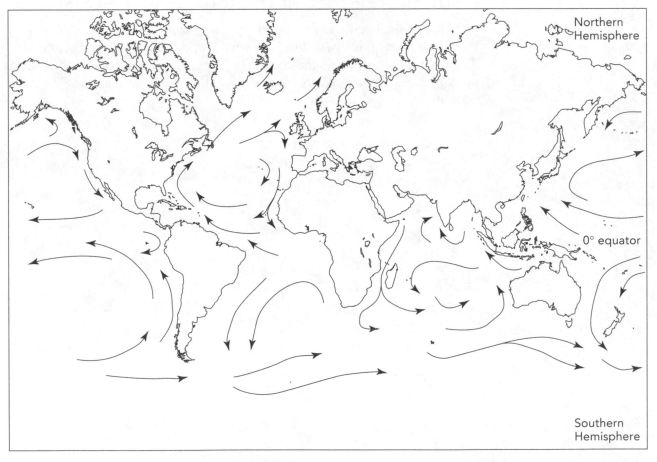

As the water moves past land, it affects the climate since the temperature of water doesn't change as quickly as the temperature of land. In cold weather, the air over the ocean warms the land. In hot weather, the ocean cools the land.

Waves

In addition to currents, winds produce the waves that are almost always present in any ocean area. Waves have two parts: the high point, or **crest**, and the low point, or **trough**. The height of a wave is measured from the top of the crest to the bottom of the trough. The wavelength is from the top of the crest to the top of the next crest.

MEASUREMENT OF A WAVE

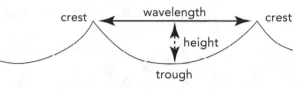

When waves approach shallow water near the shoreline, the bottom of the wave slows down as it rubs against the seafloor. The crest of the wave, however, continues at the same speed. The change in speed makes the crest curl farther and farther in front of the trough. Soon it breaks. Usually, the water then rushes back into the ocean, carrying sediments with it.

Lake to Land

Like rocks, lakes and ponds don't last forever. When a lake first forms, its water is clear and contains little living matter. Lake Tahoe is such a lake. Almost immediately, the lake begins to fill with microscopic organisms, seeds, and bits of decayed plants and animals. The increase in life forms may be very rapid. Soon larger animals, such as insects, fish, and birds, will inhabit the area. Inevitably, debris collects at the bottom of the lake. Buildup is slow but steady—perhaps no more than a foot in 100 years. Eventually, plants take root in the sediments and speed the formation of new soil within the area. Eventually, the lake fills in completely. How long a lake lasts depends on its size, water supply, and the local climate.

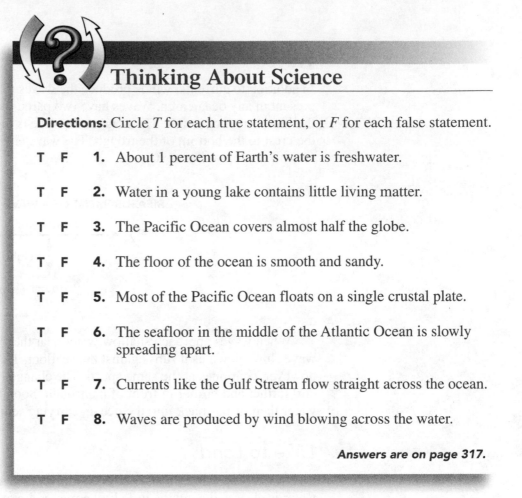

Thinking About Science

Directions: Circle *T* for each true statement, or *F* for each false statement.

T F **1.** About 1 percent of Earth's water is freshwater.

T F **2.** Water in a young lake contains little living matter.

T F **3.** The Pacific Ocean covers almost half the globe.

T F **4.** The floor of the ocean is smooth and sandy.

T F **5.** Most of the Pacific Ocean floats on a single crustal plate.

T F **6.** The seafloor in the middle of the Atlantic Ocean is slowly spreading apart.

T F **7.** Currents like the Gulf Stream flow straight across the ocean.

T F **8.** Waves are produced by wind blowing across the water.

Answers are on page 317.

PRE-GED PRACTICE

Directions: Choose the <u>one best answer</u> to each question.

Questions 1 and 2 refer to the information on pages 248–251.

1. Which of the following <u>cannot</u> be inferred about ocean surface currents?

(1) Surface currents stir up the waters below and help to shape the mountains on the ocean floor.
(2) Surface currents are caused by the wind moving across wide expanses of water.
(3) Winds exert a force on the ocean surface, setting the surface water in motion.
(4) Surface currents usually follow patterns similar to those of wind systems.
(5) Surface currents affect the climate of any land area they move past.

2. Where is most of the world's freshwater found?

(1) oceans
(2) ice
(3) lakes and rivers
(4) water table
(5) rivers

3. How is a wavelength measured?

(1) from the top of the crest to the bottom of the trough
(2) from the crest of one wave to the crest of the next
(3) from the crest of one wave to the trough of another
(4) from the middle of one wave to the middle of the next
(5) from one trough to the next

Answers are on page 317.

Earth's Atmosphere and Weather

Meteorology is the study of Earth's atmosphere and the changes in it that produce our weather. By analyzing data that have been collected from the atmosphere, meteorologists can predict weather conditions with a fair degree of accuracy.

Scientists think that at one time, almost all the gases in our **atmosphere**, the layer of air that surrounds Earth, were trapped inside Earth. Over billions of years, the main gases in our atmosphere—water vapor, carbon dioxide, nitrogen, and hydrogen—escaped when volcanoes erupted. The atmosphere that now surrounds Earth makes life possible. It supplies the air that we breathe and protects us from some of the Sun's rays. It also controls extremes in temperatures that would otherwise make life on Earth impossible.

The atmosphere is made up of five main layers: the troposphere, which extends up to about 7 miles from the ground; the stratosphere, which extends from about 7 miles to 31 miles from the ground; the mesosphere, which lies from about 31 miles to 50 miles above the ground; the thermosphere, which lies from about 150 miles to 370 miles from Earth's surface; and the exosphere, the top layer of the atmosphere. This layer sits from about 370 miles above Earth and extends into space.

The troposphere is the only layer in which living things can breathe normally. It's also the layer in which weather conditions occur. Airplane travel is limited to the troposphere.

The Nitrogen Cycle

Nitrogen is the most abundant gas in our atmosphere. Although humans need nitrogen to stay alive, the body cannot use the nitrogen that is inhaled with every breath. Animals can only get nitrogen from plants. Unfortunately, plants cannot make direct use of nitrogen either. They depend on bacteria in the soil to convert nitrogen into a substance that the roots can absorb. The nitrogen from the atmosphere reaches the soil only because it is washed into the ground with rain. As organisms decay, the nitrogen is released back into the atmosphere. This process is called the **nitrogen cycle**.

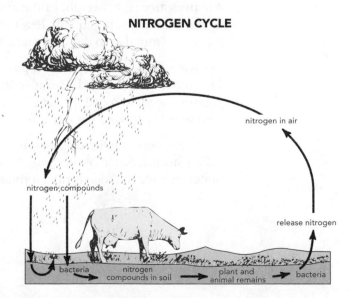

NITROGEN CYCLE

nitrogen in air

nitrogen compounds

release nitrogen

bacteria   nitrogen compounds in soil → plant and animal remains → bacteria

Other Gases in the Atmosphere

Oxygen, which all animals need to survive, and carbon dioxide, which plants use to make their food, are also abundant in the atmosphere. These gases—along with water—cycle through the atmosphere. In the atmosphere, these gases are in balance. The amount of each remains almost constant.

Moisture enters the atmosphere as water vapor, mainly through evaporation from the ocean. The more water vapor there is in the air, the higher the humidity. The amount of moisture air can hold depends on its temperature. Warm air can hold more moisture than can cold air. As moist air cools, the water vapor condenses, either in the form of clouds or as raindrops.

Scientists have noticed that in recent years, the amount of carbon dioxide in the atmosphere has increased slightly. Most think that burning fossil fuels, such as coal and oil, has upset the balance of gases in the atmosphere. No one knows for sure what the results of that imbalance will be.

The Greenhouse Effect

The heat in the atmosphere comes from the Sun. Some heat comes directly from the Sun in the form of rays. Some is indirect; it bounces back into the atmosphere from Earth. Our atmosphere traps the Sun's heat and prevents it from escaping into space. This is called the **greenhouse effect.** Without the greenhouse effect, our planet would freeze.

Not all radiation from the Sun is good for us. Some, such as ultraviolet radiation, can cause skin cancer. A type of oxygen in the Earth's atmosphere, called **ozone**, protects us from the Sun's ultraviolet radiation. The ozone layer is located in the stratosphere. Scientists have discovered that chemicals called CFCs (chlorofluorocarbons), used to propel the contents of aerosol spray cans, destroy ozone when CFCs escape into the atmosphere. Refrigerants, such as Freon, used in refrigerators and air conditioners, also are known to break down ozone. These products now are being replaced with hydrocarbons that do not destroy ozone.

Wind and Storms

Air pressure is the weight of the atmosphere as felt on Earth. Warm air is lighter than cool air and puts less pressure on Earth. Air pressure rarely stays the same from day to day and place to place.

Air moves from places of high air pressure to places of low air pressure. This moving air is **wind**. Because Earth is turning, the areas of high and low pressure seem to move. In the Northern Hemisphere, areas of high pressure tend to move toward the right, from west to east.

We experience the changes in atmosphere as weather. Violent changes are called storms. Some of the types of storms that we experience in the United States include thunderstorms, tornadoes, and hurricanes.

Thunderstorms

Thunderstorms start when moist air from Earth's surface rises. When it reaches a layer of cool dry air, it condenses into tiny droplets of water. With enough moisture, puffy, white clouds form.

As the moist air cools, it releases heat energy, causing a rapid updraft of air. More and more warm moist air is pulled up into the clouds. In just a few minutes, a puffy, white cloud may grow to cover several miles. Soon winds may flatten the top of the cloud into the familiar shape of a thunderstorm cloud.

Inside the cloud, water droplets slam into each other and combine. When they get big enough, they fall as rain. Hail may also form when tiny bits of dust and ice collide with water droplets that freeze. If the wind is strong enough to toss them about, the ice bits collect more and more ice. When they are too heavy for the wind's power, they fall.

If conditions are right for the growth of one thundercloud, chances are that several thunderclouds will be produced. Thunderclouds often form in irregular rows, called **squall lines**. Each squall lasts for 15–20 minutes, dies out, and is replaced by a new one.

When clouds are charged with electricity, lightning may leap from cloud to cloud, from cloud to ground, or from ground to cloud. A lightning bolt is five times hotter than the Sun's surface. As lightning moves through the air, the air instantly heats lightning and expands rapidly. The result is the crack or rumble of thunder. Because light travels so much faster than sound, you see the lightning before you hear the thunder.

Tornadoes

Sometimes the wind in a thunderstorm begins to spin faster and faster. A tornado may form. The funnel-shaped cloud may hop across the countryside, destroying everything in its path.

Tornadoes do strange things. After a tornado, you may see pieces of paper stuck through a tree trunk. In one case, a tornado sucked up the first floor of a house, dropping the second floor, unharmed, onto the foundation.

Like a giant vacuum cleaner, the funnel picks up dirt, dust, and debris. In about 15 minutes, the funnel becomes so choked with dirt that it slows and dies.

Hurricanes

Hurricanes are like huge tornadoes that can stretch over hundreds of miles. They kill more people each year than all other storms combined. Fortunately, they are not as unpredictable nor as common as tornadoes.

Hurricanes form over warm oceans in late summer. As the warm water evaporates from the ocean surface, a tremendous amount of heat energy is pumped up into the atmosphere. The result is a huge thunderstorm. If it begins to spin, a hurricane is born.

When a hurricane reaches land, the wind may be strong enough to pull a tree right out of the ground. It may also sweep the water near shore into a wall of water called a storm surge. When the surge hits the beach, the ground can be washed away. Boats may be sunk or carried miles inland.

Like a tornado, hurricane winds spin around a low-pressure center called the **eye of the storm**. In the eye, the wind is calm and the sky is blue and clear. The ring of low pressure at the center of the storm can be more than 185 miles across. Moments later, however, as the eye shrinks to about 30 miles across, the winds begin to swirl around it at hurricane force.

Forecasting is the key to saving lives during a hurricane. Meteorologists try to find out as much as they can about the hurricane's strength and movement. They can then try to plot where the hurricane will hit land. People in communities in the path of a hurricane are warned to evacuate.

Thinking About Science

Directions: Answer the questions below in the spaces provided.

1. The most abundant gas in our atmosphere is _____.

2. Some of the gases that cycle through our atmosphere are water vapor, nitrogen, oxygen, and _____.

3. Ozone protects us from _____ radiation from the Sun.

4. Without the greenhouse effect, Earth would _____.

5. Thunderstorms begin when moist air from Earth's surface

   _____.

6. Thunder is caused by _____.

7. Tornadoes die in about _____ minutes.

8. Hurricanes are born over _____ ocean water in late _____.

9. In the eye of a hurricane, winds are _____ and the sky is _____ .

10. Earth's atmosphere is made up of _____ layers.

Answers are on page 317.

Directions: Choose the <u>one best answer</u> to each question.

Questions 1–6 refer to the information on pages 253–256.

1. Where did the gases in our atmosphere come from?

   (1) outer space
   (2) volcanoes
   (3) evaporation
   (4) plants
   (5) the Sun

2. What are the most common gases in our atmosphere?

   (1) nitrogen, argon, and carbon dioxide
   (2) oxygen, carbon dioxide, and nitrogen
   (3) nitrogen, oxygen, and carbon monoxide
   (4) carbon monoxide, sulfur dioxide, and nitrogen
   (5) oxygen, carbon monoxide, and carbon dioxide

3. What causes wind?

   A. the spin of Earth
   B. differences in air pressure
   C. a rapid change in altitude

   (1) A only
   (2) B only
   (3) C only
   (4) both A and B
   (5) both B and C

4. When does hail form?

   (1) when bits of ice are too heavy for the wind's power
   (2) when bits of dust and ice collide with water droplets and freeze
   (3) when the water vapor in warm air freezes
   (4) when microbursts carry bits of ice to Earth's surface
   (5) when snow freezes

5. What must a thunderstorm do to form a tornado?

   (1) It must grow.
   (2) It must move.
   (3) It must spin.
   (4) It must cool.
   (5) It must rise.

6. Which of the following best explains why Earth's atmosphere does not float off into space?

   (1) air pressure
   (2) gravity
   (3) nitrogen cycle
   (4) friction
   (5) greenhouse effect

Answers are on page 317.

Earth Science Review

Directions: Choose the <u>one best answer</u> to each question.

Questions 1 and 2 refer to the following passage.

The strength of earthquakes is generally reported as a number on the Richter scale. The scale, named for the scientist who developed it, begins at 1. Each increase of one whole number means the earthquake's power has increased about 30 times.

The strongest quake ever recorded on the Richter scale was 8.9. That's about 12,000 times the energy released in an atom bomb. Two quakes share the 8.9 record. The first was in Ecuador in 1906; the second, near Japan in 1933. Both of these quakes occurred in sparsely populated areas and did not cause a major disaster. In contrast, a 1976 quake in China rated only an 8.0 but left most of the city of Tangshan in ruins. It also killed over a third of the population.

The strongest earthquake in the United States measured 8.4 on the Richter scale. It occurred near Prince William Sound in Alaska on Good Friday, 1964. The quake killed 131 paople. It created a giant wave 50 feet high that destroyed the town of Kodiak. Tremors of the Good Friday quake were felt in California, Hawaii, and Japan.

Another type of scale used to measure earthquakes is the modified Mercalli scale of earthquake intensity. On a scale of I (gentle tremor) to XII (total destruction), people's reactions to the earthquake rather than the strength of the tremor are measured.

A I is felt by birds, animals, and very few people. A IV would feel like the passing of a heavy truck. At level VII, people run outdoors and find it difficult to stand up. Damage, however, is slight. At IX, buildings shift off their foundations, and there is considerable damage and panic. At XI, bridges are destroyed and fissures show in the ground. At the worst, a XII, damage is total. Lines of sight are distorted, objects are thrown up into the air, and actual waves in the ground's surface can be seen.

1. On the Richter scale, each increase of one whole number means the earthquake's power has increased about how much?

   (1) 10 times
   (2) 20 times
   (3) 30 times
   (4) 40 times
   (5) 50 times

2. On the modified Mercalli scale, how would an earthquake that was strong enough to distort sight lines and to make actual waves in the ground's surface be rated?

   (1) II
   (2) IV
   (3) VIII
   (4) X
   (5) XII

Questions 3–5 refer to the following passage.

In about 5,000 B.C., and underwater landslide of about 430 miles of rock and mud created the world's largest wave. The wave, traveling at 110 miles per hour, was over 1,000 feet high when it hit the Shetland Islands. Throughout history, giant waves, known as *tsunamis*, have caused devastation along many coastal areas.

A tsunami can occur whenever there is a sudden change in the seafloor. Earthquakes or volcanoes are frequent causes. Most tsunamis seem to start close to the plate boundaries at the edges of the Pacific Ocean.

At sea, a tsunami might be less than a meter tall. From aboard ship, the wave might not even be noticed. The wavelength, however, may be greater than 200 km, and it may be traveling at 700 km per hour. As the wave approaches land, it slows down. Like passengers in a car crash, the water in the wave keeps going even when the wave "puts on the brakes." The rushing water pushes into itself, quickly building into a high wall.

If the trough of the tsunami reaches land first, water near the shore may suddenly rush out to sea. If the crest reaches land first, there will be a sudden increase in water level. The tsunami crest may be 50 meters high. It crashes against the land with enormous power.

Only minutes after the Good Friday, 1964, earthquake in Alaska, a tsunami ripped into the Alaskan coastline. Four hours later, the wave reached California, but although there was a great deal of property damage, no one was injured. An hour and a half later, the tsunami hit Hawaii and killed 159 people. Seventeen hours after the earthquake, the wave reached Australia. After 22 hours, it crashed into Antarctica.

Early warning systems now help save many lives that might otherwise be lost to tsunamis. However, many people cannot imagine a wave crossing the entire ocean. As a result, some wave warnings have been ignored. In Japan, many people were killed when local officials failed to pass on a wave warning. In Hawaii, 61 people ignored a wave warning and were killed.

3. When does a tsunami occur?

   (1) when there is a sudden change in the seafloor
   (2) when plate boundaries shift
   (3) whenever volcanoes erupt
   (4) when the Moon and Sun align
   (5) when the wind blows too hard

4. What action should you take if water near the shoreline suddenly rushes out to sea?

   (1) You should take the opportunity to explore the seafloor.
   (2) You should go immediately to high ground because a tsunami is likely.
   (3) You can ignore it because waves behave like that.
   (4) You should prepare for an earthquake.
   (5) You should get in a boat as quickly as possible.

5. Why do early warnings for tsunamis not always work?

   (1) The trough hits land first.
   (2) The crest hits land first.
   (3) People do not believe a wave can travel such distances.
   (4) The wave dies out before it reached land.
   (5) Once a wave begins, there is no time for a warning.

Questions 6–8 refer to the following passage.

Have you ever wished for a white Christmas or wished away a rainy day? People look for different kinds of precipitation—the water that falls from the sky.

Water moves back and forth between Earth's surface and atmosphere. Water evaporates into the air from oceans, rivers, and moist land. The amount of water vapor the air can hold depends on its temperature. Warm air can hold more water than cool air.

The water eventually falls back to Earth's surface. This precipitation happens when the air can't hold the water anymore. Sometimes warm, moist air rises and cools off. Or it may meet a mass of cold air. The cold air forces the warm air up, and the warm air cools off. The cooler air can't hold all the water. The water vapor turns into the water drops that make up clouds. If the water drops get too heavy, the water falls as precipitation.

Will the precipitation be rain, snow, sleet, or hail? That, too, depends on temperature. The following table shows which precipitation is likely to reach Earth's surface at a particular temperature.

Temperature of Clouds	Temperature at Ground	Precipitation
below 32°F	up to 37°F	snow
below 32°F	37°F–39°F	sleet
below 32°F	above 39°F	hail
any temp.	above 39°F	rain

6. One day the temperature in the clouds is 30°F. Yet on the ground it's 33°F. If precipitation falls, what kind will it probably be?

   (1) sleet
   (2) snow
   (3) rain
   (4) hail
   (5) none of the above

7. Which of the following is the correct order of the events that lead to precipitation?

   (1) water vapor turns to drops and forms clouds; water evaporates into warm air; warm air cools; moist, warm air rises; water vapor becomes too heavy for air to hold; precipitation falls
   (2) water evaporates into warm air; warm air cools; water vapor turns to drops and forms clouds; warm, moist air rises; water vapor becomes too heavy for air to hold; precipitation falls
   (3) water vapor becomes too heavy for air to hold; water evaporates into warm air; warm, moist air rises; water vapor turns to drops and forms clouds; precipitation falls; warm air cools
   (4) water evaporates into warm air; warm, moist air rises; warm air cools; water vapor becomes too heavy for air to hold; water vapor turns to drops and forms clouds; precipitation falls
   (5) none of the above

8. In a summer thunderstorm, hailstones fall. The air at the ground is 75°F. How is it possible for the precipitation to be balls of ice on such a warm day?

   (1) A mass of cold air passed through as rain was falling.
   (2) The warm air rose above the cloud that caused the storm.
   (3) The clouds broke apart and fell to the ground as hail.
   (4) The air at the ground cooled off rapidly.
   (5) The temperature in the sky was below freezing.

   Answers are on page 317.

READING EFFICIENCY I

Directions: This activity will help you to improve your reading efficiency. Before you start to read, write the present time at the top of the page. When you have completed the reading and all 5 questions, write your finishing time. Subtract to find out how long you took. Score your answers. Then turn to pages 320–321 to find your E-Factor and to graph your progress.

Finishing Time	
Starting Time −	
Reading Time =	
Number of Answers Correct	

Groundwater

When rain falls and snow melts, some of the water filters through the soil. The water settles into pores and cracks of underground rock and between particles of sand and gravel. This water is called groundwater. Groundwater is the source of water for wells and springs. About 20 percent of the freshwater used in the United States comes from groundwater. It supplies the freshwater needs for people, livestock, crops, and industry.

As groundwater flows through rocks and soil, some impurities in the water are removed. Sometimes the groundwater is clean enough to use without any treatment. In other places the water must be treated to remove harmful materials.

More and more, harmful substances are getting into the soil. As water seeps through the soil, it picks up the harmful materials from these sources. Removing these materials from water to make it useable costs money.

Another problem is the amount of groundwater. The level of groundwater is called the water table. When more water is taken from the ground than can be replaced naturally, the water table drops. Many regions of the world are using more groundwater than can be replaced. In some of those places, water from other areas can be used to replace water lost from the water table.

A drop in the water table in coastal areas can be a special problem. When this happens, saltwater from the ocean enters the supply of groundwater. The salt must be removed from the water before it is useable.

READING EFFICIENCY I

1. Which of the following would <u>not</u> be a source of groundwater?

   (1) rain
   (2) snow
   (3) lightning
   (4) hail
   (5) lake

2. Which is <u>not</u> a reason why clean groundwater is important?

   (1) Groundwater supplies 20 percent of the freshwater in the United States.
   (2) As groundwater flows through soil, it picks up harmful materials.
   (3) Groundwater is used for growing crops.
   (4) Groundwater is used in industry.
   (5) Treating groundwater to remove impurities is expensive.

3. Which type of precipitation most likely would be best for replacing groundwater?

   (1) very heavy rainfall that lasts about 30 minutes
   (2) light rain for 30 minutes followed by sunshine
   (3) light rain that lasts about an hour
   (4) light rain that lasts about a day
   (5) short bursts of very heavy rain over a period of a day

4. Which of the following events most likely would not affect the quality of groundwater in an area?

   (1) An underground gasoline tank at a gas station develops a very slow leak.
   (2) A tree nursery sprays pesticide on its apple trees.
   (3) A large area of land has been opened as a dump.
   (4) A town decides to build a large park on a piece of former farm property.
   (5) An owner of a large farm uses chemical fertilizers to grow his crops.

5. Suppose you considered buying a home whose water source is a well. Which of the following factors would <u>not</u> be relevant to your decision whether to buy the house?

   (1) The house sits near an empty field that used to be a garbage dump.
   (2) A farm is located across the street.
   (3) The homes in the area use septic systems.
   (4) The soil in the area is naturally fertile.
   (5) The home is located about a mile from the ocean.

   Answers are on pages 317–318.

READING EFFICIENCY J

Directions: This activity will help you to improve your reading efficiency. Before you start to read, write the present time at the top of the page. When you have completed the reading and all 5 questions, write your finishing time. Subtract to find out how long you took. Score your answers. Then turn to pages 320–321 to find your E-Factor and to graph your progress.

Finishing Time	
Starting Time –	
Reading Time =	
Number of Answers Correct	

Wind Power

As the price of producing electricity becomes more costly, people look for cheaper energy sources. One form that is being used is wind power. People have been using wind power for centuries—to sail ships, pumpt water, and make electricity. One method of using wind power today is a windmill. If you ever blew on a pinwheel, you have used wind power to move the pinwheel.

Modern windmills are called wind turbines. One type of wind turbine is made of a propeller blade attached to the top of a high tower. The propeller must be moved around so that it points to the wind. A second type of wind turbine looks like an eggbeater. This type of turbine does not have to face the wind. In both types, the large blades run a generator to produce electricity. Wind speed and the size of the blades determine the amount of energy produced.

Places where the wind has a steady, constant speed are the best locations for wind turbines. In the United States, these locations included the Great Plains and the east and west coasts. In some windy areas, many wind turbines are clustered together in wind farms. Families can use single wind turbines as an alternate energy source for their homes.

1. What is the source of power in a wind turbine?

    (1) electricity
    (2) wind
    (3) water
    (4) blade
    (5) windmill

2. Which conditions describe a wind turbine that would produce the most energy?

    (1) small blades, strong steady winds
    (2) large blades, strong steady winds
    (3) large blades, winds that start and stop
    (4) large blades, light winds
    (5) small blades, light winds

3. Which of the following statements lists a disadvantage of wind turbines?

    (1) In order for wind turbines to operate properly, wind speed must be between 16 and 40 kilometers per hour.
    (2) Wind is a renewable energy resource.
    (3) Operating wind turbines is inexpensive.
    (4) The land surrounding wind turbines can be used for farming.
    (5) The size of the blades determines the amount of energy produced.

4. Why would using a wind turbine as the only source of energy <u>not</u> be a good idea?

    (1) Wind turbines are a renewable energy resource.
    (2) Wind turbines must be very large to operate properly.
    (3) Operating wind turbines is inexpensive.
    (4) Wind turbines depend on strong, steady winds.
    (5) Crops can be planted around wind turbines.

5. If you were considering a wind turbine as an energy source for your home, which of the following would <u>not</u> be important to know?

    (1) how the cost of using the wind turbine compares with the cost of electricity
    (2) how strong winds in your area generally blow
    (3) how constant winds in your area generally blow
    (4) the amount of sunshine in your area
    (5) how much noise the turbine makes

Answers are on page 318.

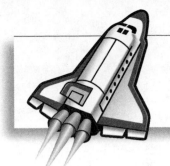

CHAPTER 9

Space Science

People have always gazed into the skies with a sense of wonder, astonished by the vastness of space. **Astronomy**, the oldest science, is the study of the movement and composition of the Sun, Moon, planets, and stars in space.

Astronomers are scientists who study these celestial bodies. Through their study, astronomers hope to learn more about the creation and the evolution of the universe. Some astronomers believe that the universe may be 10 to 20 billion years old. Astronomers have developed many theories to explain how the universe came into existence. One widely accepted idea is called the **big bang theory**. This idea suggests that the entire universe began as a single, densely packed particle. The particle exploded, spewing all matter—stars, planets, and gas—into space. Researchers have found enough evidence of the big bang that most scientists now agree with a version of this theory.

There is less agreement on what will eventually happen to the universe. Some astronomers think the universe will keep expanding forever. This is called the **open universe theory**.

Other astronomers believe that when the universe was created, it was pretty much the same composition throughout. However, as the universe expanded, the matter inside it became compressed. Gravity brought more and more matter together, leaving areas of empty space in between. These regions of matter ultimately gave birth to stars and galaxies, such as the Milky Way. These astronomers think that the force of gravity will eventually cause the universe to collapse upon itself, until it once again forms a tiny, incredibly dense particle. In that case, the big bang may start all over again. This is called the **closed universe theory**.

Still other astronomers believe that the universe will continue to expand until some future time when it reaches a size and stays at that size. This is called the **flat universe theory**.

Many different types of scientists are involved in the continued technological development of space vehicles, space stations, and Earth-orbiting telescopes. Such technological advancements will assist astronomers in their studies and lead to a better understanding of the movement, composition, and origin of our universe and the world beyond.

The Milky Way Galaxy

A **galaxy** is a large group of stars. Almost everthing you can see in the night sky (without a telescope) is part of the Milky Way galaxy. Our home in the universe is the Milky Way galaxy. It contains the Sun and about 200 billion other stars shaped into a giant spiral. The Milky Way is so large that it would take approximately 100,000 light-years to cross it. (A **light-year** is the distance that light travels in one year, about 6 trillion miles.) Scientists think that the center of our galaxy may be a star that is thousands of times more massive than our Sun.

Earth is only one tiny part of the Milky Way galaxy. In his science fiction book, *A Hitchhiker's Guide to the Galaxy,* Douglas Adams describes our location in this galaxy:

> Far out in the uncharted backwaters of the unfashionable end of the Western spiral arm of the Galaxy lies a small unregarded yellow Sun. Orbiting this at a distance of roughly ninety-eight million miles is an utterly insignificant little blue-green planet whose ape-descended life-forms are so amazingly primitive that they still think digital watches are a pretty neat idea.

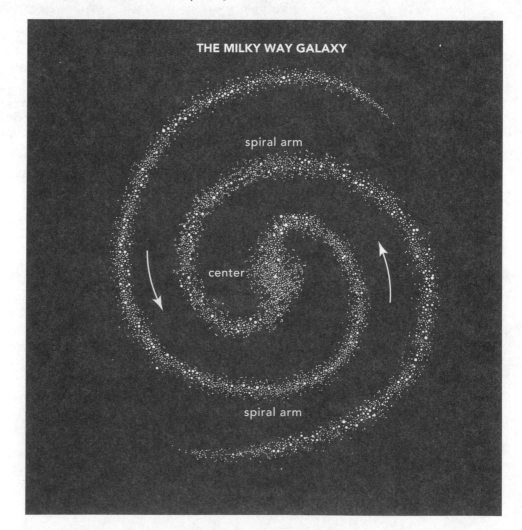

THE MILKY WAY GALAXY

spiral arm

center

spiral arm

Thinking About Science

Directions: Complete each sentence below by filling in the blanks.

1. Most scientists agree that the beginning of the universe is best described by the _____ theory.

2. The _____ theory states that the universe is collapsing and that eventually another big bang will occur.

3. The _____ theory states that the universe will continue to expand.

4. A _____ is a large group of billions of stars.

5. The Milky Way galaxy contains approximately _____ stars and is about _____ light-years across.

Answers are on page 318.

PRE-GED PRACTICE

Directions: Choose the one best answer to each question.

Questions 1 and 2 refer to the information on pages 265 and 266.

1. Which of the following can you infer from the illustration of the Milky Way on page 265?

   A. The Milky Way is one of millions of galaxies.
   B. The Milky Way is spiral shaped.
   C. All of the objects in the Milky Way revolve around the center.
   D. Spiral galaxies have arms.

   (1) A and B only
   (2) A, B, and C only
   (3) A, B, and D only
   (4) A, C, and D only
   (5) B, C, and D only

2. What is the "blue-green planet" mentioned in Douglas Adams's description?

   (1) the Sun
   (2) Jupiter
   (3) Saturn
   (4) Earth
   (5) Venus

   Answers are on page 318.

The Solar System

The **solar system** consists of the Sun, nine planets, many moons, and smaller bodies such as asteroids and comets. At the center of our solar system is the Sun. The huge mass of the Sun—and the gravity produced by that mass—keeps all the objects in the solar system orbiting the Sun. The nine planets revolve around the Sun in a regular and predictable motion. It is due to this regular motion that we experience such events as days, years, phases of the Moon, and eclipses. The Sun also is the major source of energy that creates Earth's winds, seasons, and ocean currents.

OUR SOLAR SYSTEM

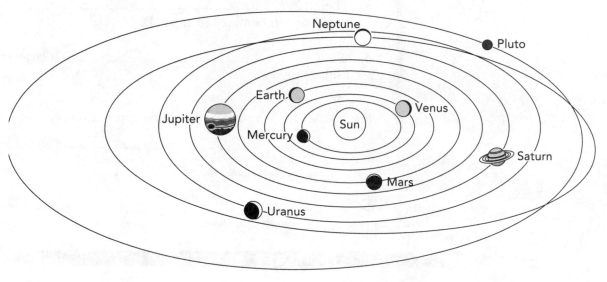

The Sun is a star, a huge ball of a gas-like substance that radiates heat and light. Although a million Earths could fit into the Sun, the Sun is only about one-fourth as dense as Earth.

At the center of the Sun, temperatures are believed to be about 15 million°C. It is in this core that hydrogen fuses into helium and the other elements in nuclear fusion reactions. The energy produced during these reactions radiates out of the core in such forms as light energy and heat energy.

The Planets

The planets shine only when they reflect light from the Sun. Most of these planets have their own satellites, or moons, orbiting them like miniature solar systems. The planets that are closest to the Sun are similar in size and in chemical makeup. Mercury—the planet closest to the Sun—together with Venus, Earth, and Mars are called the inner planets. Jupiter, Saturn, Uranus, Neptune, and Pluto—the planet farthest from the Sun—are called the outer planets.

Between the inner planets and the outer planets is a belt of rocky objects called **asteroids**. Like the planets, asteroids orbit the Sun. No one knows the origin of these asteroids, but many astronomers think they are the remains of a planet that was destroyed.

Four of the outer planets, Jupiter, Saturn, Uranus, and Neptune, are also the largest planets. These planets are the cold giants of the solar system. Most scientists agree that the cold giants have small, solid rock cores. The cores are surrounded by thick layers of liquid and gas. Each of the cold giants also has one or more moons. Jupiter has several planet-size moons. Saturn has moons and huge, bright rings. Uranus has a few moons and several small rings. Neptune has two moons.

The planet on the outer edge of our solar system is Pluto. Very little is known about Pluto except that its tilt is not the same as the other planets. Pluto also has an odd orbit that sometimes brings it closer to the Sun than is its nearest neighbor, Neptune. Some scientists think that Pluto may have been a moon that broke away from its orbit.

Comets are small objects made of dust and frozen gas that orbit the Sun. Comets look like fuzzy stars, consisting of a head and a long tail that extends far into space. Periodically seen from Earth, comets become visible only when they are near the Sun and the tail reflects sunlight. Halley's comet is one of the most famous comets. It becomes visible every 76 years. The very first recorded sighting of Halley's comet was in 240 B.C., when Chinese astronomers reported seeing a "broom star."

? Thinking About Science

Directions: Answer the questions below in the space provided.

1. The force that holds the planets in orbit around the Sun is

   _____ .

2. Our solar system consists of _____ planets.

3. The four planets closest to the Sun are called the

   _____ .

4. The five planets farthest from the Sun are called the

   _____ .

5. _____ and _____
   are smaller objects in space that orbit the Sun.

   Answers are on page 318.

PRE-GED PRACTICE

Directions: Choose the <u>one best answer</u> to each question.

Questions 1 and 2 refer to the information on pages 268–269.

1. What can you infer about the planets known as the cold giants?

   (1) They are eight times larger than the other five planets in our solar system.
   (2) They are cold because their great distance from the Sun and any heat radiating from it.
   (3) The other five planets are known as the hot dwarfs.
   (4) Their cores are hot liquid and gas.
   (5) The moons of each planet look like Earth's Moon.

2. Which of the following can you infer about objects in our solar system?

   (1) Pluto is the largest of the outer planets in the solar system.
   (2) Nuclear reactions are rare events that occur at the center of the Sun.
   (3) All nine of the planets shine all of the time.
   (4) Pluto and Neptune are likely to crash into each other in the future.
   (5) Comets move through our solar system in regular and predictable orbits.

   Answers are on page 318.

The Planet Earth

Earth is the third planet in the solar system. Every 24 hours, Earth rotates, or turns on its axis. The Sun shines on only half of Earth at a time. As each point on Earth turns toward the Sun, it begins its day. As each point turns away, it begins its night.

Earth makes one revolution around the Sun each year, moving at a speed of about 67,000 miles per hour. As it revolves, part of Earth tilts toward or away from the Sun, as shown in the illustration. It is this tilt that produces the seasons.

Winter occurs in the Northern Hemisphere when the northern half of Earth is tilted away from the Sun. The tilt makes the Sun's rays less direct. The Northern Hemisphere has summer when that hemisphere is tilted toward the Sun. The Sun's rays are then more direct.

TILT OF EARTH'S AXIS

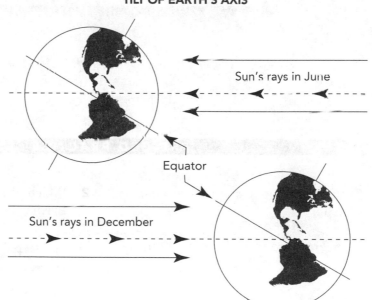

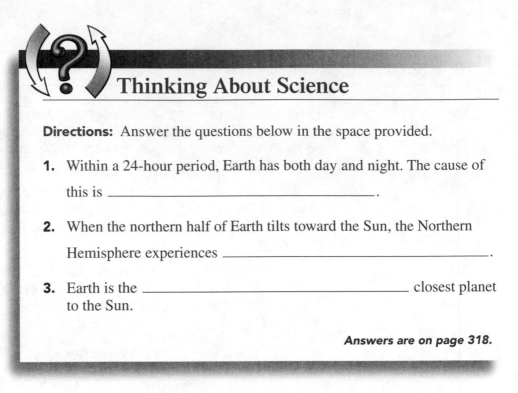

Thinking About Science

Directions: Answer the questions below in the space provided.

1. Within a 24-hour period, Earth has both day and night. The cause of this is _____.

2. When the northern half of Earth tilts toward the Sun, the Northern Hemisphere experiences _____.

3. Earth is the _____ closest planet to the Sun.

Answers are on page 318.

PRE-GED PRACTICE

Directions: Choose the <u>one best answer</u> to each question.

Questions 1 and 2 refer to the information on page 271.

1. Which of the following can you infer from the information about Earth's rotation?

   (1) When the Sun is setting in New York, it has already set in Los Angeles.
   (2) When the Sun is rising is New York, it has already risen in Chicago.
   (3) When the Sun is setting in Chicago, it has already set in New York.
   (4) When the Sun is rising in Chicago, it is setting in New York.
   (5) When the Sun is setting in Los Angeles, it is rising in Chicago.

2. Which of the following statements about Earth is false?

   (1) Earth makes one rotation each year.
   (2) Earth's rotation cause day and night.
   (3) The curved path or orbit of Earth around the Sun is called a revolution.
   (4) Seasons are caused by the tilt of Earth on its axis.
   (5) When a part of Earth is tilted toward the Sun, that part receives more direct rays from the Sun and experiences summer.

Answers are on page 318.

The Moon

The Moon is our closest neighbor in space. It's a dusty, rocky ball with no water and no atmosphere. The Moon's surface is spotted with huge craters produced when asteroids hit the surface. The dark areas that are sometimes called "seas" are really vast plains of hardened lava. Because the Moon has no water and no air, it also has no erosion. The Moon looks now just the way it did billions of years ago.

The Moon has no internal energy and does not really shine. It only reflects light from the Sun. The position of Earth, the Moon, and the Sun determine what the Moon looks like from Earth. These different appearances are called the **phases of the moon**.

When the Moon is between Earth and the Sun, we see no reflected light. This phase is called a new moon—even though the Moon is not visible. When the Earth is between the Moon and the Sun, the Moon is completely lighted. We say the Moon is full. Crescent moons are formed when a sliver of the Moon is lighted and the rest is dark. Gibbous moons occur when most but not all of the Moon is reflecting light.

PHASES OF THE MOON AS SEEN FROM EARTH

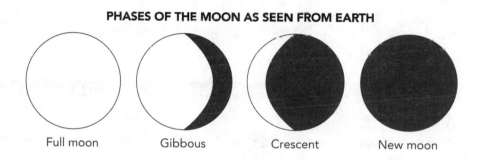

| Full moon | Gibbous | Crescent | New moon |

During a full moon, Earth is between the Sun and the Moon. In that position, Earth's shadow may sometimes cover the Moon. This event is called a lunar eclipse. Because Earth's shadow is so large, a lunar eclipse may be visible for more than an hour.

Tides

As between all other objects, Earth's gravity pulls on the Moon and the Moon's gravity pulls on Earth. The force of Earth's gravity on the Moon is strong enough to keep the Moon in orbit. The force of the Moon's gravity is strong enough to pull Earth toward it just a bit. Water, however, moves more than solid land does. The result is tides.

When the Moon is on one side of Earth, water bulges out toward the Moon. It is high tide. High tide also forms on the far side of Earth because Earth is pulled toward the Moon more than is the water on that side. Those areas of Earth that are at right angles to the Moon experience low tides. As Earth rotates and the Moon orbits, the areas of high and low tide change.

Thinking About Science

Directions: Answer the questions below in the space provided.

1. The craters that form the "Man in the Moon" were caused by

   _____.

2. We are able to see the Moon only when it

   _____ light from the Sun.

3. The phase of the Moon when we cannot see it at all is called

   _____.

4. Earth's tides are caused by the force of the _____.

Answers are on page 318.

PRE-GED PRACTICE

Directions: Choose the <u>one best answer</u> to each question.

Questions 1 and 2 refer to the information on page 273.

1. Which of the following best explains the statement "The Moon has no internal energy and does not really shine"?

   (1) The Moon has no gravity.
   (2) Only objects with internal energy can shine.
   (3) The Moon has external energy that makes it shine.
   (4) The Moon is not composed of gas-like substances that radiate heat and light.
   (5) The Moon that we see from Earth is an optical illusion.

2. When can a lunar eclipse occur?

   (1) anytime the Moon passes between Earth and the Sun
   (2) only during a full moon
   (3) at the same time a new moon occurs
   (4) when the tides on Earth are low
   (5) when a sliver of the Moon is lighted and the rest is dark

Answers are on page 318.

Studying the Universe

Until the first manned lunar landing, humans were not able to closely examine any other object in the universe. Astronomers' only tool was vision. Until recently, advances in astronomy have been closely tied to advances in telescopes.

Optical telescopes help astronomers to see distant objects more clearly. The goal of these telescopes is not to make objects appear closer. Instead, the aim is to increase the amount of light collected by the telescpe, to bring the light into focus and to produce an image. By examining the different colors of light from an object in space, astronomers learn what the objcct is made of and how hot it is.

In addition to studying the visible light from objects in space, astronomers also study the other types of radiation given off by celestial objects. This radiation includes everything from ultraviolet light and X rays to infrared and radio waves. By studying a variety of radiation, astronomers have vastly increased our understanding of the universe.

Distance in Space

Because objects in space are so far away, astronomers use the speed of light to measure distance. Light travels at about 186,000 miles per second. That's about a million times faster than a jet. Light from the Moon reaches us in about a second. Light from the Sun takes almost eight minutes. The distance to stars and other galaxies is measured in light-years—the distance light travels in one year. Each light-year is about 6 trillion miles.

Space Travel

People have always dreamed of traveling through space. In recent years, the dream has become reality. Research spacecraft have repeatedly landed on the Moon. They have touched down on Mars and entered the swirling mass of Venus's atmosphere. They have passed within camera range of the giant planets and given us a glimpse of Pluto. One spacecraft is even hurtling through the empty space outside our solar system. This spacecraft contains greetings from Earth.

In time, people may indeed travel through space with the help of spacecraft like the shuttle. However, at this time it is not even remotely possible for any human to visit another star system. The distances are simply too great. The nearest star, named Proxima Centauri, is about 26 trillion miles away. The only galaxy (other than ours) that can be seen without a telescope is about 1.5 million light-years away from us.

Thinking About Science

Directions: Answer the questions below in the space provided.

1. The historical event that first allowed humans to inspect an object in space up close was the first _____.

2. Optical telescopes use _____ to form an image.

3. Astronomers use the _____ to measure distance in space.

Answers are on page 318.

PRE-GED PRACTICE

Directions: Choose the <u>one best answer</u> to each question.

Questions 1 and 2 refer to the information on page 275.

1. Which of the following is <u>not</u> true about optical telescopes?

   (1) Optical telescopes increase the amount of light.
   (2) Optical telescopes produce an image.
   (3) Optical telescopes help astronomers to see distant objects.
   (4) Optical telescopes make objects in space appear closer.
   (5) Optical telescopes bring an image into focus.

2. Which of the following can be inferred from the information on space travel?

   (1) Space travel will become a tourist attraction within five years.
   (2) A manned spacecraft will soon land on Mars.
   (3) Proxima Centauri is the brightest star in our solar system.
   (4) Our galaxy in the only one in our solar system.
   (5) Some astronomers are trying to communicate with intelligent life outside our solar system.

   Answers are on page 318.

Space Science Review

Directions: Choose the <u>one best answer</u> to each question.

Question 1 is based on the following passage.

From *War of the Worlds* to *Star Trek*, science fiction writers suggest that there may be intelligent life on other planets. Reports of UFOs (unidentified flying objects) lend excitement to the common belief that Earth is routinely visited by creatures from outer space. Although no one has offered a reasonable explanation for how space creatures could get here, millions of people remain convinced that UFOs may be of extraterrestrial origin. Of course, at one time, millions of people were also firmly convinced that the deep channels on Mars were canals made by Martians.

Although few scientists take UFOs seriously, many take the question of whether life may exist in outer space very seriously. Just in case there are intelligent beings trying to communicate through outer space, scientists listen in on the universe's radio waves. Advanced radio telescopes, continuously monitored by computers, allow scientists to listen to about 130,000 radio channels simultaneously. Maybe someday they will pick up a message from an "ET" phoning home.

1. Why do scientists listen to radio waves from outer space?

(1) to keep track of UFOs
(2) to listen for signs of intelligent life forms from outer space
(3) to record information about Martians
(4) to keep track of our satellites
(5) all of the above

Question 2 refers to the following passage.

The temperature of the surface of Venus is 475°C. The weight of its atmosphere is one hundred times greater than that of Earth. Venus is covered with dense clouds of sulfuric acid that make its surface invisible to scientists on Earth. Carbon dioxide and other gases in Venus's atmosphere trap sunlight. This "greenhouse effect" makes the planet's surface extremely hot.

2. Which of the following statements best describes Venus?

A. Though hidden from view, Venus has many features similar to Earth
B. Trapped sunlight spreads over the surface of Venus.
C. Because of its dense atmosphere and heavy cloud cover, Venus is hot.

(1) A only
(2) B only
(3) C only
(4) B and C only
(5) A, B, and C

Question 3 refers to the following information.

A news article reporting the discovery of a galaxy gives the following information: the galaxy is about 12 billion light-years—the distance a light ray travels in a year—from Earth. Analysis of the light from this galaxy reveals that it is composed mainly of hydrogen gas and a few young stars.

3. A person who knows very little about astronomy reads this article and thinks that the galaxy is actually forming today. Which of the following statements helps explain that he does not fully understand the report?

   (1) Analysis of light from a long distance is not a reliable technique.
   (2) The new galaxy can be seen using only very powerful optical telescopes.
   (3) The galaxy formed 12 billion years ago, and its light is only now reaching Earth.
   (4) Stars are formed primarily from hydrogen gas.
   (5) Most galaxies formed billions of years ago.

Questions 4 and 5 refer to the passage below.

Sunspots are dark, relatively cool (4,500°C) areas on the Sun's surface that are regions of intense magnetic activity. The number of sunspots increases and decreases at fairly regular intervals. Whenever the number of sunspots is highest, solar flares erupt on the sun's surface and shoot out particles and radiation that can reach Earth's atmosphere and interfere with radio transmissions and electrical power.

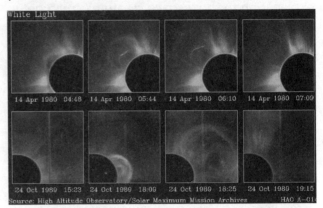

4. What happens when solar flares erupt on the surface of the Sun?

   (1) The number of sunspots decreases.
   (2) Solar matter and radiation are sent into space.
   (3) Sunspots become cooler and smaller.
   (4) The Sun becomes even hotter than normal.
   (5) The Sun loses some of its magnetism.

5. According to the passage, when are radio broadcasts likely to be interrupted by static?

   (1) when sunspots become cool
   (2) when the sunspot cycle is at its highest
   (3) when magnetic activity on the Sun decreases
   (4) when flares explode on Earth
   (5) when the Sun darkens

Questions 6 and 7 refer to the following passage and graph.

A meteor is usually a small rock from space that enters Earth's atmosphere and burns up, causing a bright streak of light across the sky. The graph shows the number of meteors a group of amateur astronomers observed during one night.

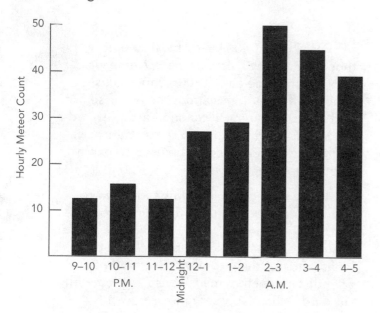

6. Which of the following statements best summarizes the information in the graph?

(1) Many more meteors were sighted during the hours after midnight.
(2) Midnight to 1:00 A.M. is the peak hour for sighting meteors.
(3) Fewer than 50 meteors were sighted each hour.
(4) The number of meteors varies greatly from hour to hour.
(5) No pattern is apparent in the number of meteors that can be sighted in a single evening.

7. An amateur astronomer counts meteors each night during mid-August when the Perseid Meteor Shower is known to occur each year. She then sends all her data to the American Meteor Society. Several of her reasons for doing this are listed below. Which of the following statements indicates that values are involved in her hobby?

(1) The origin of a meteor shower can be determined most accurately if it is observed from several different locations on Earth.
(2) When data gathered by amateurs at many different places are put together, facts not apparent to an individual observer can be determined.
(3) An experienced amateur can determine the peak time of shower activity.
(4) An amateur's reward is knowing that he or she has made a useful contribution to science.
(5) The hourly counts of meteors observed by amateurs indicates the density of the meteor cloud.

8. Gravity is a force that exists between all objects in the universe. It is measured as the force of attraction between objects. When two objects approach each other, their gravity affects their motion. The more mass an object has, the greater its attraction.

If a planet in our solar system did not follow a predicted orbit around the Sun, which of the following explanations could account for this?

(1) The planet is larger than expected.
(2) An unknown object is passing close to it.
(3) The force of gravity is not strong enough to hold the planet in orbit.
(4) The planet is moving quickly away from the Sun.
(5) The planet has no moons.

Answers are on page 319.

READING EFFICIENCY K

Directions: This activity will help you to improve your reading efficiency. Before you start to read, write the present time at the top of the page. When you have completed the reading and all 5 questions, write your finishing time. Subtract to find out how long you took. Score your answers. Then turn to pages 320–321 to find your E-Factor and to graph your progress.

Finishing Time	
Starting Time	−
Reading Time	=
Number of Answers Correct	

Models of the Universe

People have been studying the universe for thousands of years. But most of the tools that scientists use to study the universe today are less than 100 years old. Computers have been a big help to scientists studying the universe. How did people gather information about the sky without these tools? They used their eyes and what they already knew.

Ptolemy was one of the greatest astronomers of ancient times. He lived in the second century A.D. He thought that the universe was made up of the solar system and about 1,000 stars. In Ptolemy's universe, Earth was at the center of everything. The Sun, planets, and stars orbited it. Like others of the time, Ptolemy thought that he sky hung just above Earth. Four mountains at the corners of the world held up the sky.

For almost 1,400 years, most people thought Ptolemy's view of the universe was right. Then in the early 1500s Copernicus developed other ideas about the universe. He said that the planets, including Earth, orbited the Sun. Earth, he said, also spins on its axis. This motion of Earth could be used to explain what people see in the sky.

Today seeing how Ptolemy's ideas were wrong is easy. But he used the same processes that modern scientists use. He made observations, gathered information, tested ideas, and put them together. He made a scientific model that made sense at the time. His model changed over time as new information was discovered. The model of the universe that we have today is very different from Ptolemy's model. It does share many of the basic ideas of Copernicus. But the current model is changing too as new facts as learned.

1. According to the passage, which of the following statements is true?

   (1) People have been studying the universe for only the last 100 years.
   (2) Today's model of the universe is not at all like that of Copernicus.
   (3) Today's model of the universe will not change.
   (4) People didn't believe Ptolemy's ideas for very long.
   (5) Scientists use observation to make models.

2. Which part of Copernicus's model of the universe is the same as Ptolemy's model?

   (1) Earth orbits the Sun.
   (2) The universe has planets, a Sun, and stars.
   (3) Earth revolves on its axis.
   (4) The spinning of Earth on its axis can be used to explain what we see in the sky.
   (5) The Sun is the center of the universe.

3. Which of the following is <u>not</u> something Ptolemy used to make his model?

   (1) observation
   (2) reason
   (3) knowledge
   (4) computers
   (5) ideas of others

4. According to the passage, which statement below would <u>not</u> be true about a scientific model?

   (1) A new model must be very different than an old model.
   (2) A model uses the information that scientists know at the time.
   (3) A model can change with new information.
   (4) A good model makes sense at the time.
   (5) A model puts many ideas together to explain something.

5. Which of the following would be important in deciding if a model is right?

   (1) Others disagree with the model.
   (2) The model is different than other models.
   (3) The model uses ideas from several scientists.
   (4) Scientists continue to test the model.
   (5) New observations can be explained using the model.

Answers are on page 319.

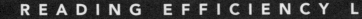

READING EFFICIENCY L

Directions: This activity will help you to improve your reading efficiency. Before you start to read, write the present time at the top of the page. When you have completed the reading and all 5 questions, write your finishing time. Subtract to find out how long you took. Score your answers. Then turn to pages 320–321 to find your E-Factor and to graph your progress.

Finishing Time	
Starting Time −	
Reading Time =	
Number of Answers Correct	

The Sun's Light

The Sun is much larger than the other objects in the solar system. In fact, it makes up more than 99 percent of all the mass in the solar system. About a million Earths could fit into the Sun. The Sun's great mass produces a very strong force of gravity. This gravity keeps the planets, moons, and millions of smaller objects made of rock and ice circling the Sun.

The Sun has been shining on Earth for about 4.6 billion years. The Sun is a very hot ball of gas that gives off energy. Scientists think that the temperature in the center of the Sun is about 15 million °C. Where does all this heat come from? In the center of the Sun, hydrogen nuclei join together to form larger nuclei with more mass. During the process, which is called fusion, a lot of energy is given off. The energy produced in the center of the Sun takes millions of years to reach the Sun's surface. Once the energy leaves the Sun as light, it takes only a little more than 8 minutes to reach Earth.

Earth and eight other plants circle around the Sun. From Earth, the other planets might seem to give off light too. But the light you see coming from the planets is reflected light. The light comes from the Sun, hits the planets, and then bounces off.

Some of the light from the Sun is absorbed by the planets. The absorbed sunlight heats the planets. The distance of a planet from the Sun affects the planets surface temperature. Mercury, the closest planet to the Sun, has a temperature above 400°C. By contrast, Pluto is 40 times as far from the Sun as Earth is. Its temperature is -236°C.

READING EFFICIENCY L

1. What is the source of heat in the Sun?

   (1) its mass
   (2) its temperature
   (3) fusion
   (4) gas
   (5) the planets

2. When was the energy that reaches Earth now produced in the Sun?

   (1) millions of years ago
   (2) 8 minutes ago
   (3) billions of years ago
   (4) 4.6 billion years ago
   (5) 8 million years ago

3. What is the reason that Earth's gravity is not as strong as that of the Sun?

   (1) Earth is cooler from the Sun.
   (2) Earth has less mass than the Sun.
   (3) Earth orbits the Sun.
   (4) Earth absorbs energy from the Sun.
   (5) Earth is younger than the Sun.

4. Some of the planets have moons. What causes the moons of the planets to stay in an orbit around them?

   (1) the mass of the moon
   (2) the gravity of the planets
   (3) the Sun's mass
   (4) fusion
   (5) the planet's temperature

5. Suppose you wanted to do an experiment to test how distance from a source of light affects temperature. You plan to place several objects at different distances from a source of light. You will take the temperature of each object at regular intervals. Which of the following would be an important part of the experiment?

   (1) The objects should all be the same size..
   (2) The source of light should be a 100-watt bulb.
   (3) The objects should be white.
   (4) The objects should round.
   (5) The light should shine on the objects from above.

Answers are on page 319.

This Posttest will help you evaluate whether you are ready to move up to the next level of GED preparation.

Directions: Choose the <u>one best answer</u> to each question. The questions are based on reading passages, charts, graphs, and maps. Answer each question as carefully as possible. If a question seems to be too difficult, do not spend too much time on it. Work ahead and come back to it later when you can think it through carefully.

Posttest Answer Grid

1 ① ② ③ ④ ⑤	18 ① ② ③ ④ ⑤	35 ① ② ③ ④ ⑤
2 ① ② ③ ④ ⑤	19 ① ② ③ ④ ⑤	36 ① ② ③ ④ ⑤
3 ① ② ③ ④ ⑤	20 ① ② ③ ④ ⑤	37 ① ② ③ ④ ⑤
4 ① ② ③ ④ ⑤	21 ① ② ③ ④ ⑤	38 ① ② ③ ④ ⑤
5 ① ② ③ ④ ⑤	22 ① ② ③ ④ ⑤	39 ① ② ③ ④ ⑤
6 ① ② ③ ④ ⑤	23 ① ② ③ ④ ⑤	40 ① ② ③ ④ ⑤
7 ① ② ③ ④ ⑤	24 ① ② ③ ④ ⑤	41 ① ② ③ ④ ⑤
8 ① ② ③ ④ ⑤	25 ① ② ③ ④ ⑤	42 ① ② ③ ④ ⑤
9 ① ② ③ ④ ⑤	26 ① ② ③ ④ ⑤	43 ① ② ③ ④ ⑤
10 ① ② ③ ④ ⑤	27 ① ② ③ ④ ⑤	44 ① ② ③ ④ ⑤
11 ① ② ③ ④ ⑤	28 ① ② ③ ④ ⑤	45 ① ② ③ ④ ⑤
12 ① ② ③ ④ ⑤	29 ① ② ③ ④ ⑤	46 ① ② ③ ④ ⑤
13 ① ② ③ ④ ⑤	30 ① ② ③ ④ ⑤	47 ① ② ③ ④ ⑤
14 ① ② ③ ④ ⑤	31 ① ② ③ ④ ⑤	48 ① ② ③ ④ ⑤
15 ① ② ③ ④ ⑤	32 ① ② ③ ④ ⑤	49 ① ② ③ ④ ⑤
16 ① ② ③ ④ ⑤	33 ① ② ③ ④ ⑤	50 ① ② ③ ④ ⑤
17 ① ② ③ ④ ⑤	34 ① ② ③ ④ ⑤	

When you have completed the test, check your work with the answers and explanations on pages 300–301. Use the evaluation chart on page 302 to determine which areas you need to review.

POSTTEST

Question 1 is based on the following diagram.

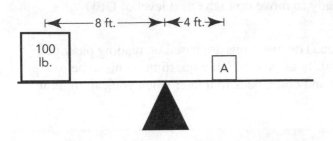

1. In order to balance the lever in the above diagram, how much must object A weigh?

(1) 50 pounds
(2) 100 pounds
(3) 200 pounds
(4) 500 pounds
(5) 1,000 pounds

Questions 2–4 refer to the following passage.

Ants have very small brains but, as a species, they are amazing. Some kinds of ants carry large quantities of food to their nest, where the food is stored or fed to developing ants. Some ants grow their own food. Others keep herds of tiny insects that they milk for food. Scientists have been very interested in how the small-brained ants communicate enough to carry out these tasks. One possibility is that ants use a chemical language. When one ant discovers food, for example, the ant becomes very excited and lays down a tiny chemical trail as it returns to the nest. Other ants can follow that trail back to the food.

2. Which of the following is a method used by ants to get food?

(1) milking small insects
(2) raiding other ant colonies
(3) stealing food
(4) saving food
(5) storing food

3. What do scientists speculate about how ants can communicate?

(1) simple words
(2) movement of their body parts
(3) chemicals
(4) their antennae
(5) all of the above

4. Which of the following is the best title for this passage?

(1) "Amazing Ants"
(2) "Ants Have Small Brains"
(3) "Ants Talk"
(4) "Ants Smell"
(5) "Ants Communicate"

POSTTEST

Questions 5–7 refer to the following passage.

The human brain is divided into three main parts. Each part has a job to do. The first part is the brain stem. This structure makes sure that all basic body functions are working. It keeps the heartbeat and breathing regular. The cerebellum is the part of the brain that coordinates balance and movement. The cerebrum includes the outer portion of the brain that appears to be folded into a tight package. The cerebrum controls senses, conscious movement, and the ability to think or read a book.

5. According to the passage, which of the following is a part of the brain?

   (1) nerves
   (2) spinal cord
   (3) backbone
   (4) cerebrum
   (5) medulla

6. As you read this passage, which part of your brain helped you to understand the words?

   A. brain stem
   B. cerebellum
   C. cerebrum

   (1) A only
   (2) B only
   (3) C only
   (4) both A and B
   (5) both B and C

7. If you run up and down the stairs, which part of your brain keeps your body balanced?

   A. brain stem
   B. cerebellum
   C. cerebrum

   (1) A only
   (2) B only
   (3) C only
   (4) both A and B
   (5) both B and C

Questions 8–10 refer to the following passage.

Chemists have discovered a new form of the element carbon. This substance, called buckminsterfullerene (C_{60}), named after the American engineer Buckminster Fuller, contains 60 carbon atoms shaped like soccer balls. The "buckyballs," as chemists call them, have some very interesting properties. First, unlike other molecules, buckyballs shot against a silicon surface are not smashed. Instead, they bounce back like rubber balls. Second, buckyballs can trap other small molecules within their round structure. Third, at cold temperatures, buckyballs lose almost all of their resistance to the flow of electric current. They become superconductors. This superconductivity of an organic material is surprising. Currently, chemists have not been able to explain the phenomenon.

8. Why might scientists call C_{60} "buckyballs"?

   A. They are shaped like a ball.
   B. They bounce.
   C. The structure resembles a ball with buck teeth.

   (1) A only
   (2) B only
   (3) C only
   (4) both A and B
   (5) both B and C

9. According to the passage, what are scientists are most surprised by?

   (1) the shape of C_{60}
   (2) the number of atoms in C_{60}
   (3) the superconductivity of C_{60}
   (4) the bounce in C_{60}
   (5) none of the above

10. Why are buckyballs termed organic?

   (1) because of the shape of carbon
   (2) because of the properties of buckyballs
   (3) because of the discovery of C_{60}
   (4) because of the bounce of carbon
   (5) because of superconductors

POSTTEST

Questions 11–13 refer to the following passage.

In recent years, scientists have been able to save the lives of thousands of people. The cause of the good news is not some new miracle drug. Its cause is an improved method of forecasting a volcanic eruption. Mount Pinatubo in the Philippines was dormant for 600 years; then small but unexpected changes occurred near the top of the volcano. Scientists began studying the volcano and soon noted that several minor earthquakes were occurring deep under the volcano. In addition, sulfur dioxide emissions were increasing. As the earthquake activity moved closer and closer to the top of the volcano, scientists became convinced that magma under the mountain was on the move. They sent out a general warning, and 58,000 people were evacuated from land near the volcano. A short time later, the volcano exploded.

11. What were the first signs that Mount Pinatubo was waking from dormancy?

    (1) small, but unexpected, changes near the summit
    (2) increased sulfur dioxide emissions
    (3) earthquake activity closer to the summit
    (4) all of the above
    (5) none of the above

12. In this passage, what does *magma* mean?

    (1) earthquake activity
    (2) molten rock
    (3) sulfurous rock
    (4) metals
    (5) boiling water

13. What does this passage imply about how scientists saved many lives?

    (1) by encouraging the local population to evacuate
    (2) by telling the local population about increased volcanic activity
    (3) by stopping the volcanic activity
    (4) by rescuing people from lava flows
    (5) none of the above

Questions 14 and 15 refer to the following passage.

Each year, despite warnings against improper disposal, over a million and a half nickel-cadmium batteries end up in landfills or in incinerators. Since cadmium is a highly toxic substance that can cause cancer and kidney damage, manufacturers have been looking for a substitute for the chemical. One of the most promising is a battery made of a nickel alloy. The battery is not only environmentally safe, but it can be used in existing electrical circuits.

14. According to the passage, why are battery manufacturers looking for alternatives to the traditional nickel-cadmium battery?

    (1) because cadmium is highly toxic
    (2) because cadmium is highly explosive
    (3) because cadmium is increasingly scarce
    (4) because cadmium is expensive
    (5) all of the above

15. According to the passage, why do battery manufacturers hope that the nickel-alloy battery will succeed?

    A. The new battery will not require any changes of electrical circuits.
    B. It will be cheaper to produce than the nickel-cadmium battery.
    C. They'll be able to sell a lot of new batteries.

    (1) A only
    (2) B only
    (3) C only
    (4) both A and B
    (5) both B and C

POSTTEST

Questions 16 and 17 refer to the following passage.

Tyrannosaurus rex was a fierce dinosaur, but it wasn't the last terrible monster. *Purussaurus brasiliensis* may have been the largest carnivore to ever live on Earth. The creature, which resembled a huge crocodile, lived in the Amazon River basin about 8 million years ago. Based on the size of its jaw, researchers estimate that *P. brasiliensis* was about 40 feet long and 8 feet high. Its weight has been estimated at 22,000 pounds.

16. Which of the following is the best title for this passage?

    (1) "The Amazon's Dinosaur"
    (2) "T. Rex's Competition"
    (3) "Mighty Jaws"
    (4) "An Ancient Crocodile"
    (5) "The World's Largest Carnivore"

17. According to the passage, *P. brasiliensis's* height is comparable to which of the following?

    (1) a two-story house
    (2) a bush
    (3) a room's ceiling
    (4) a station wagon
    (5) a sheep

Questions 18–20 refer to the following passage.

Although researchers have made great advances in the struggle against acquired immunodeficiency syndrome (AIDS), no one has yet answered the question of how the disease got started. Researchers think they have a possible answer, however. A virus similar to HIV (human immunodeficiency virus) is present in nonhuman primates. From the 1920s to the 1950s, a number of people took part in a research study to find out if malaria parasites from primates would also affect humans. As part of the research, some humans received blood from nonhuman primates. The nonhuman primates may have been infected with the HIV-like virus. Scientists speculate that the virus may have mutated and infected a human, causing the disease AIDS.

18. Based on the facts in the passage, how is the HIV virus spread?

    (1) through monkeys
    (2) through malaria patients
    (3) through mosquitoes
    (4) through saliva
    (5) through blood

19. Which of the following do scientists assume because the HIV virus that affects nonhuman primates is not the same as the HIV virus that affects humans?

    (1) A mutation occurred.
    (2) An accident occurred.
    (3) The human HIV virus is more dangerous.
    (4) The human HIV virus is not curable.
    (5) The two are not related.

20. What is acquired immunodeficiency syndrome better known as?

    (1) HIV
    (2) ACDU
    (3) IDS
    (4) PTU
    (5) AIDS

Questions 21–23 refer to the following passage and illustration.

Visible light is the light that people are able to see, such as sunlight or candlelight. It is a small part of the electromagnetic spectrum that also includes X rays, ultraviolet rays, and radio waves. While humans cannot see the invisible part of the spectrum, they have found numerous ways to use it. Gamma rays are used by doctors to treat cancer and to locate disorders inside the body. Ultraviolet rays are used in sunlamps. Infrared rays are used to treat skin diseases and to dry paint on cars. Radio waves, like the one shown below, are used in radio and television broadcasting.

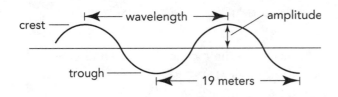

The differences among the colors of the spectrum lie in their wavelengths. A wavelength is measured by the distance between the crests or troughs of a wave. Wavelengths range from less than 10 trillionths of a meter (gamma rays) to more than 10,000 kilometers (long radio waves). Visible light has a wavelength of between 400 and 730 millimicrons. (There are a million millimicrons in a millimeter.)

The visible light spectrum, or white light, can be broken down into its component colors, as in a rainbow. Although light coming from the Sun looks colorless, it is actually a mixture of different wavelengths. The wavelengths range from violet (the shortest wavelength) to deep red (the longest wavelength).

21. Which of the following is the shortest wavelength visible to humans?

   (1) red
   (2) violet
   (3) orange
   (4) yellow
   (5) blue

22. What can you conclude from the passage about the lengths of electromagnetic waves?

   (1) They are always long.
   (2) They are unimportant to human vision.
   (3) They are determined by pigment.
   (4) They are always the same.
   (5) They vary greatly.

23. When light passes through a glass prism, it emerges and displays the colors of a rainbow. This is due to which of the following?

   (1) The ultraviolet rays disrupt the visible light waves.
   (2) The pigment of the glass absorbs the lighter colors.
   (3) White light is broken down into its different component colors.
   (4) White light is absorbed by the prism.
   (5) The light creates an optical illusion.

POSTTEST

Questions 24–26 refer to the following passage.

Because controlling the process of fusion on Earth would solve the world's energy problems for all time, many researchers are working hard to solve the many problems associated with fusion research. One of the biggest problems is that, as far as we know, fusion only occurs when temperatures are about as hot as the interior of the Sun. No known container could hold the fusion reaction without melting.

In the last decade, scientists were astonished when two researchers announced that they had achieved fusion, at room temperature. Their process, called cold fusion, was immediately found suspect by many in the scientific community. Suspicion grew when other scientists were unable to replicate the experiment. Then a well-respected international team of scientists confirmed the cold-fusion results. The race for cold fusion was on. Unfortunately, the only result so far is that several scientists have been injured and one killed in laboratory explosions related to cold-fusion testing.

24. Which of the following is the only known place where fusion occurs?

   (1) in magnetic fields
   (2) in fluorescent lightbulbs
   (3) in laboratories
   (4) inside stars
   (5) around atomic bombs

25. This passage implies that the argument over whether or not cold fusion is a realistic energy alternative is fueled by the inability of many scientists to do which of the following?

   (1) to understand the details of the experiment
   (2) to repeat the experiment
   (3) to accept another scientist's success
   (4) to drop their fusion research
   (5) to get research funding

26. According to the passage, what is a major problem of hot-fusion research?

   A. The reaction occurs at temperatures as hot as the interior of the Sun.
   B. No container can hold the fusion reaction without melting.
   C. Scientists do not know what kind of fuel to use for the reaction.

   (1) A only
   (2) B only
   (3) C only
   (4) both A and B
   (5) both B and C

Questions 27–29 refer to the following passage.

The effects of smoking on the unborn fetus are not good. The fetus of a mother who smokes two packs of cigarettes a day loses 40 percent of the oxygen that is normally present. A lack of the oxygen needed to grow at a normal rate may explain why babies born to smokers average six to seven ounces lighter at birth than the babies of nonsmokers.

Lower birth weight is not the only adverse effect of smoking on babies and their mothers. Women who smoke less than a pack a day increase the chances of their babies dying by 20 percent. Those who smoke more than a pack a day are 36 percent more likely to have their babies die. Smokers are twice as likely to have miscarriages and will also suffer more complications during their pregnancy, more premature births, and a greater chance of having a stillbirth.

Even if a woman stops smoking before delivery, smoking during pregnancy makes it more likely that her baby will have malformations of the heart or other organs. Smoking during pregnancy doubles the chances of abruptio placentae—a premature separation of the placenta from the uterine wall that may result in the death of the fetus.

Difficulties do not end at birth. The children of smokers are 52 percent more likely to die of crib death and twice as likely to develop a lung illness, such as bronchitis or pneumonia.

27. On the average, how much lighter are the newborn babies of women who smoke during pregnancy than the newborns of nonsmokers?

(1) less than two ounces
(2) two to three ounces
(3) four to five ounces
(4) six to seven ounces
(5) eight or more ounces

28. What is abruptio placentae?

(1) a minor complication occurring only during the first trimester of pregnancy
(2) a birth defect involving an underdeveloped digestive tract
(3) a condition in which the fetus receives a diminished supply of oxygen
(4) another term for sudden infant death syndrome, or crib death
(5) premature separation of the placenta from the uterine wall

29. Which of the following is not mentioned as a possible adverse effect of a pregnant woman's smoking?

(1) increased risk of miscarriage
(2) more premature births
(3) greater possibility of a stillbirth
(4) lower birth weight
(5) severe brain damage

POSTTEST

Questions 30–32 refer to the following passage.

Humans have long marveled at the phenomenon of lightning. It was the ultimate weapon of the gods of ancient civilizations. Today, lightning is subjected to scientific scrutiny, but it is no less awesome, and it still deserves respect.

National Center for Health Statistics data for recent years show that lightning kills about 125 Americans per year and injures more than 500. Property loss is estimated in the hundreds of millions of dollars each year.

Lightning is an effect of electrification within a thunderstorm. As the thunderstorm develops, interactions of charged particles produce an intense electrical field within the cloud. A large positive charge is usually concentrated in the frozen upper layers of the cloud, and a large negative charge, along with a smaller positive area, is found in the lower portions and tries to escape to the ground.

Earth is normally negatively charged with respect to the atmosphere. But as the thunderstorm passes over the ground, the negative charge in the base of the cloud induces a positive charge on the ground below and for several miles around the storm. The ground charge follows the storm like an electrical shadow, growing stronger as the negative cloud charge increases. The attraction between the positive and negative charges makes the positive ground current flow up buildings, trees, and other elevated objects in an effort to establish a flow of current. But air, which is a poor conductor of electricity, insulates the cloud and ground charges, preventing a flow of current until huge electrical charges are built up.

Lightning occurs when the difference between the positive and negative charges—the electrical potential—becomes great enough to overcome the resistance of the insulating air and to force a conductive path for current to flow between the two charges. Potential in these cases can be as much as 100 million volts.

Lightning strokes proceed from cloud to cloud, cloud to ground, or, where high structures are involved, from ground to cloud.

30. What inhibits the flow of electricity between the massed negative charge in the base of the storm cloud and the positive charges on the ground?

   (1) air
   (2) water vapor
   (3) raindrops
   (4) step leaders
   (5) conductive paths

31. What causes the positive charges on the ground to flow up elevated objects?

   (1) The raindrops are charged as they fall to the ground.
   (2) Electrical ions are carried downward by the cold winds that accompany thunderstorms.
   (3) Elevated objects are the best conductors of electricity and provide a path for positive charges to follow.
   (4) Conductive channels between the clouds and the ground carry electrical charges.
   (5) There is an attraction between the negative ions in the cloud and the positive ions on the ground.

32. If you were caught in a thunderstorm, which of the following would be the safest?

   (1) lying in a drainage ditch
   (2) standing under a tall tree
   (3) sitting in a boat on a large lake
   (4) walking along a railroad track
   (5) standing in an open field

Questions 33–35 refer to the following passage.

The advent of synthetic shampoos in the past several decades has revolutionized cleansing and cleaning chores. The major advantage of synthetic detergents over soap is how they function in hard water. Soap, an alkali salt of fatty acids, removes dirt and grease from surfaces. However, soap's foaming and cleansing action is reduced according to the degree of hardness of the water. Also, in hard water, which contains a relatively high amount of calcium in solution, the calcium reacts with the soap to form a scum. The familiar ring in the bathtub is composed of these deposits, to which dirt and other undissolved matter in the water may adhere. Shampooing with soap and hard water can result in scum forming on the hair. The result is a dull luster and difficulty in combing the hair. A rinse with a substance that will redissolve the scum is needed. Today, soap is seldom used for hair washing. In days prior to synthetic shampoos, the scum that dulled the hair's luster was often reduced or eliminated by rinsing with an acidic substance, such as vinegar or lemon juice.

Synthetic detergents do not react with the calcium in water, and scum deposits do not form, even in the hardest water. However, the detergent or cleaning action may vary depending on the kind of synthetic detergent used and the kind of dirt to be removed. Synthetic detergents are classified as anionic, cationic, nonionic, or amphoteric, depending on the way their ions behave in water. All work by breaking down the resistance between the water and the dirt, oil, or other material on the surface to be cleaned and allowing the dirty material to be rinsed away. Synthetic detergent shampoos sold for adults are usually of the anionic type. Those for babies and children are usually of the amphoteric type or amphoteric mixed with anionic. Cationic synthetic detergents are not usually included in shampoos as detergent agents.

33. A manufacturer claims that the anionic synthetic shampoo that she produces is suitable for babies and small children. From the information in the passage, which of the following is probably the mildest type of synthetic cleansing agent?

(1) anionic
(2) cationic
(3) nonionic
(4) amphoteric
(5) all of the above

34. According to the passage, which of the following is needed to dissolve the scum formed by synthetic detergents?

(1) vinegar
(2) protein derivatives
(3) alkali salt
(4) conditioner
(5) none of the above

35. What does a bathtub that has a film of an oily, yet gritty, substance containing particles of hair suggest that the bather washed his or her hair with?

(1) soap
(2) an anionic type of synthetic shampoo
(3) a cationic type of synthetic shampoo
(4) a nonionic type of synthetic shampoo
(5) an amphoteric type of synthetic shampoo

POSTTEST

Questions 36–38 refer to the following passage.

Radiation can kill or damage cells. If enough cells die, the organ they form will die. If crucial organs die, the organism will die. Thus, one consequence of radiation is death.

To be immediately lethal, radiation exposure to the whole body must exceed 1,000 rems over a brief period of time—minutes or hours. Such exposures occurred at the Hiroshima and Nagasaki bombings during World War II. A dose of 500 rems, delivered at one time to the whole body, will cause death in about 50 percent of the cases.

In the range from 500 rems down to 100 rems, radiation sickness occurs, and some individuals will die. At lower radiation levels, the consequences are more difficult to predict and detect.

For low radiation doses, it is cell damage, not cell death, that is harmful. A dead cell can be replaced. A damaged cell, however, can replicate itself and multiply. The type of damage depends on the nature of the stricken cell. If it is an ordinary cell—bone tissue or flesh, for instance—the damage is confined to the stricken organism. This is called somatic damage. The most feared type of somatic damage is cancer or leukemia. If, however, a reproductive cell is damaged, then a mutation can be caused and the damage can be transmitted to future generations.

That radiation can cause cancer or genetic mutation is not questioned. What is questioned is the relationship between the dose— particularly doses below 1 rem—and the number of resulting cancers or mutations. For both types of damage, the latency period—the time between exposure and the effect—is long. It is 25 or more years for cancer and a generation or more for genetic damage.

36. Which of the following is the best title for this passage?

   (1) "The Biological Effects of Radiation"
   (2) "The Legacy of Hiroshima"
   (3) "Somatic Diseases"
   (4) "The Atomic Bomb"
   (5) "The Nuclear Winter"

37. What is the danger when a reproductive cell is damaged?

   (1) The cell could die.
   (2) Subsequent exposure to high levels of radiation could be lethal.
   (3) There would be an increase in the incidence of multiple births.
   (4) Genetic damage can be transmitted to future generations.
   (5) The danger is no different than when other types of cells are damaged.

38. Why is it difficult to predict the long-term effects of low levels of radiation?

   (1) There are no long-term effects of low levels of radiation.
   (2) There are not enough people who have been exposed to low levels of radiation.
   (3) The Pentagon has suppressed all of its data on radiation exposure.
   (4) We have never had a thermonuclear war.
   (5) The latency period can be 25 years for cancer and can be generations for mutations.

POSTTEST

Questions 39–41 refer to the following passage.

On Earth, all life of every kind, from the tiniest viroid to the largest whale, from the blue-green algae to the giant sequoia, including the human species itself, is fully and precariously dependent on the Sun. All life on Earth originated and evolved in the Sun's light and warmth.

Life on Earth would be forever extinguished with even a minor change in the Sun's radiance. A drop of only 2 percent in the Sun's 10,000°F surface temperature would initiate a global glacial advance. The new ice age would turn our beautiful blue planet into a giant, uninhabitable snowball in only fifty years. A rise of 2 percent would melt the ice caps of Greenland and Antarctica, flood the continental coasts, and eventually sear the land masses of Earth to a Saharan stillness and sterility.

Today, there are books, articles, television specials, news reports, and bumper stickers—all concerned with something presumably just recently discovered—about solar energy. The fact is that our Earth and all the life on its surface and in its seas have always been powered by solar energy. In fact, there are only a few kinds of energy on our planet that are not solar. Geothermal energy (heat from the deep interior of Earth), tidal (the ebb and flow of the tides caused by the gravitational pull of the Moon), and nuclear energy are the usual examples. Oil, gas, and coal all come from the fossils of plants which grew by converting sunlight to energy. Wood and "biomass" are from the same source but more recent. Hydroelectric power is possible only because the Sun evaporates Earth's standing water and pours it back in rainfall into the sources of the rivers that drive the water turbines. Even the wind that turns our windmills (a clean, renewable energy source) is born out of the uneven heating of Earth's atmosphere by the Sun.

In ultimate confirmation of the closeness of their relationship, Earth and the Sun will one day die together as they were born together. About 5 billion years from now, the Sun will begin to exhaust the hydrogen fuel in its deep interior. The fusion process will move outward,

expanding the Sun into a red-giant star, which will engulf and incinerate the inner planets. Earth will probably be incinerated, too. But there is no comfort in that "probably," because even if it is not physically swallowed by the swollen Sun, our planet will be just a charred and lifeless cinder swinging through space.

39. What creates wind?

  (1) the gravitational pull of the Moon
  (2) the evaporation of water
  (3) the movement of clouds
  (4) the uneven heating of Earth's atmosphere
  (5) the movement of the jet streams

40. Before the Industrial Revolution, animals provided power and transportation. How was this work style dependent on energy from the Sun?

  (1) The Sun dried the ground so that it would be dry enough to work.
  (2) The uneven heating by the Sun created breezes that cooled the laborers.
  (3) Wood, which grew through the conversion of sunlight, was burned to keep the animals warm in the winter.
  (4) The animals derived their energy from plants, which had used the Sun's energy for their own growth.
  (5) This was not dependent on the Sun.

41. If the surface temperature of the Sun were to decrease to about 9,800°F, or 2 percent below its present temperature, which one of the following would be the most likely long-term effect?

  (1) The level of the oceans would rise.
  (2) The surface of Earth would be covered by ice masses.
  (3) The surface of Earth would become desert-like.
  (4) Desert regions would be transformed into lush, tropical rain forests.
  (5) The average daily temperature would drop a degree or two.

POSTTEST

Questions 42 and 43 refer to the following passage and illustration.

The interior of Earth is hot enough to melt rock and boil water, but this heat is seldom felt or noticed until a cataclysmic event, such as a volcano spewing melted rock into the atmosphere.

In the state of Wyoming, however, there are at least two hundred reminders of Earth's hot interior. The reminders are geysers—jets of hot water and steam that explode out of holes in Earth's surface. The most famous geyser is "Old Faithful" in Yellowstone National Park. This geyser got its name because it erupts just about every hour and has been doing so for over a hundred years.

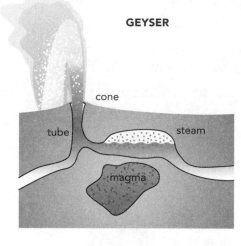

GEYSER

cone

tube

steam

magma

42. What does a geyser consist of?

   A. melted rock
   B. hot water
   C. steam

   (1) A only
   (2) B only
   (3) C only
   (4) both A and B
   (5) both B and C

43. What does the passage suggest that geysers are proof of?

   (1) Earth's interior is hot enough to boil water.
   (2) Earth's interior is hot enough to melt rock.
   (3) Hot water can rise against the force of gravity.
   (4) Hot water can melt holes in Earth's surface.
   (5) Geysers are as powerful as volcanoes.

Questions 44 and 45 refer to the following passage.

Socks removed from a hot drier often cling together. In the dark, you may even notice a tiny spark when the socks are pulled apart. The cause of this phenomenon is static electricity.

As the socks rub together in the drier, electrons are rubbed from one atom to another. The result is atoms that are no longer electrically neutral. Instead, they have either a positive or a negative electrical charge. The socks stick together because opposite electrical charges attract.

44. According to the passage, what causes static electricity?

(1) when atoms gain electrons
(2) when atoms lose electrons
(3) when atoms are heated
(4) either when atoms gain or lose electrons
(5) none of the above

45. According to the passage, when will atoms that are electrically charged attract each other?

(1) when they are heated
(2) when they gain electrons
(3) when they lose electrons
(4) when they have the same electrical charge
(5) when they have opposite electrical charges

Questions 46–48 refer to the following passage.

We now recognize that there are millions of species of organisms. However, there are obvious differences in the body structures of these organisms. One of the smallest, a one-celled amoeba, has a very simple digestive process. It simply absorbs food through its cell walls. On the other hand, the more advanced animals, such as cats, dogs, and monkeys have very complex digestive processes, with specialized groups of cells that form the different parts of the digestive tract. In these animals, cells are grouped together to form organs that function together as systems.

Despite the differences in their structures, all living things are made up mostly of protoplasm. This substance is called "the basic substance of life."

46. Which of the following is usually considered an advanced organism?

(1) the digestive tract
(2) a mouse
(3) an amoeba
(4) a mold
(5) protoplasm

47. What substance is common to all organisms?

(1) protoplasm
(2) photosynthesis
(3) blood
(4) skeletal systems
(5) wings

48. What is the main idea of the passage?

(1) The structures of different species vary from simple to complex, but all are mostly made up of protoplasm.
(2) Animals must develop more complex digestive systems.
(3) There are many kinds of organisms.
(4) There are more than 1 million species of animals.
(5) The level of complexity of an organism is determined by its protoplasm.

POSTTEST

Questions 49 and 50 refer to the following illustration and passage.

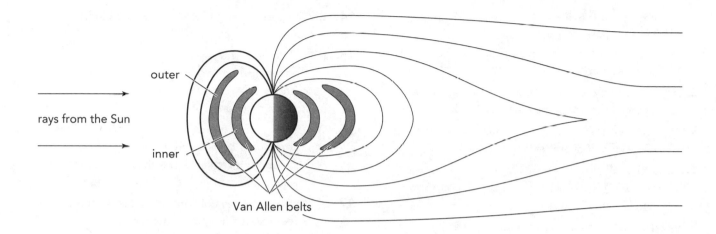

Three hundred miles above the surface of Earth are two circular, magnetic shields, or belts. These zones that encircle Earth are called the Van Allen belts. The zones are named after the scientist James Van Allen, who discovered them in 1958. These belts of intense radiation protect Earth from blasts of dangerous X rays and ultraviolet rays that erupt from the Sun.

The Van Allen belts are held in place by Earth's magnetic field. They also trap incoming high-energy charged particles and funnel them in at the poles, creating brilliant displays of shimmering lights called auroras in regions near the North and South Poles.

49. From what do the Van Allen belts protect Earth?

(1) auroras
(2) nuclear fallout
(3) X rays and ultraviolet rays
(4) meteorites
(5) infrared rays

50. What holds the Van Allen belts in place?

(1) intense radiation
(2) Earth's magnetic field
(3) radiation from the Sun
(4) X rays and ultraviolet rays
(5) the auroras

Answers are on pages 300–301.

Answer Key

1. (3) If object A is half the distance from the middle of the lever as the 100-pound weight, then in order to balance the lever, object A must weigh twice as much, or 200 pounds.

2. (1) The fourth sentence states that ants keep herds of tiny insects that they milk for food.

3. (3) The passage states that scientists think ants use a kind of chemical language.

4. (5) Although all choices are linked to the passage, choice (1) is too general and choices (2), (3), and (4) are too specific.

5. (4) The last part of the passage discusses the cerebrum, which is the outer gray portion of the brain.

6. (3) According to the passage, the cerebrum controls the ability to think or read a book.

7. (2) The passage states that the cerebellum coordinates balance and movement—both required for navigating the stairs.

8. (4) Although the passage does not specifically state why buckminsterfullerene is called a buckyball, the reader could infer that it is due to both the shape and the behavior of the molecule.

9. (3) The next-to-last sentence states that the superconductivity of an organic material is surprising.

10. (2) Buckyballs are termed organic because of the chemical properties they exhibit.

11. (4) All three signs were mentioned in the passage: that there were small, but unexpected, changes near the summit, increased sulfur dioxide emissions, and earthquake activity closer to the summit.

12. (2) The passage says that magma under the mountain was on the move. The only choice that suggests movement and is characteristic of volcanic activity is choice (2), molten rock.

13. (1) Although choices (1) and (2) are both possible, the passage states that a warning was issued. Because the population responded by evacuating, we can conclude that the warning was more specific than choice (2) would suggest.

14. (1) The passage states that cadmium is highly toxic.

15. (1) Although all choices are possible, choice (1), that the new battery will not require any changes of electrical circuits, is the only one actually mentioned in the paragraph.

16. (5) The second sentence of the passage describes *Purussaurus brasiliensis* as the largest carnivore to ever live on Earth, so choice (5) is the most appropriate title of the passage.

17. (3) Choice (3) is the only option that is close to 8 feet tall, the height mentioned in the passage.

18. (5) The passage mentions that humans received blood and implies that the blood may have been contaminated.

19. (1) The last sentence of the passage mentions that the HIV virus may have mutated (changed).

20. (5) Choice (5), AIDS, is the only one that fits the letters of the disease.

21. (2) The last sentence states that the visible spectrum wavelengths vary from the shortest—violet, to the longest—deep red.

22. (5) The third paragraph mentions wavelengths ranging from 10 trillionths of a meter to 10,000 kilometers. From this you could conclude that the lengths of electromagnetic waves vary greatly.

23. (3) The third paragraph mentions that white light can be broken down into its component colors, as in a rainbow. It is reasonable to conclude that the glass prism can break down light into its component colors.

24. (4) The first paragraph states that as far as we know, fusion only occurs when temperatures are as hot as inside stars.

25. (2) The second paragraph mentions that suspicion grew when scientists were unable to replicate (repeat) the experiment.

26. (4) Choices (1) and (2), that the reaction occurs at temperatures as hot as the interior of the Sun, and that no container can hold the experiment without melting, are mentioned in the passage.

POSTTEST

27. (4) The last sentence of the first paragraph states that babies born to smokers are an average of six to seven ounces lighter at birth.

28. (5) Abruptio placentae is described in the third paragraph.

29. (5) Choice (5), severe brain damage, is the only one not specifically mentioned. All of the other choices can be found in the second paragraph.

30. (1) The fourth paragraph states that air is a poor conductor and insulates the cloud and ground charges. This prevents a flow of current until the electrical potential becomes great enough to overcome the resistance of the air.

31. (5) The passage states that the bottom of a storm cloud is dominated by negative charges, inducing a positive charge on the ground below. It also mentions that the attraction between negative and positive ions makes the ground current flow up buildings and trees.

32. (1) The fourth paragraph mentions that the attraction between the positive and negative charges makes the positive ground current flow up elevated objects. Choice (1) is the only one that does not include an object that is elevated above the surrounding area.

33. (4) Since shampoos for babies are usually amphoteric, and baby shampoos are usually mild, it is reasonable to assume that this is the mildest type of synthetic detergent.

34. (5) Nothing is used to dissolve scum   because the passage states that synthetic detergents do not produce scum.

35. (1) The passage states that when soap is used in hard water, soap scum forms and that the familiar ring in the bathtub is composed of this substance, along with dirt and other matter. This is not true of the synthetic shampoos.

36. (1) While choices (2), (3), and (4) contain items mentioned in the passage, only choice (1), "The Biological Effects of Radiation," covers the main idea.

37. (4) The fourth paragraph states that when a reproductive cell is damaged, a mutation can be caused, and the damage is transmitted to future generations.

38. (5) From the passage you can infer that it is difficult to predict the long-term effects of low levels of radiation because the latency period is so long.

39. (4) The end of the third paragraph states that wind is created by the uneven heating of Earth's atmosphere by the Sun.

40. (4) The energy the animals used in their work came from plants (oats, corn, barley, and hay), which had used the Sun's energy for growth.

41. (2) The passage states in the second paragraph that a drop of only 2 percent would start a glacial advance that would turn Earth into a giant snowball. The drop in Earth's temperature would be much greater than a couple of degrees.

42. (5) The second sentence of the second paragraph defines a geyser as a jet of hot water and steam.

43. (1) That Earth's interior is hot enough to boil water is stated in the first paragraph of the passage.

44. (4) Rubbing electrons from one atom to another will remove electrons from some atoms and add them to others.

45. (5) The last sentence states that opposite electrical charges attract.

46. (2) Of the organisms mentioned, only the mouse has a complex organ system.

47. (1) This is stated in the last paragraph.

48. (1) Choice (1) brings together the main points of both paragraphs. Choices (2) and (5) are not stated in the passage, and choices (3) and (4) are too specific.

49. (3) The first paragraph states than Van Allen belts protect Earth from X rays and ultraviolet rays.

50. (2) The fact that Earth's magnetic field holds Van Allen belts in pace is stated in the second paragraph.

POSTTEST
Evaluation Chart

On the following chart, circle the number of any item you answered incorrectly. Under each theme and subject area, you will see the pages you can review to learn how to answer the items correctly. Pay particular attention to reviewing themes and subject areas in which you missed half or more of the questions.

Theme / Subject Area	Fundamental Understandings	Unifying Concepts and Processes *(pages 15–30)*	Science as Inquiry *(pages 31–70)*
Life Science *(pages 75–172)*	10 questions 2, 5, 7, 17, 18, 20, 27, 28, 37, 47,	7 questions 3, 16, 29, 36, 38 46, 48	3 questions 4, 6, 19,
Physical Science *(pages 175–236)*	8 questions 1, 9, 14, 21, 24, 26, 34, 44	6 questions 8, 10, 22, 23, 35, 45	3 questions 15, 25, 33
Earth and Space Science *(pages 239–283)*	8 questions 12, 13, 30, 31, 39, 42, 49, 50	3 questions 32, 40, 43	2 question 11, 41

Answer Key

Chapter 1

Thinking About Science, page 18

1. Observing, identifying, describing, experimenting, explaining, and communicating
2. Scientists examine small units of investigation called *systems*.
3. Our world has predictable properties and behaviors.
4. organization or classification

Pre-GED Practice, page 18

1. (2) Systems can be organized according to many different traits.
2. (5) In this example, mail is organized according to similarities and differences—a type of classification.

Thinking About Science, page 20

1. H
2. F
3. O
4. O
5. F

Pre-GED Practice, page 21

1. (3) This is not reliable evidence. The scientist has not done anything to determine if sodium chloride is present.
2. (3) The ride will let a person experience a real event without the dangers of the real event.
3. (2) This is an opinion based on the scientist's values and beliefs.

Thinking About Science, page 24

1. a. Change: the shape of the tire; the amount of air in the tire
   b. Remain constant: the materials in the tire; the color of the tire
2. a. Change: the shape of the cube; the phase of the cube (from solid to liquid)
   b. Remain constant: the amount of water; the volume of water

Pre-GED Practice, page 24

1. (4) The tide continually rotates between high and low based on the Moon's gravitational force.
2. (1) This enables scientists to be more accurate in their predictions.

Thinking About Science, page 26

1. The statement "organisms evolve" means that living things change over time.
2. Equilibrium is a physical state in which forces and changes occur in opposite and offsetting directions.

Pre-GED Practice, page 26

1. (4) Cloud formations change because of atmospheric conditions, not because of evolution.
2. (4) While all molecules strive to attain equilibrium, it does not always occur.

Thinking About Science, page 28

1. The tail of a monkey: to have an extra limb to use when swinging from trees
2. The neck of a giraffe: to reach food high in trees
3. The bill of a pelican: to capture fish

Pre-GED Practice, page 28

1. (4) While a seagull uses its wings for flying, a penguin uses them for swimming.
2. (3) Many animals have physical characteristics that are unique to their needs. For example, a beaver has strong, sharp front teeth to help it cut tree branches to form a shelter.

Concepts and Processes in Science Review, pages 29–30

1. (4) A coin does not consist of many parts that work together to form a whole.
2. (3) A rain shower occurs randomly. While the shower can be predicted, the rain itself does not fall in any particular order.

3. (1) Organization helps scientists to be more accurate in their predictions.
4. (4) The phases of the moon are a never-changing cycle. You can always predict when each phase will occur.
5. (5) The color of each moth most likely resulted from a need to blend into its environment.
6. (1) Since the Sun appears every day, this is an example of a daily change.
7. (1) Oparin was not able to prove his suggestion.
8. (2) Miller only demonstrated that Oparin's suggestion was possible. He did not prove it to be a scientific fact.

Chapter 2

Thinking About Science, pages 32–33

Part A
1. (4) The entire passage builds to sentence 4, which contains the main idea: as we get older, we get fewer colds.
2. (1) The main idea is stated in the first sentence: cactuses are remarkable plants, made to live in one of nature's harshest environments. The rest of the paragraph gives details about how they are made specially to survive harsh conditions.

Part B
1. (4) The passage deals primarily with research activities at Woods Hole. Choices (2) and (3) are too general. Choice (1) is not relevant to the passage.
2. (1) This statement summarizes the main idea of the passage. Choices (3) and (4) are never stated. The passage never implies that there are too many scientific activities, choice (2).

Pre-GED Practice, pages 34–35

1. (1) The passage discusses the advantages and uses of solar energy. Choices (2), (3), and (4) are supporting details. Choice (5) is not mentioned.
2. (4) The passage shows how solar energy could meet our energy needs. Choices (1), (2), and (3) are too general. Choice (5) is not mentioned.

3. (3) The passage details the advantages of solar energy, stated in the third sentence of the first paragraph.
4. (4) The main idea of this passage is that air pollution is a health hazard. Choice (1) introduces the passage. Choices (2) and (3) are supporting details. Choice (5) is a conclusion.
5. (2) While the passage asserts that air pollution is a health hazard, it also suggests that an emphasis on stronger measures to protect the environment could lessen the danger.
6. (4) The last sentence expresses the main idea, which is that air pollution is a health hazard that requires strong measures to protect the environment.

Thinking About Science, page 37

Part A
  The third sentence states that: "Climate is another important influence because stone decays faster in moist air than in dry air."

Part B
1. Sentence 4 contains the answer, high-frequency sounds. Since high-frequency sounds are between 900 and 5,000 hertz, 900 would be the lower limit for these sounds.
2. the frequency of sound and the intensity of a sound. The words: "Loudness depends upon two factors. . ." in the first sentence help you to quickly find the answer.

Pre-GED Practice, page 38

1. (4) The passage states that since dioxin bonds itself to soil, the chances that it will seep into water supplies are minimized.
2. (1) This supporting detail is stated in the passage.
3. (1) The main idea is stated at the beginning. The rest of the passage supports this main idea.

Thinking About Science, page 40

(4) Ptolemy thought that Earth was stationary. He thought that the movement of the other heavenly bodies proved his theory. What he did not realize was that Earth was also in motion. Information found in the last sentence shows that choices (1), (2), and (3) are incorrect.

Pre-GED Practice, pages 40–41

1. (4) According to the passage, one of the most important characteristics of aluminum is its resistance to corrosion. You can infer that this makes it an attractive metal to use in the manufacture of cars and airplanes.

2. (2) The passage points out that while other metals are affected adversely by oxygen, aluminum is not. This ability to combine with oxygen to form a tough, protective film enables aluminum to resist corrosion.

3. (1) The passage states that Earth's surface is changing and describes several processes that slowly cause alterations in Earth's crust. Choices (2), (3), and (5) are incorrect. Choice (4) is true only some of the time. The word *always* should make you cautious.

4. (5) The passage states that the Hawaiian Islands are being formed by erupting volcanoes, choice (2). From that, you can infer that choices (1), (3), and (4) are also correct.

Thinking About Science, page 43

Part A

1. unwanted substances or chemicals. The entire paragraph defines the word *antigen*. The first two sentences refer to the body's ability to recognize and attack its enemies. The third sentence mentions "unwanted chemicals." Finally, you were told that the body recognizes the antigens.

2. enemies. These are described as foreign bodies such as those found in bacteria, viruses, and other microscopic organisms.

Part B

1. liquid. The strongest clue to the meaning of *liquify* is its similarity to a word you already know—*liquid*. Context clues prove that these two words are related.

2. melted by heat. The context clues indicate that *liquify* and *molten* are related. If iron ore becomes molten at 2,800 to 3,000°F, a tremendous amount of heat is needed. It is reasonable to think that *molten* means "melted by heat."

3. to become solid. A clue to the meaning of *solidify* is its similarity to the word *solid*.

4. a hole, dent, or hollow. The description of a tub of margarine helps to explain what *indentation* means.

Pre-GED Practice, page 44

1. (5) The first sentence speaks of the danger of depleting the ocean's food supply. Choice (2) is a danger. Since the rest of the passage is not about pollution, (5) is the better choice.

2. (1) We know that the ocean's supplies are in danger of being used up. If scientists are growing conchs in laboratories, they must be working to replace them.

3. (4) You may know that the word part *aqua* means "water," or you could have inferred its meaning from the passage. Since *agriculture* means "cultivating the soil for food production," *aquaculture* means "using the ocean for food production."

4. (4) Cuts stop bleeding when the blood clots. The passage tells you that when a hemophiliac gets cut the bleeding does not stop. You can infer that *coagulate* means to "clot."

5. (3) The passage tells you that a hemophiliac is someone whose blood does not coagulate. *Coagulate* means "to clot," so a hemophiliac is someone whose blood does not clot.

Thinking About Science, page 46

1. 30°C. If you find 90°F (between 80 and 100) on the Fahrenheit side of the thermometer, you will see that the closest Celsius equivalent is just above 30°.

2. 0°Celsius.

Pre-GED Practice, page 46

1. (3) This is the number on the Celsius thermometer that corresponds with 98.6° on the Fahrenheit thermometer.

2. (4) This is the number on the Celsius thermometer that corresponds with 137° on the Fahrenheit thermometer.

Thinking About Science, page 48

Part A

The correct answer is (3). The passage shows that Salk used inductive reasoning to produce an effective polio vaccine. To do so, he first grew viruses in laboratory cultures.

Part B

1. (1) Sentence 1 contains the generalization that the elements in Earth's crust do not represent the composition of the entire planet.

2. (1) If the composition of Earth's crust does not represent the makeup of the entire planet, you could deduce that different layers of Earth must contain different proportions of elements.

Pre-GED Practice, page 49

1. (4) The passage states that water and salt cause rust. Rain and snow are forms of water, plus salt is used to melt snow on snow-packed streets. Areas near the ocean have salt in the air as salt evaporates from the ocean. Choice (4) is the only option that has no rain, snow, or salt.

2. (3) Only answer (3) is a logical conclusion for this paragraph. You can use inductive reasoning to generalize from the specific items listed in the passage.

3. (5) While all of the choices are true statements about the Earth, they serve to support the main idea, choice (5), of this passage.

Comprehending and Applying Science Review, pages 50–52

1. (4) The first sentence suggests that there are many causes of dizziness. The paragraph goes on to discuss a variety of these causes. Choices (1), (2), and (3) are all too specific to be correct.

2. (2) Of all the possible causes of dizziness, ear wax and eyeglasses are the easiest to correct. In addition, the passage refers to them as less serious than other causes.

3. (4) Airplanes and rockets need powerful engines to overcome gravity.

4. (4) The prefix *over-* means "too much," so a tire that is overinflated has too much air in it.

5. (1) The passage says that both overinflation and underinflation can cause tire problems.

6. (3) A relatively comfortable thermostat setting that would also conserve heat would be 68°F or 20°C.

7. (4) The equivalent of the normal body temperature of 98.6°F is approximately 37°C.

8. (4) The passage states that the scarred liver cannot absorb and process substances in the blood. Some of those substances would be nutrients. The passage refers to this process as life-sustaining work.

9. (1) Alcohol provides calories but few nutrients. Its lack of nutrients may account for the malnourished condition of many alcoholics.

Chapter 3

Thinking About Science, page 54

1. Peyer's patches. The third sentence states that the typhoid bacilli travel to the small intestine and settle in the lymphatic tissue known as Peyer's patches.

2. The typhoid bacilli are in the alimentary canal before entering the small intestine.

3. (4), (3), (1), (5), (2) is the correct order.

Thinking About Science, page 55

1. (2) and (3) are effects and should have *E* in front of them.

2. (3) The passage says that a parasitic protozoan causes toxoplasmosis.

Thinking About Science, page 56

(3) Sentence 2 states that scientists can use fossils to date rocks. It is logical to conclude that scientists can tell what varieties of life existed at different times in Earth's history. There is not enough information to draw the conclusion offered in choices (1), (2), and (5). Choice (4) is not correct, because sentence 2 states that paleontologists can determine the age of rocks.

Pre-GED Practice, page 57

1. (3) Disease-causing organisms and predators limit population growth. You could conclude from the passage that populations that are kept in balance by limiting factors would shrink if these two limiting factors increased greatly. Choices (1), (2), (4), and (5) could not be concluded from this passage.

2. (4) Predators limit the growth of the prey animal population. If the predators are removed, then one of the limitations on growth will be removed. Initially, an increase in the number of prey animals could be expected.

3. (4) The passage states that, in higher-level animals, the embryo grows in the uterus and is nourished by the mother until it is mature enough to be born.

4. (4) The passage discusses the protective function of the embryo's covering. You can conclude that an injury to the protective covering could result in damage to the embryo.

Thinking About Science, page 59

Statements (1), (2), (4), and (5) would be relevant to your deciding that the word *chemical* does not necessarily mean anything bad. The reason that statement (3) is not relevant is that carbon tetrachloride is a hazardous chemical that is not commonly used by most people. Therefore, it could not help you to decide whether or not the word *chemical* has a negative connotation.

Pre-GED Practice, page 59

1. (1) This is interesting information, but it does not have to be known in order to make a decision about buying the house.

Thinking About Science, page 61

1. F 4. T
2. F 5. T
3. F

Pre-GED Practice, page 62

1. (3) Choices (1) and (2) do not provide enough information for a comparison to be made between automobile safety and air safety. Choices (4) and (5) may be true but are not supported by details in the passage and chart.

Thinking About Science, page 64

1. power that is needed
2. individual rights
3. community
4. what is considered murder
5. right to privacy, or individual rights

Pre-GED Practice, page 65

1. (4) All of the other headlines do represent a conflict in values.

Thinking About Science, page 67

1. (3) and (6)—ingredients list of your favorite foods and a journal, notebook, or diary would be relevant to the experiment.
2. Items (1), (3), (4), and (5) would introduce additional variables other than an allergy to wheat into the experiment.
3. Actions (1), (2), and (3) could help you decide whether wheat is causing the allergy.

Pre-GED Practice, page 68

1. (5) This is the only choice that offers a possible explanation of the information you heard.
2. (2) Statements (1), (3), (4), and (5) are outside the range of the experiment and cannot be concluded from this experiment.

Analyzing and Evaluating Science Review, pages 69–70

1. (3) The graph shows that tamoxifen users have an improved breast-cancer survival rate.
2. (1) A large number of patients (30,000) were surveyed.
3. (2) The tamoxifen advantage is more pronounced the longer the patient lives.
4. (3) The graphs show that tamoxifen improves long-term survival.
5. (3) The results would not be affected if two batches were laundered at different times of the day.
6. (4) To draw a conclusion, it would be important to note the appearance of the stain spots after laundering.
7. (2) To control the experiment, only one variable, the detergent itself, could be used.

Chapter 4

Thinking About Science, page 75

Part A
1. F **3.** T
2. F **4.** F

Part B

1. (c) 4. (e)
2. (f) 5. (b)
3. (a) 6. (d)

Pre-GED Practice, page 76

1. (5) The passage mentions that all of the signs of life were examined.
2. (2) The passage notes that something in the soil seemed to make "food" out of sunlight and carbon dioxide.
3. (1) The passage says that the tests neither proved nor disproved the question of life on Mars. This means that the results were inconclusive.

Thinking About Science, page 78

1. (c) 4. (b)
2. (d) 5. (a)
3. (e)

Thinking About Science, page 80

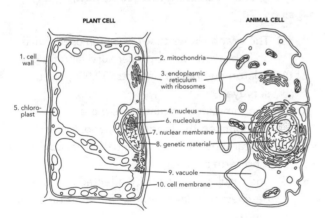

Thinking About Science, page 81

1. (a) active transport
   (b) diffusion
2. filter
3. diffusion
4. active transport

Pre-GED Practice, page 82

1. (2) A plant cell's chloroplasts are the site of food production, or photosynthesis.
2. (5) This strength helps a plant support itself.
3. (3) Excessive waste in a cell causes harm to the parts of a cell.

4. (1) Since the iodine is moving from an area with less iodine (the seawater) to an area with more iodine (the sea plants), active transport is needed.

Thinking About Science, page 86

Part A

1. an organism that is too small to be seen without a microscope
2. (a) no cell wall/ability to move
   (b) chloroplasts
3. bacuase they are not complete cells

Part B

1. P 4. P
2. M 5. P
3. M

Thinking About Science, page 90

1. virus   5. yes
2. cell wall 6. no
3. yes   7. no
4. multicell 8. in nucleus

Pre-GED Practice, page 91

1. (1) This is mentioned in the chart.
2. (1) This is mentioned in the "Symptoms" column of the chart.
3. (4) This is mentioned in the "Symptoms" column of the chart.

Thinking About Science, page 94

Part A

PARTS OF A FLOWERING PLANT

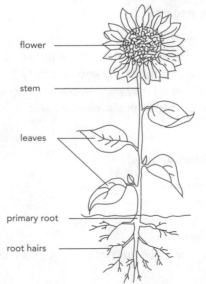

Part B

3. The function of stomates is to provide an opening for gases to enter and exit the leaf.

Thinking About Science, page 97

Part A

1. (3)
2. (2)

Part B

1. pistil
2. genetic information

Pre-GED Practice, page 98

1. (1) During respiration, the lungs take in the oxygen released by plants.
2. (4) This is mentioned in the passage.
3. (1) Plants do not respond to a stimulus as quickly as animals do.

Thinking About Science, page 104

1. (d)   4. (a)
2. (e)   5. (b)
3. (c)

Thinking About Science, page 111

1. a. fish
   b. amphibians
   c. reptiles
2. Both insects and amphibians undergo metamorphosis.
3. a. cartilaginous
   b. bony
   c. jawless
4. It changes with the surounding temperature.
5. a. birds
   b. mammals
6. It is kept constant by energy released from food.

Pre-GED Practice, page 112

1. (2) This is mentioned in the last paragraph.
2. (5) Koko displays all three traits.

Thinking About Science, page 115

1. producers
2. Nutrients would not be returned to the soil, and dead organisms would cover the earth.
3. Voles would decrease.

Thinking About Science, page 117

1. (f)   4. (d)
2. (a)   5. (e)
3. (c)   6. (b)

Thinking About Science, page 120

1. More people need more food, water, space, and resources.
2. Although trees are renewable, the process takes a long time. Old growth takes hundreds of years to replace, by which time species that live only in old-growth forests would be extinct.

Pre-GED Practice, page 121

1. (1) Farmers use these pesticides to protect plants from insects and to enhance plant growth.
2. (1) These women might have been exposed from a different source that was not relevant to the experiment.
3. (5) Developed countries have more access to technological advancements, such as pesticides.

Thinking About Science, page 125

1. (c)
2. (a)
3. (d)
4. (b)

Thinking About Science, page 126

1. Mutation is the result of a mistake in an individual's DNA. Adaptation suggests that several organisms have increased their survival potential.
2. Disease-causing microbes are mutating, resulting in an organism that is resistant to penicillin.
3. A chromosomal mutation occurs when pieces of chromosomes that contain some genes are lost or enter the wrong nucleus. A genetic mutation occurs after exposure to X rays, nuclear radiation, or chemicals.

Thinking About Science, page 129

1. Bacteria and other organisms can't get at it.
2. trilobites
3. bacteria and blue-green algae

4. by determining the age of the rocks in which a fossil is found and by measuring the amount of carbon-14 a substance contains

5. fishes

Pre-GED Practice, page 130

1. (2) Evolution supports the idea that species have changed over time.
2. (2) Because of this, organisms must compete for food in order to survive.
3. (2) These events interrupt periods of stability and cause change.
4. (3) This has not been proven as a scientific fact. It is merely a hypothesis.

Plant and Animal Science Review, pages 131–135

1. (2) This theme is the focus of the branch of life science known as ecology.
2. (3) All living things are made of one or more cells.
3. (3) These are the five main "kingdoms" in the classification system.
4. (1) This is one main difference between plant and animal cells. The other difference is that plants contain special structures called chloroplasts.
5. (4) Bacteria is essential to the production of yogurt.
6. (4) Photosynthesis is the process by which plants transform the Sun's energy into food energy.
7. (3) This is the reason why a warm-blooded animal's temperature remains constant.
8. (4) This is the only disease caused by a virus. Choices (1), (2), and (3) are caused by bacteria. Choice (5) is caused by a mutated gene.
9. (5) Humans use fungi for many things, including as a form of food.
10. (3) A plant takes in carbon dioxide for photosynthesis and releases oxygen as a waste product of forming glucose.
11. (4) A grasshopper egg does not enter the pupa stage and change form. It grows into a nymph that looks like a small adult grasshopper.
12. (3) This was proposed by Darwin as a hypothesis for how organisms developed over time.
13. (5) Without a microscope it would have been difficult to examine the bacteria that caused different diseases.

14. (3) This is mentioned in the fourth paragraph.
15. (3) This is mentioned in the fifth paragraph.
16. (2) The mercury from industrial wastes polluted the environment where it was produced.
17. (2) This happened in the case of Minamata.
18. (3) Since the people of Minamata didn't pay attention to the dead fish in the early stages of mercury poisoning, enough poison accumulated to harm human cells.
19. (1) This is mentioned in the fifth paragraph.
20. (4) This is mentioned in the fourth paragraph.
21. (1) The males have adapted to their different environments.
22. (1) The orangutans have adapted to their environment in order to increase the chances of producing surviving offspring.

Reading Efficiency A, page 136

1. (2) Von Frisch tested bees response to various shades of similar and different colors.
2. (5) Von Frisch wanted to start with more obvious differences in color and work towards less obvious differences.
3. (3) In the experiment, Bees seemed to have the easiest time finding yellow over the other choices.
4. (1) Bees were able to see shades of blue and yellow.
5. (2) This would test one variable only—shape—and have one constant—color.

Reading Efficiency B, pages 137–138

1. (3) Cells have many different functions and shapes.
2. (1) This is illustrated in the illustration.
3. (5) Since the nucleus holds important genetic information, it is important that it is well protected.
4. (3) These cells need more energy and would need more mitochondria to produce it.
5. (4) The area near the sunny window must contain less water molecules than the shady area.

Chapter 5

Thinking About Science, page 143

Part A
1. bone marrow
2. cardiac, smooth

Part B

1. (c) 4. (b)
2. (a) 5. (e)
3. (d)

Thinking About Science, page 148

1. T
2. F
3. T
4. T
5. F
6. F
7. F
8. T
9. F
10. T

Thinking About Science, page 151

1. a. eyes
   b. ears
   c. nose
   d. mouth
   e. skin
2. reflex
3. right
4. chemicals (or hormones), blood

Thinking About Science, page 153

1. testes, ovaries
2. two weeks
3. during the first three months
4. at the end of two months
5. labor

Pre-GED Practice, page 154

1. (4) The skeleton does not provide nourishment for the body. That function takes place through the digestive system.
2. (1) You have to think about jumping in order to do it. The other actions happen automatically.
3. (5) The digestive system is responsible for the breakdown of food and absorption of nutrients.
4. (3) The heart pumps blood throughout the body. It is not responsible for excretion.

Thinking About Science, page 157

1. T
2. F
3. T
4. F
5. F

Pre-GED Practice, page 158

1. (2) Since a plant appears short only if it has two t genes, it is recessive.
2. (4) Most of the next generation will have at least one T gene and will therefore be tall.
3. (2) This is mentioned in the second paragraph
4. (2) This is done to prevent PKU from harming children who have the disease.

Thinking About Science, page 161

1. (g)
2. (e)
3. (f)
4. (d)
5. (a)
6. (h)
7. (c)

Thinking About Science, page 163

1. It advises that some foods are better for you than others.
2. grains
3. 2–4 servings per day
4. 3–5 servings per day
5. fats, oils, and sweets

Thinking About Science, page 165

1. They slow it down.
2. malnutrition, sleeplessness, nervousness, fatigue, or depression
3. psychosis
4. It produces seizures and slows breathing to the point of coma or death.
5. the lungs, liver, brain, and kidneys

Pre-GED Practice, page 166

1. (3) A low-fat diet will actually help decrease the risk of cardiovascular disease.
2. (1) Ice cream is high and fats and sugar. The body only needs a moderate amount of these nutrients.

Human Biology Review, pages 167–168

1. (5) As bones age, they become less flexible and more brittle, which makes them more likely to break.
2. (4) The skeleton is what gives humans their form.
3. (4) The brain is protected by the skull, not the ribs.
4. (2) Ligaments connect bones and hold them in place in the body.
5. (5) The skeletal muscles are not involuntary. You can move them by thinking about them.
6. (2) When stomach acids break down part of the stomach wall along with the foods in the stomach, an ulcer occurs.
7. (3) The excretory system is responsible for removing all wastes from the body.
8. (1) Adrenaline does not cause muscles to hurt. It provides them with increased blood flow so the body can react quickly.
9. (5) This is the best way to prevent against Fetal Alcohol Syndrome.
10. (1) As a child's brain develops, any mental disabilities will become apparent.
11. (2) If the woman stops drinking alcohol immediately, she will have a greater chance of having a healthy baby.

Reading Efficiency C, pages 169–170

1. (1) Since Dallas has the highest temperatures of all the cities listed in the chart, it would have the greatest decrease in temperature if the temperature dropped to 23°F.
2. (2) When the blood vessels expand to carry more blood, it uses up heat inside the body.
3. (1) Since heat causes the heart to beat faster, a person with heart conditions is at a higher risk for complications from extreme heat.
4. (4) This would cause sweat to remain around the body instead of evaporating, which would not help the body cool off. Humidity has the same effect.
5. (2) Age does not have anything to do with this study.

Reading Efficiency D, pages 171–172

1. (1) Minerals are made of molecules that are small enough to pass through cell membranes. This is mentioned in the second paragraph.

2. (5) Since blood carries nutrients to the cells via blood vessels, a blockage of vessels leading to an organ would prevent nutrients from reaching the organ.
3. (4) Villi cause the small intestine to have a greater surface area so it can absorb more nutrients.
4. (2) Water is the only substance listed that can pass directly through cell membranes without having to be broken down.
5. (1) The student will not get the necessary nutrients that are provided by different types of food.

Chapter 6

Thinking About Science, page 177

1. Physical properties can be examined without changing the matter. Chemical properties cannot be examined without producing a new material with new properties.
2. the simplest type of matter

Pre-GED Practice, page 178

1. (4) This is mentioned in the second paragraph of the section on matter.
2. (4) An element is the smallest type of matter. It cannot be broken down into simpler substances, but it can be combined with other elements to form new substances.
3. (2) Stars are a form of plasma and are larger than any of the other objects mentioned.
4. (5) All of these features are mentioned in the section on matter.
5. (1) When ice melts to water, it changes form but does not change in chemical structure.
6. (2) When sodium and chlorine combine to form salt, they create a new substance with different chemical and physical properties.
7. (4) The Sun is a star, and scientists consider stars to be plasma.
8. (1) When something evaporates, it changes from a liquid to a gas. This is a physical change, not a chemical change.

Thinking About Science, page 184

1. (a) electron
   (b) neutrons

(c) protons

(d) electron

2. Instead of being in a specific orbit, the electron has a chance of being anywhere within a wavy cloud.

3. (a) +   (d) 0
   (b) 0   (e) + or −
   (c) −

Pre-GED Practice, page 185

1. (2) This is the definition of an atom.
2. (1) This is mentioned on page 180.
3. (3) Since helium has two protons, its atomic number is 2.
4. (4) This is mentioned on page 181.
5. (2) An element can be broken down into atoms, which display the same traits as the original element.

Thinking About Science, page 189

1. F   5. F
2. T   6. F
3. F
4. T

Pre-GED Practice, page 189

1. (2) One molecule of sand would be written as SiO_2 (one atom of silicon and two atoms of oxygen). Therefore three molecules of sand would be written as $3SiO_2$.
2. (4) There is one atom of carbon and four atoms of chloride (CCl_4).

Thinking About Science, page 191

1. (b)   5. (d)
2. (a)   6. (f)
3. (c)   7. (g)
4. (e)

Pre-GED Practice, page 192

1. (2) An element with eight electrons in its outer shell is said to be inert, or stable. It does not need to bond with another element to complete its outer shell.
2. (1) Atoms that form a covalent bond share electrons in their outer shells.
3. (4) Carbon dioxide has one atom of carbon (C) and two atoms of oxygen (O_2), or (CO_2).

4. (4) This is the definition of the law of conservation of matter.

Thinking About Science, page 194

1. one substance dissolved in another
2. an atom with a (+) or (−) charge
3. salt and water
4. metal alloys
5. the substance that dissolves
6. the substance in which the solute is dissolved

Pre-GED Practice, page 194

1. (3) This is the definition of a solution.
2. (2) An electrolyte is a substance with ionic bonds that, when dissolved in water, create a solution that can conduct an electric current.

Thinking About Science, page 196

1. All known forms of life contain carbon.
2. They combine with oxygen in the air.
3. a. plants
   b. photosynthesis
   c. carbon dioxide
   d. respiration
   e. organic

Pre-GED Practice, page 197

1. (2) Organic chemistry is the study of carbon and its compounds.
2. (4) Once hydrocarbons are used as fuels, they remain in the environment and cause many types of pollution.
3. (3) Coal is formed when carbon atoms become trapped under the earth and is cut off from oxygen.

Chemistry Review, pages 198–200

1. (3) Aspirin is a drug based on a natural remedy used by Native Americans to lower fevers.
2. (2) Ellagic acid combines with benzopyrene and causes it to split into noncancer-causing components.
3. (1) The first paragraph mentioned that ellagic acid is found naturally in nuts. Almonds are a type of nut.
4. (2) For example, if a positron and electron meet, both particles are destroyed.

5. (2) Tetrachloroethylene evaporates more quickly than water, so the fibers of the fabric don't need to swell to absorb it.
6. (1) This is mentioned in the second paragraph.
7. (4) When ethanol and water are heated and passed through zeolite, a chemical reaction occurs in which the oxygen in the ethanol combines with hydrogen to form water, and the remaining hydrogen and carbon form gasoline.
8. (4) It does not provide an efficient amount of energy.

Reading Efficiency E, pages 201–202

1. (1) The nucleus is made of protons and neutrons, which each have a mass of 1. The electrons have virtually no mass.
2. (5) This atom has the greatest number of particles in its nucleus. Therefore, it has the most mass.
3. (3) Thompson discovered electrons, which proved that atoms could be broken down into smaller particles.
4. (2) Electrons from a scanning electron microscope bounce off the surface of the object being viewed, which creates an image of the object's surface.
5. (4) This statement indicates that electrons from a SEM only make it to the surface of the object.

Reading Efficiency F, pages 203–204

1. (5) Carbon dioxide is not a pure form of carbon. It is a molecule composed of carbon and oxygen.
2. (1) Carbon can form with a variety of atoms to create a variety of compounds.
3. (3) While the passage states that fullerine was first made in the laboratory in 1985, it does not state whether it existed in nature prior to 1985.
4. (2) Because of this, graphite used to make pencils.
5. (3) This is an opinion and is not based on scientific information.

Chapter 7

Thinking About Science, page 207

1. Friction slows moving objects.
2. People should use seat belts because once they (as passengers in a vehicle) are in motion, they will stay in motion even if the vehicle is rapidly slowed by brakes or impact.
3. It takes more energy to move a larger mass than a smaller mass.
4. Because there is an equal reaction for every action, the force of the hot air out the back of the rocket will force the spacecraft forward.

Pre-GED Practice, page 208

1. (1) The field of optics deals with the behavior of light. This has led to improvements in many types of lenses, including eyeglass lenses.
2. (1) The field of mechanics deals with motions and the application of forces to material objects. This would be very important in the design of an airplane.
3. (4) Seatbelts in a car prevent a passenger from continuing to move forward as a car stops.
4. (4) Momentum is related to both speed and mass. Since a golf ball has more mass than a Ping-Pong ball, the golf ball would have more momentum than the Ping-Pong ball when hit at the same speed.
5. (2) The amount of momentum an object has is related to the object's mass. Therefore a refrigerator's momentum depends on its mass. Momentum increases as mass increases. Therefore as a person grows and gains mass, he gains momentum.

Thinking About Science, page 210

1. the force that attracts one object to another
2. anything that can affect the motion of an object
3. the drag produced when two objects rub against each other
4. the state in which objects experience identical forces
5. force x distance

Thinking About Science, page 214

1. gear
2. inclined plane
3. wheel and axle
4. pulley
5. lever

Pre-GED Practice, page 215

1. (1) A lever can be made from a rigid bar with a small support for a fulcrum.
2. (2) A pulley changes the direction of a force. For example, a person can lift an object by pulling down on it.
3. (4) Gears can change the direction of a force and can either increase the force or change its speed.
4. (2) Work is performed on an object if a force is exerted on the object and moves the object a certain distance. A parent holding a child is exerting a force on the child but is not moving the child any distance. Work would only be performed if the parent lifted the child.
5. (5) All the simple machines that make up a compound machine work together to function. If one machine is broken, the others will not work.
6. (1) As the hockey puck moves across the ice, friction is created which slows down the puck.
7. (1) A clock consists of many simple machines. Therefore, it is a compound machine.

Thinking About Science, page 217

1. Kinetic
2. potential
3. Friction
4. electric
5. nucleus of the atom

Pre-GED Practice, page 217

1. (5) The nuclear energy will not perform work until it is converted into another form of energy as in the other examples.
2. (3) While energy can change from potential to kinetic or vice versa, the original amount of total energy never changes.
3. (2) The chemical reaction that occurs when a log is burned turns chemical energy into heat and light energy—the fire.

Thinking About Science, page 219

1. expand; contract
2. conduction
3. conductors
4. rises; sinks
5. Dark; light

Pre-GED Practice, page 220

1. (2) Conductors transfer heat as their molecules move about and bump into each other.
2. (4) Shiny clothing will reflect radiant energy and light-colored clothing will not absorb as much radiant energy as dark-colored clothing.

Thinking About Science, page 223

1. gamma rays, X rays, ultraviolet rays
2. infrared waves, microwaves, radio waves
3. particles, waves
4. shadow
5. short, long

Pre-GED Practice, page 223

1. (2) As the different wavelengths that make up white light pass through a prism, they bend at different angles and split into individual colors.
2. (2) Light is produced when an atom releases a particle of energy called a photon.
3. (1) Red has the longest wavelength and bends the least as it passes through the prism.

Thinking About Science, page 224

1. F
2. F
3. T
4. T
5. T

Pre-GED Practice, page 225

1. (4) The sound wave bounces off an object. This is called an echo.
2. (1) Since sound travels faster in water than in air, it is easier to hear sound across a body of water than across land and air.

Thinking About Science, page 228

1. (b)
2. (d)
3. (a)
4. (e)
5. (c)

Pre-GED Practice, page 228

1. (3) A circuit breaker or fuse prevents too much electricity from flowing through a circuit.
2. (4) This is mentioned on page 271.

Physics Review, pages 229–232

1. (1) This is mentioned in the third paragraph of the passage.
2. (3) This keeps the contents of the refrigerator cool.
3. (3) Heat is released so the gas can absorb more heat when it moves into the evaporator. The condenser is locates at the back or bottom to keep heat away from the contents of the refrigerator.
4. (3) This is mentioned in the first paragraph of the passage.
5. (4) Lasers have been used for scientific research (measuring the distance to the Moon), for practical procedures (guiding missiles), and for medical procedures (eye surgery).
6. (1) Since the like poles of the magnets are placed next to each other in the illustration, the poles will repel each other and push the magnets apart.
7. (3) Wires 4 and 5 will not affect the other lights, since they are beyond the other lights.
8. (2) This is mentioned in the first sentence of the second paragraph in the passage.
9. (4) This is mentioned in the last paragraph of the passage.

Reading Efficiency G, pages 233–234

1. (4) Thermal pollution occurs when thermal energy enters a body of water as heated water.
2. (2) Heat flows from a warmer substance to a cooler one. Therefore, heat would flow from the warmer hand to the cooler ice cube.
3. (1) After a substance is heated, it has a higher temperature, or average kinetic energy.

4. (1) As the solid is heated, it gains thermal energy. The resulting liquid has more thermal energy than the original solid.
5. (3) The other reasons are based on scientific fact. Whether the factory is unattractive is based on a person's values.

Reading Efficiency H, pages 235–236

1. (1) This can be observed in the diagram.
2. (2) Since the waves that make up laser light do not spread out like ordinary light, a laser light would be effective in lighting up a room.
3. (2) The waves that make up regular light consist of many different wavelengths that spread out in different directions.
4. (1) The focused beam created by a laser makes it effective as a cutting tool.
5. (3) As scientists learned more about laser light, they discovered its many uses.

Chapter 8

Thinking About Science, page 244

Part A

1. the thick layer of rock beneath the crust
2. intense pressure
3. the mantle
4. continental drift, or plate tectonics

Part B

1. (c)
2. (c)
3. (a)
4. (a)
5. (b)
6. (b)

Thinking About Science, page 246

1. Your completed diagram should look like the one on page 245.
2. 100,000 years or more
3. humus

Pre-GED Practice, page 247

1. (1) The continents are found on the surface, or crust, of Earth.

2. (2) Continental drift, or plate tectonics, is the name of the theory that describes the movement of the continents.

3. (5) The development of a volcano begins when crustal plates rub against each other, which heats up molten rock. The pressure caused by the heated molten rock builds up until the volcano erupts.

4. (2) The rock cycle is the process by which rock turns from one form to another form.

5. (3) This can be determined from the diagram on page 245.

6. (3) Weathering is caused by many different factors, including water, ice, plants, animals, and chemical changes.

Thinking About Science, page 252

1. T
2. T
3. T
4. F
5. T
6. T
7. F
8. T

Pre-GED Practice, page 252

1. (1) This cannot be inferred from the information presented in the passage.

2. (4) Approximately 62.5 percent of Earth's freshwater is located in groundwater.

3. (2) The length of a wave is measured from crest to crest.

Thinking About Science, page 256

1. nitrogen
2. carbon dioxide
3. ultraviolet
4. freeze
5. rises
6. rapidly expanding air
7. 15
8. warm; summer
9. calm; clear
10. five

Pre-GED Practice, page 257

1. (2) Scientists believe the gases in our atmosphere were trapped inside Earth and escaped as volcanoes erupted over billions of years.

2. (2) Nitrogen is the main gas in Earth's atmosphere, followed by oxygen and carbon dioxide.

3. (4) The spin of Earth causes the movement of air from areas of high pressure to areas of lower pressure, which causes wind.

4. (2) Hail is formed from bits of dust and ice that collide with water droplets and freeze. When the ice bits get too heavy for the wind to carry, they fall to the ground.

5. (3) Tornadoes and hurricanes are spinning thunderstorms.

6. (2) Earth's gravity keeps the atmosphere from floating off into space.

Earth Science Review, pages 258–260

1. (3) This is mentioned in the first paragraph of the passage.

2. (5) This is mentioned in the last paragraph of the passage.

3. (1) This is mentioned in the second paragraph of the passage.

4. (2) When the trough of a tsunami reached land first, the water near the shore may suddenly rush out to sea.

5. (3) This is mentioned in the last paragraph of the passage.

6. (2) According to the table, snow will fall when the temperature in the clouds is below 32°F and the temperature at the ground is below 37°F.

7. (4) These effects are explained in the fourth paragraph.

8. (5) The hailstones were formed in the clouds in the sky, where it must be below freezing.

Reading Efficiency I, pages 261–262

1. (3) Lightning occurs during a rain storm, but it has nothing to do with replenishing groundwater.

2. (5) This reason has nothing to do with the importance of having clean groundwater. It has to do with the cost of treating groundwater to make it clean.

3. (4) A light rain that lasts for about a day will have plenty of time to be absorbed into the ground.

4. (4) Building a park would not create any disturbances to the groundwater in the area.

5. (4) This factor would not affect your decision to buy the home. The other factors would be serious considerations because they could lead to possible contamination of groundwater.

Reading Efficiency J, pages 263–264

1. (2) Power in a wind turbine is created when wind moves the blades, which run a generator that produces electricity.

2. (2) The larger the blades on a turbine, the greater the energy produced. Turbines run best in areas with steady, strong winds.

3. (1) If the wind in an area is not strong enough, the turbine will not be able to generate electricity.

4. (4) There may not always be enough wind to power the turbine, so an alternate source of energy is necessary as a back-up.

5. (4) The amount of sunshine in an area does not affect how much energy a wind turbine can produce.

Chapter 9

Thinking About Science, page 267

1. big bang
2. closed universe
3. open universe
4. galaxy
5. 200 billion; 100 thousand

Pre-GED Practice, page 267

1. (5) These three statements can be inferred by looking at the illustration.

2. (4) All of the references to the "blue-green planet" are to Earth.

Thinking About Science, page 270

1. gravity
2. nine
3. inner planets
4. outer planets
5. Asteroids; comets

Pre-GED Practice, page 270

1. (2) This is the only statement that can be inferred. The other statements have either been proven as fact or are opinions with nothing to back them up.

2. (5) According to the information discovered about comets over the years, it seems likely that comets move in predictable orbits.

Thinking About Science, page 272

1. Earth's rotation
2. summer
3. third

Pre-GED Practice, page 272

1. (3) Because of the way Earth rotates, by the time Chicago is turning away from the Sun, New York has already turned away from it.

2. (1) Earth makes one revolution around the Sun each year. It makes one rotation every 24 hours.

Thinking About Science, page 274

1. asteroids hitting the Moon's surface
2. reflects
3. new moon
4. Moon's gravity

Pre-GED Practice, page 274

1. (4) If the Moon were composed of gas-like substances, it would be like the Sun.

2. (2) A lunar eclipse only occurs during a full moon.

Thinking About Science, page 276

1. manned lunar landing
2. light
3. speed of light

Pre-GED Practice, page 276

1. (4) Optical telescopes help to make objects in space appear clearer, not closer.

2. (5) This could be inferred because of the sentence in the passage about the spacecraft with the message that is traveling beyond our solar system.

Space Science Review, pages 277–279

1. (2) Scientists are trying to discover whether Earth is the only planet that contains forms of life.
2. (3) The words *atmosphere*, *cloud*, and *hot* are key words in the description of Venus.
3. (3) The galaxy is 12 billion light-years from Earth. This means it has taken the light from the galaxy 12 billion years to reach our planet. Therefore, we are seeing this galaxy as it looked 12 billion years ago. There is no way of knowing what is occurring in the galaxy right now.
4. (2) This information is in the third sentence.
5. (2) According to the passage, when the number of sunspots is highest, solar flares shoot out particles that can interfere with radio transmission.
6. (1) Only this statement both accurately summarizes the graph and determines that there is a pattern.
7. (4) The amateur enjoys her hobby because she values making a scientific contribution. All other options are facts and do not involve values.
8. (2) Gravity is the attraction between two objects. If the planet does not follow its expected orbit, it must be attracted by another object. No other option takes into account the effect of gravity on the planet's orbit.

Reading Efficiency K, pages 280–281

1. (4) People believed Ptolemy's ideas for almost 1,400 years.
2. (2) Both Copernicus and Ptolemy believed the model of the universe contained planets, a sun, and stars.
3. (4) Computers were not around in Ptolemy's time.
4. (1) A new model is not necessarily different than an old model. It is just an improved version of the old model.
5. (5) As more and more observations are made and can be explained by the new model, then the new model remains correct.

Reading Efficiency L, pages 282–283

1. (3) The Sun's heat occurs when hydrogen nuclei join together to form larger nuclei with more mass. This process is called *fusion*.
2. (1) While energy that leaves the Sun as light takes only 8 minutes to reach Earth, energy produced in the center of the Sun takes millions of years to reach the Sun's surface.
3. (2) The larger an object's mass, the larger its gravitational pull. The Sun has a larger mass than Earth; therefore, it has a larger gravitational pull.
4. (2) The gravity of the planets is greater than the gravity of their moons, which keeps the moons in orbit around the planets.
5. (1) The objects should be the same size so they will all need the same amount of time to heat according to their distance from the light.

Assessment

Using the Reading Efficiency Activities

Contemporary's Reading Efficiency Activities will help increase your reading speed and your comprehension accuracy. The activities are similar to the reading passages and questions you will find on the GED Test.

Your goal is to complete each exercise in less than 10 minutes. You should also answer at least 4 of the questions correctly. If you can always score within this range (within the shaded areas of the Efficiency Factor Chart), you should be successful with the readings and the number of questions on each GED Test.

Once you know the amount of time it took you to complete the activity and the number of questions you answered correctly, look at the Efficiency Factor Chart below. Find your time along the left side and your number of correct answers along the top. If your time falls between two of the times on this chart, round up to the higher time. Move across and down until your time and number correct meet. This is your E-Factor.

Find where your E-Factor fits on the Efficiency Factor Grid on the next page. Make a dot to the right of that number on the line below the letter of the Reading Efficiency Activity you completed.

As you read other Activities, mark your E-Factor and connect the dots to create a line graph. You should see a line that moves upward as it crosses the grid. If your E-factor is not improving, ask your instructor what you can do to increase either your speed or your accuracy.

EFFICIENCY FACTOR (E-FACTOR) CHART

Correct

Time	0	1	2	3	4	5
6.0	0	33	67	99	133	167
6.5	0	31	62	92	123	154
7.0	0	29	57	86	114	143
7.5	0	27	53	80	107	133
8.0	0	25	50	75	100	125
8.5	0	24	47	71	94	118
9.0	0	22	44	67	89	111
9.5	0	21	42	63	84	105
10.0	0	20	40	60	80	100
10.5	0	19	38	57	76	95
11.0	0	18	36	55	73	91
11.5	0	17	35	52	70	87
12.0	0	17	33	50	67	83

READING EFFICIENCY

EFFICIENCY FACTOR (E-FACTOR) GRID

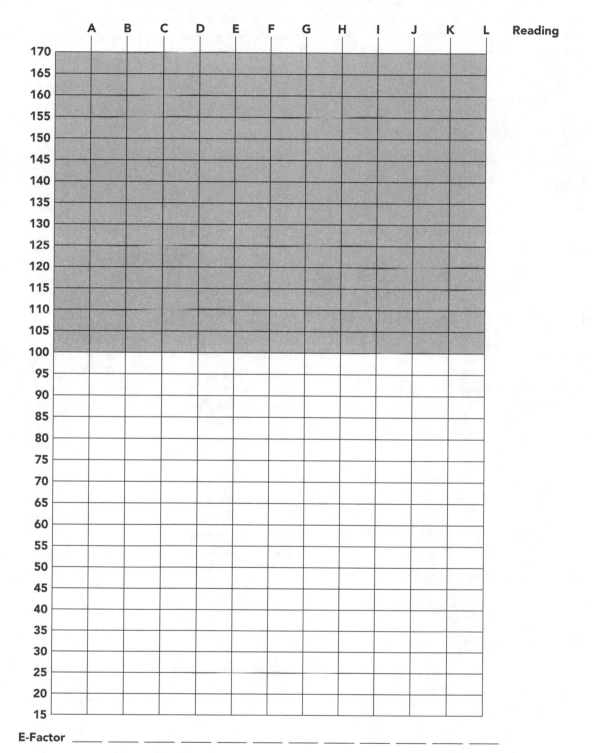

E-Factor ___ ___ ___ ___ ___ ___ ___ ___ ___ ___ ___ ___

Glossary

A

acid   a substance that has a sour taste, such as lemon juice or vinegar, and that produces salt and water when added to a base

active transport   process in which cells move molecules from less crowded areas outside the cell to more crowded areas inside the cell

adaptation   a change in a species in response to its environment that improves its chances of survival

air pressure   a measure of how strongly the atmosphere pushes against Earth

algae   the simplest nonflowering plants

alloy   a solid solution made by using heat to fuse two or more metals

amino acids   the building blocks of proteins

amphibians   a group of vertebrates that undergo metamorphosis

anatomy   the study of the structure of living things

arthropods   invertebrates with legs that bend and an exoskeleton

asteroids   a circle of rocky objects between the inner planets and the outer planets

astronomy   the study of all objects in the Universe other than our Earth

atmosphere   the layer of air that surrounds Earth

atom   the smallest particle of an element that retains the characteristics of that element

autonomic nervous system   the part of the nervous system that works automatically and enables the body to perform actions involuntarily

B

base   a substance that has a soapy or slippery feel, such as a detergent, and that produces salt and water when added to an acid

big bang theory   the idea that the whole universe was once a single, densely packed particle that exploded, creating the universe

biochemistry   the study of the atoms and molecules that form cells

biotechnology   the use of microbes to make useful materials for human consumption

biological process   a fundamental property that is common to all living organisms

biome   a large group of ecosystems that have similar climates

biosphere   the part of Earth in which life exists

birds   a group of vertebrates that fly

botany   the study of plants

C

calorie   a unit used to measure the energy value of different foods

carbohydrates   starches and sugars that are the main energy source for the body

cardiac muscles   involuntary muscles that control the heartbeat

cartilage   a tough, flexible material that covers bones and joints

cause-and-effect relationship   a relationship in which a certain action leads to a specific result

cell   the basic unit of all living things

cell membrane   the flexible outer surface of a cell

cell wall   the outermost structure just outside the cell membrane

cerebellum   the part of the brain that controls muscle coordination and balance

cerebrum   the outer portion of the brain that is responsible for thought

chemical energy   energy released when two substances are combined in a reaction

chemical properties   those things that describe how a substance reacts with another substance

chlorophyll   the green pigment in plants that is central to the food-making process

chloroplast   a cell structure that contains chlorophyll

chromosome   genetic material that determines the traits of an organism

chronological order   an arrangement of events in the order in which they happen

circuit   the path that electrons follow; it must be complete if electricity is to flow

classify   to organize organisms into groups based on their structure, growth, and function

closed universe theory   the theory that the force of gravity will eventually cause the universe to collapse upon itself

comet   a small object made of dust and frozen gas that orbit the Sun

communicating   sharing your experimental results and conclusion with others

community   all the organisms living in a certain area

compound   two or more elements combined chemically to form a single substance

compound machine   a machine that is made of two or more simple machines

compression wave   a sound wave of high pressure that vibrates in the direction of a line

conduction   the method in which heat is transferred by objects that are in contact with each other

conservation   the practice of saving nonrenewable resources

continental drift   the theory that describes the movement of Earth's crustal plates

continuity the process by which life continues as it is

constancy the tendency for things to remain unchanged

contract to get smaller as a result of being cooled

control a standard against which the effects of an experiment are compared

convection the process by which heat moves through air or water

covalent bonding the bonding of elements by sharing electrons

crest the top of a wave

crust the thin outer layer of Earth

crustal plate a part of Earth's outer surface that shifts during an earthquake

cytoplasm living material in the cell

D

decomposers bacteria, fungi, or protozoa that feed on dead organisms

deductive reasoning using a generalization about one thing to draw a conclusion about another

describing determining what you already know about the subject and researching more information about it

diffusion movement of molecules in and out of cells without the use of the cell's energy

diversity the idea that living things look different on the outside but often have many similarities on the inside

DNA deoxyribonucleic acid—the chemical basis for heredity in humans

dominant tending to overpower the effects of, as a dominant gene for brown eyes over blue eyes

drug a kind of chemical that affects the body, mind, or behavior

E

echo a reflected sound wave

ecology study of how organisms interact with one another and with the world around them

ecosystem the system of interacting organisms and their environment

electrical energy the movement of electrons within matter

electrolyte a liquid that conducts electric currents

electromagnet a part of an electric motor used to change electric energy to mechanical energy

electromagnetic spectrum waves arranged according to length that carry energy throughout the universe

electron a negatively charged particle orbiting the nucleus of an atom

element a substance that cannot be broken down into a simpler form

embryo a vertebrate in its early stage of development

endoplasmic reticulum a cellular structure that leads from the cell membrane to the nucleus

engine a compound machine that has a source of energy other than human muscle

environment the living and nonliving surroundings of an organism

equation an expression that shows the elements that combine in a chemical reaction and the products that are formed

equilibrium a physical state in which forces and changes occur in opposite and offsetting directions

evidence the observations and data from experiments

evolution the theory that complex forms of life develop from simpler forms

exoskeleton an outer skeleton that is made of nonliving material

expand to increase in size as a result of being heated

experimenting testing your explanation using orderly steps

explaining gathering results from your experiment and drawing conclusions from them

explanation a consistent, logical statement that includes existing scientific facts and new evidence from observation, experiments, and models

extinct no longer present on Earth

eye of the storm the low-pressure center of a hurricane

F

fact a conclusion, based on evidence, that scientists agree on

fat oily or greasy matter that provides a concentrated dose of energy

ferns a group of simple, nonflowering plants that have true roots, stems, and leaves but no true seeds

fetus a developing human from three months after conception to birth

fish a group of vertebrates that live in water

flat universe theory the theory that the universe will continue to expand until some future time when it reaches a size and stays at that size

food chain a group of organisms arranged in an order showing how each organism feeds on and obtains energy for the one before it

food web the many food chains within a community

force anything that affects the motion of an object

form the physical characteristics of an object

formula a symbol consisting of letters and numbers

fossil the preserved remains of an organism

frequency the number of waves that pass a point in a given amount of time

friction the resistance to motion between two surfaces moving over each other

fulcrum the point around which a lever turns

function the purpose served by a form

fungi a group of multicelled organisms that are rooted in one place like plants but lack the chlorophyll necessary to produce food

fusion a process in which two or more atomic nuclei combine to form a single nucleus and to release energy

G

galaxy a large group of stars forming a system

gas a substance that has no definite volume and no definite shape

gears a compound machine that can change the direction of a force and can either increase the force or change its speed

gene each small section of DNA; genes determine eye color, the shape of blood cells, and control whether the right or left side of the brain is dominant

generator a machine that uses mechanical energy and magnets to produce electricity

genetics the study of the inherited characteristics of plants and animals

geology the study of Earth; how it was formed, what it is made of, its history, and the changes that occur on it

gravity the force that attracts one object to another

greenhouse effect a condition in which the atmosphere traps the Sun's heat and prevents it from escaping into space

H

habitat a place where a person or group lives

hermaphrodite an animal that contains both male and female reproductive organs

hormones chemicals produced by endocrine glands; hormones control growth, how the body uses energy, and the ability to reproduce

humus decayed plant and animal matter; it helps the soil hold water and increases fertility

hydrocarbons compounds, such as fuels, that are made up of hydrogen and carbon

hypothesis a reasonable explanation of evidence or a prediction based on evidence

I

identifying asking a question about what you have seen and proposing a possible explanation for it

igneous a type of rock that forms from melted rock material

immunity protection from disease

inclined plane a simple machine that consists of a flat surface that has one end higher than the other to magnify force

inductive reasoning making a generalization based on a specific experience and then applying that generalization to another experience

inert condition of atoms that do not form compounds with other elements

inertia the tendency of an object to not change its state of motion

inference an educated guess

inner core the part of Earth that extends about 800 miles to Earth's center

insulator a material that does not conduct heat quickly; a material that does not carry electric current

interdependence the dependence of one living thing on another living thing

invertebrates animals without backbones

ion an atom with either a positive or a negative charge

ionic bond a bond formed when atoms give up or gain electrons

irrelevant information facts that have no bearing on a judgment or decision

isotope an atom of the same element that has different numbers of neutrons

K

kinetic energy the energy of a moving object

L

labor the contraction and relaxation of the smooth muscles of the uterus resulting in birth

laterite deep red soil

law of chance a description of the probability of something happening

law of conservation of energy the idea that the total amount of kinetic and potential energy remains the same

law of conservation of matter a fundamental scientific principle stating that matter cannot be created or destroyed in a chemical reaction

law of nature a property of nature that does not change

leaves the part of a plant in which glucose is made

lever a simple machine consisting of a rod or bar that turns around a point to move a load

life science the study of living things

ligaments tough strands of tissue that connect bones

light-year the distance light can travel in a year (9.5 trillion km)

liquid a substance that has a definite volume but no definite shape

logical order an arrangement of events based on logic

M

magnet an object that attracts iron and a few other elements

main idea a short summary of what a passage is about

mammals a group of vertebrates that have hair and give birth to live young

mantle a thick layer of very dense rock that lies under Earth's crust

marrow the jellylike substance consisting of nerves and blood vessels inside human bones

marsupial a type of mammal that nourishes its live-born young in a pouch

matter anything that has mass and occupies space

measurement an expression of an amount of change

mechanical energy energy that comes from motion; it can be either kinetic or potential

medulla the part of the brain that controls involuntary actions such as the heartbeat, breathing, and digestion

menstrual cycle a period resulting in the growth and release of a mature egg

metamorphic sedimentary or igneous rock that changes due to high pressure and high temperature

metamorphosis   the change in an organism from one life stage to another

meteorology   the study of the atmosphere

microbe   an organism (or near-organism) that, because of its size, cannot be seen without the help of a microscope

microbiology   the study of microbes

mitochondria   sausage-shaped structures that trap the energy from food and release it to the cell

model   a drawing, physical object, or plan that stands for the real thing

molecule   the smallest particle of any material that has the chemical properties of that material

mollusks   a group of invertebrates that have an outer shell

molting   process in which arthropods shed their exoskeletons to grow

monerans   the smallest and simplest group of organisms that do not have a separate nucleus

mosses   a group of simple, nonflowering plants that have a two-stage life cycle

mutate   to change, as a gene changes

mutation   a change in the genetic information within a cell

mutualism   beneficial association between different kinds of organisms

N

natural resources   those things in the environment, such as air, water, and food, that people need and use to survive

natural selection   the theory that nature acts as a selective force in which the least fit die and the most fit survive

neutron   a particle found in the nucleus and that has no electrical charge

nitrogen cycle   the process that maintains the nitrogen content of the atmosphere fueled by bacteria in the soil and decaying organisms

nonrenewable resources   resources that cannot be easily replaced, such as topsoil, oil, and coal

nuclear energy   energy derived from splitting or changing the nucleus of an atom

nucleic acids   the substances that control a cell's activities

nucleolus   a dense, round body that makes specialized cell structures called ribosomes

nucleus   the control center in a cell

nutritionist   one who studies what foods the body needs to stay healthy

O

observing   noticing things around you and thinking about what you see

oceanography   the study of the oceans

open universe theory   the theory that the universe will keep expanding forewver

opinion   a personal belief that is often based on a person's own value system

optics   the study of how light behaves

order   properties and behavior that are predictable

organization   classifying systems to better show their similarities and differences

organ   a group of tissues working together to perform a complex function

organ system   a group of organs that work together to perform a life process

organic chemistry   the study of carbon compounds present in life forms

organic compound   any compound containing carbon

organism   any living thing

outer core   the layer of Earth that is about 1,400 miles thick and is made up of melted iron and nickel

ozone   a form of oxygen that protects us from the Sun's ultraviolet radiation

P

parasitism   the harmful attachment of organisms, such as ticks, fleas, and lice, to other creatures

periodic table of the elements   the organization of the elements according to mass and the number of electrons in their outermost shell

phases of the moon   the repeating position of the moon in relation to Earth and Sun from month to month

photon   a bundle of energy released by an atom

photosynthesis   the process by which plants use light energy to make food

physical properties   those things that can be examined without changing the identity of the matter

physiology   the study of the functions and vital processes of organisms

pistil   the female reproductive structure of the flower

pitch   the measure of the frequency at which a note vibrates

placebo   a dosage in an experiment that lacks the ingredient being tested in the experiment

placenta   a membrane by which a fertilized egg attaches itself to the uterus

plasma   a light-colored watery liquid that contains some proteins, minerals, vitamins, sugars, and chemicals; it provides transport throughout the body; the fourth state of matter

plate tectonics   the theory that describes the breakup of one land mass into the seven continents

platelets   tiny particles in the blood that form blood clots

pollen   the male reproductive material of flowering plants

pollination   the process by which plants transfer reproductive materials from one plant to another

pollution   the contamination of the environment with substances in a quantity great enough to affect an ecosystem

population   all of the organisms of one type

potential energy energy that is stored

predators life forms that live by eating other life forms

prey organisms predators hunt and kill for food

prism clear piece of glass or plastic with triangular ends that split light

producers green plants that manufacture food by photosynthesis, directly or indirectly

proteins nutrients that are broken apart in the body into amino acids

protists a group of single-celled organisms with a nucleus

proton a positively charged particle found in the nucleus of an atom

pulley a simple machine that changes the direction of a force

punctuated equilibrium the suggestion that the history of life on Earth shows times of stability interrupted by rapid change

R

radiant energy nuclear energy that travels through space as waves

radiation heat from the Sun that comes to us in waves

recessive tending to be suppressed, as a recessive gene for blue eyes vs brown eyes

reflex a type of reaction in which signals are immediately transmitted to the spinal cord and the brain

relevant information facts that have a bearing on a judgment or decision

renewable resources resources that can be replaced within an average lifetime, such as animals, crops, and trees

reptiles a group of vertebrates related to the dinosaurs that once roamed Earth

ribosomes tiny dots on the endoplasmic reticulum that combine amino acids into proteins

roots the part of a plant that anchors it into the ground

S

salt a compound that results when an acid is mixed with a base

scientific method a systematic method of investigation that scientists follow

sedimentary rock formed from loose material that becomes tightly packed over time

simple machine a machine that performs a single function

skeletal muscles voluntary muscles that allow humans to change the position of their body

smooth muscles involuntary muscles that are controlled by the nervous system

solar system the system consisting of the Sun, nine planets, their moons, and smaller bodies of asteroids and comets

solid a substance that has a definite shape and a definite volume

solute the substance that dissolves in a solution

solution a mixture formed by one substance dissolving in another

solvent the substance in which a solute is dissolved

species the smallest group in the classification of organisms that can interbreed

spectrum all the wavelengths of light broken up into seven colors

sponges the simplest of the invertebrates

squall lines irregular rows of thunderclouds

stamen the male reproductive structure of a flower

stem the part of a plant that provides support and transports food and water

system a small unit of investigation used by scientists to gain a better understanding of a larger concept

T

tissue a group of like cells working together

traits characteristics displayed by an organism

trough the lowest part of a wave

V

vacuoles cellular organs that have a variety of functions, such as digesting food and disposing wastes

variable a changeable element that affects the quality or reliability of an experiment's outcome or result

vertebrates animals that have backbones

virus a nonliving structure that contains genetic material surrounded by protein and that can cause disease

W

wheel and axle a simple machine that combines a wheel with the idea of a lever

wind the movement of air from places of high pressure to places of low pressure

work the result of energy that can be defined as force multiplied by distance

worms a complex invertebrate with a simple brainlike structure and digestive tract

Z

zoology the study of animals